To. Isla.
Happy 25th birthday.
Best wishes
Maria xx.

THE PUNCH BOOK OF HEALTH

Also published by Grafton Books

The Punch Book of Cricket
The Punch Book of Golf

THE PUNCH BOOK OF

Compiled by
Susan Jeffreys

Foreword by
Alan Coren

GRAFTON BOOKS
A Division of the Collins Publishing Group

LONDON GLASGOW
TORONTO SYDNEY AUCKLAND

Grafton Books
A Division of the Collins Publishing Group
8 Grafton Street, London W1X 3LA

Published by Grafton Books 1987

British Library Cataloguing in Publication Data

The Punch book of health.
1. Medicine – Anecdotes, Facetiae,
Satire, etc.
I. Jeffreys, Susan
610'.207   R705

ISBN 0-246-13160-8

Printed in Great Britain by
Butler & Tanner Ltd,
Frome, Somerset

*The articles by Richard Gordon appear by
permission of Curtis Brown, London*

*The article by John Wells
is copyright John Wells 1979*

Contents

List of Contributors

Foreword

by Alan Coren

Since *Punch's* last birthday was its 145th, there was a not unsurprising surge of media frenzy – these are health-obsessed times – as to how, exactly, we had not only arrived at this milestone at all, but how we had arrived there in such remarkable nick and fettle.

The short answer given to the gawping lenses and clamouring microphones of a hundred different international networks was that we owed it all to booze, sex, and nicotine. The longer answer was that we also owed it to marriage, temperance, well-kept gardens, and God. The absolutely interminable answer was that we owed it, in addition, to desert islands, crooked politicians, beds of nails, talking dogs, oak-limbed pirates, intergalactic missions, psychiatric couches, cars, punk rockers, account executives, turkeys, trains, diving boards, fish soup, aeroplanes, things sticking to your shoe, queen mothers, manholes, boats, thermonuclear devices, hard drugs, lager, changeling frogs, office politics, encounter groups, romantic novelists, war, roofing contractors, dirty old men, computers, tea ceremonies, vests, binliners, student unrest, ventriloquists, flying saucers, secondhand furniture. . .

We owed our continuing comic health, in short, to living life to the full by taking every conceivable constituent of life and extruding therefrom its comic possibilities. If you could laugh about something, you stood a fair chance of dealing with it.

And perhaps the most fertile comic seed-bed of all was, with an irony appropriate to our trade, sickness. Not only could individual pain and gloom be turned to mass enjoyment on the part of the callous healthy, it could also assuage the glum suffering of the lonely individual himself. Stuck in some fearful pesthouse with a throbbing tonsil, a plastered leg in the air, a boil erupting on the conk, an appendix in a bucket, and a polythened finger poking into anything that yielded, the image of any or all such horrors filtered through the comic spectroscope and, turned to laughter, could do you more good than a golfcourseful of doctors.

This book is about feeling good about feeling lousy. Or perhaps, such is the engaging quiddity of our delightful language, feeling funny about feeling funny.

1

To Be or Not To Be

'Oh, that reminds me, dear –
I had a boy this morning.'

DOC BRIEF

Robert Buckman on
CHILDBIRTH

GYNAECOLOGISTS

To begin at the beginning. A gynaecologist is a doctor who specialises in women's complaints e.g. 'You never take me out any more.' It is interesting to note that there is no male equivalent of a gynaecologist. There isn't such a thing as an 'andrologist', which would be a specialist in male problems. Certainly, there are trained people who have enormous knowledge and skill in discussing such masculine problems as impotence and baldness, but these people are not called doctors as such; they are called hairdressers.

What is even more curious is that for decades there have been pressure groups campaigning for women to have female conditions treated exclusively by women doctors. This principle was widely accepted and then extended to having, for example, Italian patients treated by Italian doctors, short patients treated by short doctors etc. In fact when, a couple of years ago, I developed appendicitis, I insisted on being operated on by a famous Jewish neurotic doctor/writer who had appendicitis himself. The hospital eventually located one (it was Jonathan Miller actually), but by the time they got to him, he was being operated on by a gynaecologist. Anyway, the general rule still applies and this is

'We warned you about smoking when you were pregnant, Mrs Roth.'

why to this day our National Health Service is full of bad-tempered patients being looked after by bad-tempered doctors.

However, to return to gynaecologists – these dedicated persons attend to feminine problems and were, for example, the first clinicians to describe a variant of feminine itching due to plastic seat-covers in new Swedish cars (*pruritus volvo*). It is often said that because of the nature of their calling, gynaecologists are narrow-minded and, according to ancient legend, when they re-decorate their houses, paint the front hall from the outside through the letter-box. These stereotyped assertions are denigratory, unworthy and despicable, though they are often good for a laugh at parties (but not the kind gynaecologists go to. Which I wouldn't go to anyway. Even if I was invited).

The only time I was looked after by a gynae-cologist myself was when I was in a car accident outside a Gynaecology clinic in Lisson Grove. I was bleeding from the nose and was led inside where a gynaecologist used the only kind of padded dressing available to him to wrap around my face. He was very apologetic but couldn't help pointing out the poetic irony, given the fact that not only did I usually act like one, I now looked like one, too. It occurred to me at the time that in some respects, gynaecology is part of the divinity that shapes our ends.

OBSTETRICIANS

Obstetricians deliver babies and all obstetricians have trained as gynaecologists and wear bow-ties while doing both jobs, a fact that I can explain but would rather not. The word 'obstetrician' is actually derived from the Latin prefix 'ob-'

meaning 'in the way', 'stet' meaning 'he stands', and 'rician' is just tacked on the end to make it seem grander, like an OBE really, which is why so many obstetricians have got one of those for just standing around. Mind you, it takes over ten years of training to learn how to stand around looking grand, and not just how, but also where e.g. Kensington Palace, particularly if you want that OBE.

Of course, the rewards of obstetrics are not just in delivering crowned heads, there is the utterly wonderful joy of assisting at the start of a brand-new life, though it must be hell if forty years later you realise that what you pulled out all pink and gurgling innocence grew up into Norman Tebbit or something. Nowadays, of course, many babies are delivered in high-tech units by what might appear to be a rather soulless and mechanical method (mind you, quite a lot of them are conceived in the same sort of style as well).

Fashions in child-birth (*see below, but hurry*) are apt to change, and these changes often place obstetricians in a very awkward position e.g. crouching underwater. Child-birth is, of course, not a disease but a natural process, though I had my doubts hearing Esther Rantzen talk about it, and to some extent the manner of the birth is the prerogative of the participants. One of which is the baby and undoubtedly a human life capable of independent existence. Which is why it has often puzzled me that when a new fashion in child-birth crops up, there isn't a LIFE group or similar organisation campaigning to recognise the baby's right to choose e.g. their obstetrician and style of delivery. I mean, you only get born once, and it would be just typical of everything about life on earth that your mother makes all the important decisions for you.

FASHIONS IN CHILD-BIRTH

There have been many transient fashions in child-birth, some of which have been valuable to mother and child, and some to obstetrician and accountant. I've always been a great supporter of natural child-birth, which involves dealing with pain by controlled breathing and thinking about something else – a process that aided many important births e.g. the SDP (you will notice that I am avoiding any tasteless comments about Labour pains).

Then of course there was Leboyer, who wanted babies delivered in semi-darkness with soft music so that they shouldn't be traumatised. This led to an entire school of surgical thought in which, for example, gall-bladders were removed in the same gentle environment so that they shouldn't become juvenile delinquents and turn to a life of crime. I think it is a testament to the foresight and wisdom of Leboyer that of the thousands of muggers arrested annually in Paris, none have been gall-bladders. Mind you, they started doing circumcisions in the same way, with the semi-darkness and soporific music, and have now produced by Pavlovian conditioning a generation of accountants who get a psychosomatic pain in their privates whenever they go into a supermarket.

However, I digress. The latest fashions in child-birth have been of the underwater school, though personally I was put off any form of underwater life by Hans and Lotte Hass. Anyway, mothers can now produce their offspring underwater and I'm told that many yuppies are now asking to produce their yupplettes under Perrier. Or was it Buck's Fizz? I can't recall. Either way, I'm sure it'll be a vintage year for something. Obstetricians, probably.

Young Husband. 'I CAN'T STAND THIS SUSPENSE ANY LONGER. IT WILL KILL ME.'
Doctor. 'CALM YOURSELF, MY DEAR SIR. I'VE BROUGHT THOUSANDS OF BABIES INTO THE WORLD AND NEVER LOST A FATHER YET.'

BIRTH, ITALIAN STYLE

When I was a medical student, I somehow acquired a reputation for being able to speak Italian. I treated it just as I would have treated a reputation for sexual prowess – I left it alone (not wanting to dispel it altogether) and hoped that it would never be tested. Unfortunately, one day it was tested, weighed in the balance, and found missing.

Our group had been assigned to obstetrics, and were just being introduced to the complexities of the Labour Ward and Delivery Rooms, when the obstetric registrar suddenly rushed up and asked which one of us was the Italian translator. It seemed that a certain Signora Rosalino was well advanced in labour, and no-one knew the Italian for 'the cervix is fully dilated'.

I was whisked down the corridor, and pushed into the Labour Room where la Signora lay in waiting. She was an enormous, placid lady who looked as if her father had been a gigolo and her mother a Guernsey. She was lying on her back, within easy reach of the nitrous oxide pain-killing apparatus, with her legs lifted up and outwards in stirrups. Her position was catastrophically damaging to the modesty, and (doubly lethal) to my naïve sense of social propriety. Despite the fact that I had been taught always to shake hands with my patient at the beginning of any interview, I stared at the ground and got on with some serious blushing.

The registrar said a few comforting things to her in English, and then said since I was here and meant to be learning obstetrics, why didn't I put a surgical glove on, and feel the baby's head. I found a glove, and then very gingerly, I examined the baby's head, trying to remember what I'd been told about deciding what position it was in. Half-way through this, my sense of politesse and rectitude suddenly overcame me, and I came over all coy and embarrassed about doing this to a patient to whom I hadn't even said good morning. Since my right hand was on the baby's head, I was rather handicapped, and

didn't dare to try a left-handed handshake from my position at the nether end, so I compromised, and, waving at her in a rather half-hearted fashion with my free hand, I said 'Ciao!'.

Given the circumstances this was probably a bit too informal. The registrar was quick to point out that this wasn't some kind of cocktail party, or did I think it was, and, if I did, was that the way I usually behaved towards women guests?

I stopped examining the baby's head with a speed which suggested I'd burnt my fingers. It was a very bad start. The registrar said that la Signora was in the second stage of labour, and would I tell her that. I had a bash.

'Nonne le devi disturbare,' I said, 'ma questo e la secundo piano di lavoro, e pronto la bambino va andare la.' ('I don't wish to disturb you, but this is the second storey of a factory, and soon your son she will go there.')

The Signora stared at me, and then took a good long suck at the nitrous oxide. The registrar's patience was wearing thin.

'Tell her the neck of the womb is fully dilated.'

'Right,' I said trying desperately to remember whether neck was 'collo' or 'collino' and whether 'hysterectomy' was a Latin sort of word or not. I chose wrong. 'La collina de la vostra . . . er . . . istero e aperto. Totallmente.' ('The hillock of your hysteria is open. Totally.') She had three more long sucks at the nitrous oxide, and they took advantage of the temporary calm to shove her onto a trolley and wheel her to the Delivery Room.

'The baby's head is coming down quickly, tell her.' I did my best. 'La testa di bambino vieni adeso . . . er . . . down . . . er . . . zu,' rather gave the impression that the head of the baby was coming off rather than down, but my accompanying gestures gave her the general mood of the thing all right.

By now, the midwife had gowned and scrubbed. The Madonna was going to have to push hard, she said, but only when there was a contraction. We both looked in the general direction of these hoped-for contractions. Something happened. I saw a glint of white.

'Tell her to push – now!', the midwife yelled. I panicked, and the last remnants of my Linguaphone deserted me.

"Cut out the jokes, Henderson. Just show her the baby."

'Tirez!' I said, which wasn't Italian for 'push' but French for 'pull'.

The Madonna was in no position to pull anything, least of all the head of her unborn child. The midwife, who, I later found out, was Welsh but had a fluent command of abusive French and a smattering of dermatitis, pointed out my mistake. I said I was awfully sorry but when I was a kid I'd been on the car-train to Rome, and there were all those trilingual instructions everywhere and I'd got confused. Suddenly la Madonna groaned a special groan. The flash of white appeared again. The midwife bellowed 'Tell her to push – push – PUSH!'

I went to pieces. In desperation I roamed my car-train memories and plucked at random.

'Adeso – e pericoloso sporgersi!' At least it was Italian. But it didn't really mean 'push', it was more a sort of warning about the dangers of leaning out. At this dire forecast, la Signora stopped pushing and stared at me with eyes on stalks. There she was busy shelling out a *piccolino Rosalino*, and this goddam medical student was shouting at *il bambino* not to lean out. Was this the Welfare State she'd heard so much about in the Old Country?

The registrar had returned from his quiet fag and now asked, somewhat rudely, what the coitus was going on here, the baby should have been out hours ago. He had a look, and said that it would need a lift-out – a minor procedure in which obstetric forceps would be applied to the baby's head.

He scrubbed and picked up the forceps. I pointed at him.

'La forcipessa,' I explained.

If this meant anything, it meant that the registrar was the strongest of all, and that he was actually a she. La Madonna *no comprendata*.

'Questo,' I said, touching the forceps which were unfortunately sterile and thus had to be replaced *subito*, 'questo e por la testa di bambino.'

Madonna Rosalino sobbed as if I'd just told her that the baby would only walk with his head in calipers.

The *forcipessas* went on. The baby's head leant out, and the rest of the baby followed. There was an incredibly loud lusty cry, which, I remember, surprised me by not sounding in the least bit Italian. Madonna Rosalino burst into floods of tears and hugged everyone. I hugged her back, since it was a fairly emotional experience for me too.

'Auguri,' I said to the proud mother. ('Congratulations') and then, turning to the bawling baby boy (a fine boy – even *I* could spot that) I tried to say Happy Birthday. I actually wished him Joyous New Year, but by that time nobody gave a stuff what I said.

Robert Buckman 24.11.1976

'Sixty thousand pounds' worth of scientific research and you thought we were going to let you take the baby home?'

Harpur:

PREGNANT PAUSE

'I wonder how long it will be before we can start
testing its IQ?'

'I think I felt it kick just then —
don't say it's going to grow up to be
a policeman.'

'Darling, from now on I shall be drinking for two.'

'I wanted to go back to work
afterwards, but they'd found a
job-minder.'

'Jennifer's taking a **suspiciously** long time discarding last year's pregnant look . . .'

'He focused!'

'Just think — one day whoever's in there will be scorning all my little jokes.'

'What — just pick it up and walk out? That can't be right.'

THE SECRET DONORS

Leer at us, mock us; use us; but do not quite forget,
For we are the donors of England, who haven't made it yet.
There is many a doting mother with a baby on her knee,
Who wouldn't be changing nappies if it weren't for AID.
There is many a sturdy student who's prepared to be a dad,
And many more who'd do it if the wages weren't so bad.
You look at us and wonder why we are so upset:
We are the young do-gooders, and we haven't done it yet.
We hear indignant voices saying our offence is rank,
But by and large it's just the same as going to the bank,
The only difference being the odd pictures on the wall,
And thumbing through the dirty mags before we give our all.
There's little satisfaction and the money is hard-earned;
It's good to be of service, but you can't help feeling spurned.
For we are the donors of England, and we have one regret:
It's hell to mate with women that you haven't even met.

Roger Woddis 7.3.1979

ABORTION

There was once a man who was a failed abortion.

His mother, a Moslem, had been delivered of a second son only two months before she learnt of the impending arrival of another child. She had no need of a third son. She was twenty-six, and her marriage contract had already been fulfilled.

Thus, when two months pregnant, she went on a holiday to Cairo, and spent a fortnight climbing the pyramids, in the hope that the strain might rid her of the unwanted passenger she carried in her womb. This having failed, she spent some three weeks riding from dawn to dusk. She drank gin (the very rich Moslems being above their normal religious laws) and threw herself downstairs. Finally, she appealed to her husband. He sent her to Switzerland for an abortion.

This too failed, and after a further six months, she was delivered of a healthy boy.

Six years later, she tried to have another baby, and suffered a miscarriage.

As soon as the boy was old enough to understand, she explained what the position had been before his birth, for fear he might hear it from one of the servants on the estate, and see it in the wrong light. With a great depth of understanding for one so young, he accepted her explanation and tried to understand her motives, giving thanks to Allah that the operation had not been successful.

Then a friend of his mother's went to Switzerland for a similar operation, which succeeded. Then another, and another. His aunt snuffed out an unwanted life in this way. All around him, the unborn were being slain.

This set him on a curious course of thought. If such an operation was successful so often, why was it that it had not been successful in his case? He remembered the story of Clive of India, who tried to kill himself when young; if he pointed the pistol at his head, it refused to fire. When he turned it away, it exploded. In his later years, Clive always took this to mean that God, in his infinite wisdom, had some plan in store for him, and did not choose to let him die then.

From this first spark, the thought of Divine influence in his life began to obsess him. Starting first as a flickering thought, it began to grow until it filled his every waking moment, and

obsessed every second of his spared life. He looked upon himself as blessed by Allah. He would pray three times a day: 'Praise be to Allah, amen and amen.'

He regarded every second of his life as precious, and ceased to regard time as a continuous stream, but took it instead as a series of different units, made up of small happenings: the time it took to strike a match and watch it flicker out, the sound of a bird flying overhead, even the time it took to breathe in and then out again, none of these seemed to be linked any more, each was a totally separate event, and he hated to lose grip of any of them.

He treated all others as if they were below him. He had a servant beaten because her child stole one of his toys. It was a clockwork fire engine, and he had many such, but this did not worry him.

He was spoilt and intolerant. His family was descended from royalty and royalty often visited his parents. He would play with their children. They had much in common, he decided.

His parents owned the local school – they had paid for it to be built, it was theirs. He found nothing strange in wandering from room to room when he should have been working, and refusing to play with the other children.

For who would try to stop him?

Suddenly, when he was nine, his family had to move from India to Europe, and then to Britain, because of a sudden, unfavourable change of government. They settled in a small town on the south coast, the three sons were sent to the best schools in the country, and all was well.

He had been at his school for only a few weeks when it became apparent to him that things were very different from India. Cries of 'Wog', 'Nigger', and 'Coon' soon persuaded him that here he was not regarded as one of Allah's chosen. He settled down, and hoped that the remarks would grow less as time passed.

Seven years later, as he approached his GCE's, they were as strong as they had ever been, though now more sophisticated, yet cruder.

For his career, he had chosen the profession of lawyer, ostensibly, but meant this to be only a training ground for the mission that he was sure was his. He intended to bribe his way into the Indian parliament (such things are very easy, even today) with his father's money and influence, then rise to become the Prime Minister of the Indian sub-continent, and as the youngest leader ever, he would lead his country out of their ignorance and poverty into the shores of light.

He failed all his GCE's but one, and was forced to stay down an extra year to retake them all. Shocked and embarrassed, he crammed hard for three months, and retook them all the following November. Miraculously, he passed. God was with him again. The ways of Allah, he decided, were strange.

He rarely shone at work in school, nor in any extra-curricular activity. He was Pindarus in *Julius Caesar*, and played briefly in the third XV. But as he considered 'show-business' to be of little consequence, and thought all sportsmen were morons, this bothered him little. He had no loyalty to anyone, considered himself to be above such petty matters, stirred up trouble among his friends, and was universally regarded as unreliable and deceitful.

He failed to get into either Oxford or Cambridge, and had to be satisfied with a lesser university. He consoled himself with the fact that any English education held great weight abroad.

He read Sartre and became very bitter. It seemed as if God had deserted him. Where was the mission for which he had been intended? He stopped praying to Allah three times a day. He began to resent the non-presence of God. Why had he not taken more interest in this life he had saved? Where was he now?

While running up the stairs of his digs, he felt a strange pain down one side of his body. He forced himself to ignore it; he could not afford private treatment, and would not submit himself to the National Health.

He was finally admitted to hospital on the insistence of his trainee sales manageress girlfriend.

He grew weaker and weaker, and was visited by his father, mother, and a Moslem priest who convinced him that his illness was a direct result of his abandoning God.

'I have not abandoned Him!' he screamed, furious, 'He has abandoned me!'

But the priest told him to repent and be readmitted.

The disease he suffered from was a rare one, picked up in his home country; its incubation period was lengthy. It had taken four years to become apparent after a trip back in his A-level

year. The doctor thought he was unlikely to survive.

He readmitted himself to the Faith and made a miraculous recovery against all odds. Once more, he regarded himself as one of God's chosen. He read the Koran again, and prayed three times daily.

He remained in hospital for further observation. Walking on the verandah of his private room, paid for by his father, he felt a pain in his side, and suffered a relapse. He called for the nurse, and she burst into his room as he fell to the floor outside on the balcony. She rang for the doctor and pulled him back to his bed.

He heard the doctor tell his father that this time there would be no miraculous recovery. He would not believe it. From his bed he cried:

'No! No! Allah has some plan for me, He saved me twice, He will not take me so lightly now.'

That night he died.

Afterwards, someone conducted a post mortem. Inside his body, a certain kind of bacteria was found and isolated for the first time. A serum was prepared from it, and flown to India, which was suffering from an epidemic at the time.

Such are the ways of Allah. Praise be to Allah. Amen and amen.

Bruce Jones 2.7.1980

A SNIP AT THE PRICE!

I drove.

The last time we were here, the contractions had been deceptively mild and she never made the actual delivery room, giving birth instead on a handy bed along the way. We were lucky that the little sod didn't pop out as we were screeching down the road past the newsagent, forcing me to knock the poor man up and ask if he'd got any back-numbers of *Nursing Times* that would help me with the do-it-yourself maternity wing in the back seat.

This time, we were easily keeping our

appointment with the forces of life and, in a way, of death. She took my arm and guided me over the pelican crossing, through the maze of hospital buildings and in at the correct door. It was too late to back down now. I'd never find my way to the car.

It must be awful doing this unaccompanied, being half of a couple in which the chauvinist partner stays at home, or, worse, finding oneself in a single-parent situation without a permanently meaningful relationship for that particular week. Especially when you forget the porter's directions, the kind of thing I do under stress. She remembered them perfectly, leaving me to point out sights of interest along the way, such as signs to *Diabetic Foot Clinic*, surely a mistake there?

'There's a mistake there,' I said. 'Look, it says, "Ante-natal clinic". It should say, "Anti-natal clinic", meaning "Against birth", not "before birth". We did say we wanted a vasectomy, didn't we?'

'We're here,' she said. 'Give your card to the nice lady in the white coat.'

I didn't have to be here, of course. Marie Stopes had been in charge of our personal birth control campaign long ago, before the child-rearing years. The last contact I had with them was a free offer: they were trying out a new male contraceptive and would I like to go round for a fitting? Sadly, we were just at that point in paying off the mortgage when the stork says you can start a family, and had to decline.

So when we decided that, in terms of children, three's a crowd, and that a vasectomy was the best way to keep the numbers down, I rang the nearest Marie Stopes clinic to see if they had any special offers that week. Clearly I had missed my chance a decade ago. No bargains available, but a flat rate of £59, thousands of satisfied customers can't be wrong, telephone bookings accepted. It was certainly a bargain compared with the Wellington Hospital in North-West London, where they asked me, 'Are you covered by insurance?' and went on to answer their own question with, 'Oh no, you wouldn't be.' No, you wouldn't, not for a vasectomy. 'Let's see, a twin room would be £110 a night.' That's before the surgeon starts making out his bill.

Why twin beds – one for me and one for what

they take out, father and Vas Deferens doing well? Why overnight, anyway?

'We have a Day Centre in Harley Street where you can rest for four hours.'

The switchboard there seemed to be resting as well, so I tried the London Clinic instead, to learn that 'There is no price list.' Not as such, but there is in fact a price, obtained by approaching surgeons individually. '£250. We can do it at the Wellington Day Centre.' Nonsense, they'd never answer the phone to take the booking.

For £250 I could buy a brand-new racing cycle, fit it with one of those knife-edge saddles and do the job myself in commuting to work. What am I saying – *two* bikes, and still have change left over for Marie Stopes. Or I could save the entire sum by roughing it on the National Health Service.

Exactly how rough the NHS was, I had no idea. I patronise a homeopath who hands out essences of herbs plucked at midnight when the moon is right, so the state's medical practices are, or were, a totally unknown quantity. The full truth hit me as soon as I looked around from the comfort of the waiting-room chair to which my wife and the lady in white had shepherded me. I began to see why people turn in desperation to the rival establishments of the London and Wellington.

The copy of *Woman's Own* on the table beside me was ten whole days old.

I was just composing a sharp letter of complaint to the regional health authority – 'Sir, It is not for this that I pay my taxes, or would pay them if I got round to submitting my accounts' – when I was ushered off down another corridor by another white-coated angel of mercy, who asked me if this was my first visit. I was about to snap that I had only got the one set of equipment, when I recalled that King's College Hospital also does teeth, appendices, babies, ears, noses, throats and other trifles; and I also recalled that one man in a thousand (and I've always thought of myself, when no one's listening, as a man in a thousand) has an extra pair of the relevant tubes.

We sat down. My gaze dropped – it kept doing this – below waist height and I noticed with approval the cut of my trousers. They were new jeans, complementing the bold red shirt and open-toed sandals. I didn't want to look too effete in case the hospital decided that the operation was a waste of time, so there was more than a hint of lumberjack about the ensemble. My wife, in this context, was also part of the macho look.

'I had a letter from Naomi today,' said that part of the ensemble. 'She wishes you the best of luck with your op.'

'Do I need it?' I asked.

'She says her GP, who's six-foot-two-inches and ex-Captain of the English rugby team, has also had it, and he swears by it.'

'What about her husband?' I asked.

'Oh no. He declares it would make him impotent. He's Greek, you know.'

'Wait a minute,' I said, in some alarm, 'what's that got to . . .'

'Mr Sale?' It was a nurse. It shouldn't have made any difference, but I was somehow comforted by the fact of it being a male nurse. I knew he'd be familiar with the process of shaving, for a start, which he employed, once I'd hung up the lumberjack gear in a cubicle, on the undergrowth that was obscuring the view. I'd cropped some of it down that morning, but when you grow a beard you forget how to shave the chin, let alone the nether regions. He was the Vidal Sassoon of the private parts, flipping up the left testicle, racing over its environs with the razor, flipping up the right testicle, zooming under that.

'You haven't changed your mind?' The surgeon had come in and was leaning over my horizontal and clean-shaven form.

I thought: Of course, I didn't have to be here. I possessed, did I not, a copy of *The Tao of Love and Sex – The Ancient Chinese Way to Ecstasy*. This volume is full of symbolism such as blacksmith's hammers and jade gates but the basic thrust, if that's the word, is that contraception can consist of the blacksmith learning to turn off the tap (to mix symbols). There's a lot of fun in *The Tao*, but I'd feel no happier than with the Pope's recommendation to play Vatican Roulette.

He was much bigger than I, clearly a member of the front row of the scrum in the hospital's team, and he was leaning over me in a possessive sort of way, so I denied any change of mind.

'Have you had any dental work?' he asked, which seemed a strange question in the circumstances.

'My mouth is ninety per cent lead,' I replied.

'Good,' he said, 'then you will be used to local anaesthetics,' and he gave me one, though not in the gums. The two of them seemed to be making a bit of a meal of it, in my humble, non-medical opinion. All that fussing about with implements and muttering to each other, just for a local anaesthetic. What on earth would it be like when they got round to snipping the tube itself? The surgeon straightened up.

'That's one side,' he said briskly.

Unbelievable – we had already reached the halftime score of one-nil! Vasectomy was certainly a whole lot simpler than following the instructions in *A Co-operative Method of Natural Birth Control* by Margaret Nofziger which has you, or rather your wife, using thermometers and drawing diagrams. 'Don't make love until you have recorded three consecutive temperatures of $0.4°F$ ($0.2°C$) higher than your temperatures for the six days previous to the rise.'

Ms Nofziger's scheme is not, alas, as simple as that: 'You can cancel one high temperature from the six temperatures previous to the rise.' NB: 'Do not cancel if more than one temp is at that level.' In an ideal world, my wife would start the day with a thermometer sticking out of her mouth. In a slightly less than ideal world, I was lying on the operating table with the two of them shifting around for action stations on the other side.

Which side it was, I cannot now remember, but medical readers of this book will know instantly, as it is the side where the tubes are harder to find and more painful to inject. Fingers prodded a bit to the North and a fraction to the West of my geography. They were followed by the needle. Which was followed by the scalpel.

'I felt that,' I remarked, I did, too. I couldn't see it, since I myself was in the way, but I could feel it. It was the opposite of those operations on television, and in this case I couldn't change channel.

The surgeon screeched to a halt and topped up the tank of anaesthetic. Waiting for it to get me in its icy grip, we discussed the merits of branded (expensive) as against unbranded (cheaper) drugs being prescribed by doctors. A friend of mine on the *Guardian* can marshal all the arguments on the subject, but then he does not write his news stories when lying on his back with his privates under the knife. My summary did not do him justice.

The surgeon was better briefed, and the subject took us through the rest of the operation and indeed lasted such a time afterwards that my wife was beginning to wonder if something had gone terribly wrong (Leg Taken Off In Vasectomy Op Shock Horror). Finally we turned instead to sex, which, I was advised, was not a good idea for a bit and certainly did not feel like a good idea at that moment.

'I have to warn you,' said the doctor, 'because we had one chap who must have leapt straight into bed with his wife after his vasectomy and then had it off four times in five days, which led to complications. "I felt amorous," was his excuse.'

He should have stuck to his Margaret Nofziger: 'Ovulation will cause a rise of about 6/10th of one degree or six lines on your graph.' All that is behind me now, thank God, just as soon as the laboratory okays my specimens (to be presented in a couple of tiny plastic pots, like the ones containing marmalade in hotels).

She was waiting outside and offered congratulations. I would have preferred something more akin to what she had received at her births: flowers, cards, grapes, chocolates, health visitors. Still, she was very sympathetic, taking my arm and guiding me back to the car.

She drove.

Jonathan Sale November 1983

2

What's Up, Doc?

WHAT'S UP, DOC?

Heart attacks appear to have some mysterious link with fluctuations in the earth's magnetic field, according to an analysis published in the august scientific journal 'Nature'.

Guardian

'It's probably nothing at all,' I said, walking in. 'Slight nausea, bit of a temperature, it wouldn't surprise me if there were a lot of it about, as a matter of fact I really shouldn't be taking up your time, I'll be off now, it was nice talking to . . .'

'Sit down,' said my doctor, not looking up from his hurried jotting. He flicked the pages of an old leather-bound book. Motes eddied up, warmed themselves in the shaft of anglepoise.

I cleared my throat, played with my hat, stared at his stuffed alligator.

'Nothing at all, eh?' he repeated at last. He threw down his pen, picked up something brown and shrivelled with his callipers. 'Know what that is?'

I shook my head.

'It's a newt,' he said. 'Or, in precise medical terms, an ewt. I've just been looking it up in Galen. It's essential to have the exact timing for the legs, you know.'

'Is it?' I said.

'Absolutely. When they begin to curl. I had a patient once, she'd miscarried three times on the trot, I couldn't for the life of me understand why. Then it turned out she'd put the newt under her hat the wrong way round.'

'I don't see what that has to do with me,' I said. 'I'm not pregnant.'

He took off his glasses.

'It was merely a cautionary example,' he said. 'It was the confidence with which you said *Nothing at all.* I wonder, can you tell me the time of today's high tide at London Bridge?'

I shook my head.

'And yet you're prepared to say that your condition is trivial! Don't you realise that most ulcers are caused by the Moon?'

'I hadn't,' I replied, 'no.'

He sighed.

'I'll try to put it in layman's terms,' he said. 'Moon comes up, tide goes out, black bile reacts adversely with phlegm, result: ulcers. You're the seventh this morning. It's these phenomenally high tides due to melting ice, plus, of course, Krakatoa.'

'I'm sorry?'

'It's the ninety-sixth anniversary of the eruption. Ninety-six is a mystic number, if you're Sumatran. The sea remembers.'

'I'd never realised.'

'There's quite a good paper on it in this week's BMJ,' he said. 'Every year, on the anniversary, the world's sea-level rises metaphorically. This year, of course, it's phenomenal: if it weren't metaphorical, all you'd see of London would be the top three floors of the Millbank tower. It's a major duodenal crisis. I've gone on a milk pudding diet myself, and I'm not even an Aquarian.'

'I don't think mine's an ulcer,' I said. 'More of a headache, really.'

He took out my card from his file.

'You live up there,' he said, nodding. 'I'd forgotten. There's an old tin seam running under your place. Very substantial deposits, the hazel twig jumps right out of your hands if you don't watch it. Yes, that'll be it, tin.'

'You mean it's polluting the water?'

He looked at me.

'What? Didn't they teach you *anything?*' He barked a hollow laugh, and his cat jumped out of the sink, hackles fanning. 'If the tin combined with the water, my friend, you'd know it soon enough!'

'Really?'

'There'd be throats cut all over. It brings on melancholy, tin and water. I mean, the body's only got four humours to play with, start mucking about with tin and water, there'd be hell to pay. There was a bad outbreak in Rochdale last summer, it defied the best medical brains in Europe. Tried everything: burning dead mice at midnight, sticking on dung poultices, appeasing the bats with garlic, but did it work? Did it buggery! Eventually there was nothing for it, we had to hang the Pope in effigy, cleared it up in no time, but it didn't half put people's backs up. No, *your* tin problem is basically one of astral disturbance. It's electrical. I'd like you to see a good comet man.'

THE PREVAILING EPIDEMIC.

'AH! YOU MAY LAUGH, MY BOY; BUT IT'S NO JOKE BEING FUNNY WITH THE INFLUENZA.'

I looked at my watch.

'I'm afraid I've got an appointment at –'

'No problem, it so happens there's probably the country's foremost comet authority upstairs, consultant at the Middlesex.' He punched his intercom. 'Could you ask Dr Simms-Dalston to pop down here for a moment, if he's free?'

After a minute or two, the door opened, and a small man in a chalk-stripe suit came in. He was carrying an old leather globe, and a dead dog. He walked all round me slowly; he shook the dog a couple of times.

'It's not comets,' he said.

'Really?' said my GP.

'Feel his head,' said the consultant. 'I'd stake my reputation he's got no Bump of Syriax to speak of. His sort never goes down with comets. Anyway, no bishops have died this week.'

'Bishops?' I enquired.

'During exceptional cometary activity,' said the consultant, tapping the globe with his dog, 'bishops die, murrain suddenly increases, and you get sterility in pike. There's been nothing like that in North London for months.' He turned to my doctor. 'I suppose you were thinking of the tin seam?'

'The patient complained of nausea and fever, and has large cuticles,' said my doctor, 'and the cat's been funny ever since he walked in.'

The consultant sucked his teeth, walked to a corner of the surgery, beckoned my doctor across, and began murmuring. They glanced towards me once or twice.

'I'd like to dangle this lodestone over you,' said my doctor finally. 'It won't hurt.'

'Take your shoes and socks off,' said the consultant.

He got down on all fours to examine my feet, as the lodestone swung above me. After a couple of minutes, he stood up again.

'I think he ought to see a demonologist,' he said. 'They're not cloven yet, but my watch has stopped. What's the lodestone doing?'

'Not much,' said my GP. He rolled up the snakeskin thong, and put it away. 'Dr Simms-Dalston thinks you might be turning into a devil,' he said to me, 'but I don't want you to say anything to your wife until we've tried dipping a bee in your saliva.'

'You mean it could be serious?' I said.

Dr Simms-Dalston shrugged.

'It might be no more than a case of simple possession,' he said, 'in which case your best bet would probably be a good bone-man.'

'An orthopaedic surgeon, do you mean,' I said, 'or an osteopath?'

'He doesn't listen, does he?' said Dr Simms-Dalston.

'Dr Simms-Dalston said a bone-man,' snapped my doctor. 'He'll shake a few lizard ribs onto the carpet, piddle on them, throw your hat out of the window, you could be right as rain in a day or two.'

'I've just thought,' said Dr Simms-Dalston, 'it's not a leap year, is it?'

'No,' replied my doctor. 'But there could be unusual sunspot activity.'

'Irrelevant,' said the specialist, waving a dismissive hand. 'It's not as if it was his liver.'

'Quite.'

'Not that there hasn't been a lot of liver disorder recently,' said Dr Simms-Dalston, 'what with the Gulf Stream changing course.'

'Really?' enquired my doctor keenly.

'It's fairly serious. My spirit guide has been suggesting I put a sockful of rice under my arm and walk backwards for a bit,' said Dr Simms-Dalston, 'especially since if you multiply my birth-date by the circumference of my thigh, you come up with the exact height of the Great Pyramid.'

'My dear chap!' exclaimed my GP sympathetically. 'I'd no idea.'

'I can live with it,' murmured the specialist.

'What about *me?*' I cried. 'Suppose it's more serious than you think? I mean, what if I wake up one morning and my feet really are . . .'

Dr Simms-Dalston shook his head, pursed his thin lips.

'There is a strong body of professional opinion,' he said, 'which would insist upon immersing you totally in a duckpond for up to three hours, isn't there, Dr Nabley?'

'True, true,' said my doctor. 'Of course, it depends.'

'On what?' I said.

Dr Simms-Dalston smiled. He took off his glasses and wiped them on the dog.

'Were you thinking of going privately?' he said.

Alan Coren 7.3.1979

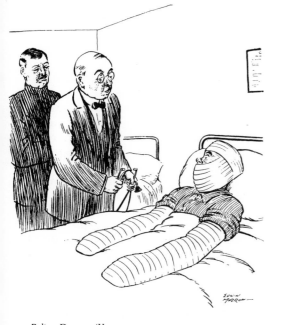

Police Doctor. 'YES, MY MAN, YOU FELL FROM THE
FOURTH FLOOR, AND I MAY AS WELL TELL YOU THAT YOU'LL BE
NO USE AS A CAT BURGLAR AGAIN.'
Patient. 'CAN'T YOU PATCH ME UP SO THAT I'LL BE ALL
RIGHT FOR GROUND-FLOORS AND BASEMENTS?'

Doctor (to lady recovering from a sprained wrist). 'WELL,
NOW, WHAT CAN YOU DO WITH IT?'
Lady. 'I CAN JUST RAISE 'ARF-A-PINT TO ME LIPS, DOCTOR, IF I
STOOPS ME 'EAD.'

Lady (who has brought her boy to the hospital). 'IT'S 'IS 'EAD,
NURSE. 'E'S 'AD IT OFF AND ON EVER SINCE 'E WAS BORN.'

DOC BRIEF

Robert Buckman on
ALLERGIES

ALLERGIES

Allergies are abnormal reactions to substances that are not normally caustic. Thus you can't call it an allergy if the substance causes irritation or inflammation to everybody e.g. sulphuric acid, rush hour, Nicholas Parsons &c. And of course there are substances which are too simple at a molecular level or too bland to cause any reaction e.g. water, tapioca, Cliff Michelmore &c. In between are the materials that cause reactions in some people and not in others and which may – as we shall see – be the cause of itching, crying, sneezing, migraine and diarrhoea or all of these (e.g. Benny Hill). However, the word 'allergy' is used very loosely by many people who really mean that they have a phobia ('I'm allergic to Thursdays'), although the difference can become academic. For example, some people are so phobic about work in any form that they become genuinely ill when confronted with any type of work, occupation or gainful employment. Such people cannot be cured by anti-allergic medicines or tablets, and have to be given a job in television.

SKIN ALLERGIES

A skin allergy is called 'eczema' if it occurs on elbows, ears, knees or Bank Holidays, and is called 'dermatitis' if it occurs on a private patient. Skin allergies can be caused by contact with rubber (e.g. gloves and tyres, particularly if run over by a lorry), with nickel (e.g. 'copper' coins, or suspenders if you're lucky), with gold (but who cares) and with funguses and mosses (e.g. Gray's allergy in a country churchyard). Skin reacts to allergic stimulation by becoming inflamed and itchy and this initiates the reflex of scratching which makes the inflammation and itching worse. Nature presumably justifies this on the grounds of productivity. Doctors can tell which substances are causing the allergy by 'patch testing', in which pieces of the suspected material are kept in prolonged contact with the skin, a handy thing to remember if you're ever caught wearing ladies' suspender belts in your hat. Another important thing to remember is that skin allergies can develop after years of trouble-free use of the allergen. One patient of mine developed a multiple allergy after ten years to mascara, lipstick, blusher, toner and hair lacquer and it got so bad he had to resign his job at the Foreign Office.

FOOD ALLERGIES

Many people claim to be allergic to various foods, additives or colourings used in modern restaurants, but immunologists from Carlisle have found that only one in ten of these is genuine. The other nine just want to get out of paying for their share of the meal. The problem is that genuine food allergies can produce many different symptoms, and sufferers claim that food allergies are the cause of their diarrhoea, stomach pains, headaches, depression, parking offences, minor embezzling and break dancing. The commonest foods associated with genuine allergies are peanuts, shellfish, strawberries and monosodium glutamate ('Chinese restaurant headache'). Interestingly, about 10% of the giant man-eating clams of the Amazon get a headache and rash after eating Chinamen, although none of them is hungry an hour later. I would advise caution before pleading a food allergy as the cause of behavioural problems. My friend Trevor was arrested in Mexico for being drunk and disorderly, and claimed that it was an

'It's all right – he's cancelled his coronary.'

HEART-ATTACK ROTA

allergic reaction to the Maraschino cherries in his pina coladas. The arresting officer beat the hell out of him and then blamed the violence on a hypersensitive reaction to his chewing-gum.

HAY FEVER

Hay fever is an allergy to pollen and, to put it simply, pollen is what happens when grass wishes to have babies. Hay fever results from raiding-parties of pollen landing on the beach-heads of your nostrils, despite withering fire from air support i.e. sneezes. When you think of how most plant seeds can grow in very adverse and hostile environments e.g. Dalston, you realise that sneezing serves a purpose i.e. if it weren't for hay fever we'd all have dandelions growing up our noses. Since pollen grains are very small relative to noses, the best treatment is to prevent contact between pollen and nostril. Nowadays, this can be done in several simple ways e.g. wearing a gas-mask or living in a submarine. I was once told that in the 18th century people sometimes had their nostrils bricked in, but maybe this wasn't to cure hay fever but to avoid the dreaded nostril tax, I can't remember. Anyway, that's where we get the phrase still used to this day, particularly by allergologists in Harley Street, 'Hay fever sufferers pay through the nose.'

THE DOCTOR ANSWERS YOUR QUESTIONS

Q: My legs keep on 'going to sleep' – what can I do?
A: Try an 'alarm clock' in your socks.

NEXT PSEUDOPATIENT, PLEASE!

'Eight perfectly normal people, by shamming symptoms of a mild kind, successfully gained admission to psychiatric wards where they remained undetected for as long as they could stand it. Once admitted, the pseudopatients' behaviour was normal in every way, but doctors and nurses continued to treat them as disturbed.'

The Observer

'Brien is engaged in writing-behaviour again,' observed the nurse fondly, looking over my shoulder as I typed the last words of my *Punch* article. I pretended not to hear.

'Possibly some hysterical deafness too,' mused the doctor, applying a match to my first page and lighting his pipe.

'Get stuffed,' I said, picking up a new sheet and beginning again. The doctor and nurse looked at each other with delight.

'Negative therapeutic reaction,' cried the doctor, slapping his hands together and dropping ash into my typewriter.

'Resentment against imagined threat to need-satisfying object,' added the nurse. 'Primary, or even secondary, narcissism leading possibly to solipsism: that is, a tendency to use oneself as a point of reference round which experience is organised.'

'Stekel speaks of it,' agreed the doctor. 'Did any other analyst ever tell you that you look pretty when you're bending over a patient?'

'You remind me of my father,' she confessed. And they wandered off, lovingly entwined.

Old Mrs A. trapped in that collapsed armchair again, waving her sticks in the air like a praying mantis. I put my hands under her elbows and helped her to her feet.

'You're no patient,' she said. 'I bet you're a journalist, or an undercover psychologist, checking up on the hospital. Are Curtis Brown still the best agents? I need some advice on my VAT.'

Before I could answer, two nurses had seized me and pinioned my arms behind my back. I was frog-marched into the doctor's office.

His face darkened as he heard their report. 'Compulsive gerontophilia now,' he muttered. 'I might make my name from this case.' He practised his signature for a while on the blotter until the flush in his cheeks had subsided.

'Characteristic revelation of suppressed Oedipal desires. Has it never seemed strange to you that you only offer assistance to members of the opposite sex old enough to be your mother? And never to members of the same sex young enough to be your son?'

He made a note. 'Have you ever been treated for latent homosexuality probably as a defence against paranoid anxiety?'

'I've always been interested in women,' I replied sullenly. 'You ask my wives.'

'Ha, Ha,' he crowed at dictation speed. 'The Casanova delusion. An unmistakeable clinical symptom of false-Don Juanism as a screen for unacceptable pederastic impulses. Double the bromide in his tea, sew up his trouser pockets and no television after 9.30 at night.'

I cut myself shaving this morning. I was just sucking the blood from my finger when the nurse appeared, without knocking as usual.

'Incipient vampirism,' she screeched. 'You are a phenomenon hitherto unknown to the science of abnormal psychology.'

'Oral sadism,' corrected the doctor, giving her an admonitory nip. 'Has the patient always displayed such an excessive growth of facial hair?'

'It is already fully covered in his record,' she replied rather tetchily, rubbing her rump. 'I hazarded a guess there that it is was a form of displacement upwards – a socially acceptable type of exhibitionism representing the pubic area.'

'Go and wash your mouth out,' he ordered. 'I'm the only one around here allowed to talk dirty in long words.'

She grovelled at his feet. 'Kick me, doctor. Please.'

He stepped over her. 'No,' he said, after a pause. 'You would only enjoy it.'

I was piling up my loose change on top of my locker last night when the doctor entered, without knocking as usual.

'What do those objects represent to you?' he demanded.

'Penury,' I replied.

'Ah. Ha,' he explained, and the nurse took the comment down in shorthand on her cuff. 'Pen, you see, is penis. Ury, you see, is urine. Money is anal satisfaction.'

'Coins are simply tokens of exchange useful for buying small comforts,' I argued.

'Worse than I thought,' he said to the nurse. 'Reification or the process of treating concepts as though they were things. But nothing would persuade you to give me those coins for a piece of paper, now would it, whatever amount was written on the paper?'

After some argument, I handed over 37 and a half pence for his cheque for £5. 'Masochistic desire for self-deprivation,' he suggested, looking not entirely pleased, I thought, with the bargain.

I only hope the bank will accept the signature 'Adolf Freud Jnr'.

The rest of the inmates are growing rather unfriendly, even Mrs A., who accuses me of having lost the manuscript of her novel, because I am monopolising the attentions of the staff. Not one believes that I am anything other than a spy.

The doctor, who has now dressed his favourite nurse in see-through plus-fours and leads her by a chain round her neck, remains convinced that I am the greatest discovery since the Rorschach Test.

In the last week, I have been identified as suffering from zoophilia because I was observed stroking the cat, of transvestism because I wear a nightshirt, of auto-eroticism because I pick my teeth, of anorexia because I refuse to eat corn-flakes, of dromomania because I go for a long walk in the evenings, of a castration complex because I hate the dentist, of deep inferiority feelings because I do not admit to feeling inadequate and conversely of megalomania because I do not claim to be always right. The diagnosis of my behaviour contains a built-in Catch 22 – either each act is in itself a clear example of mental unbalance, or it is a cover for another form of mental unbalance, probably even more severe and dangerous because concealed.

This morning I told him I was Enoch Powell. He looked disappointed. 'I'm afraid he's recovering,' he said to the nurse. 'We'll have to let him go.'

Alan Brien 31.1.1973

*'You've got to help me, doctor – I tell you
I'm desperate!'*

'Say XCIX'

'Like I always say . . . if you've got it, flaunt it.'

*'It's that deathly pallor of his that worries me . . . we're either going to
have to move him or redecorate the room . . .'*

DOC BRIEF
Robert Buckman on
FEET

VERRUCAS

Verrucas are basically the same thing as warts except that they occur on the soles of the feet and have a more up-market yuppy feel to them, which is why they are known in private dermatology clinics as 'designer warts'.

Verrucas have been known for thousands of years and were mentioned in the Bible, most notably in the Epistle of Paul the Apostle to the Chiropodists. Although the famous alternative reading mentioned in Huckstable's commentary ('. . . so BE ye clean at every hour of every day [lest] there shall be a small affliction of your sole [which] shall be with you always, and shall be visited upon those that you love, yea, and upon those that shall bathe with you, and share your [towel] also . . .') was probably a mis-translation by the Middle German Bible-scholar, Dr Scholl.

Nowadays, we know that verrucas (or more correctly *verrucae*) are not of divine origin, but are caused by the same virus that causes warts. For this reason, the Americans call verrucas 'plantar warts', which is often corrupted to 'Planter's warts'. This explains why some Americans have the impression that verrucas are transmitted in tins of peanuts and are inclined to behave fussily at cocktail parties, while others simply believe that the best verrucas are dry-roasted.

Here in the United Kingdom, due to the high level of public medical education (something in which I myself have played no small part), most people know that verrucas are caused by swimming-pools or sitting on radiators, and that they can be cured by washing in a silver bowl at midnight at a cross-roads under the gallows of a man recently hanged for doubting the recovery of our economy.

ATHLETE'S FOOT

Athlete's foot is another of those famous medical misnomers, in that it is not limited to athletes or to feet, although it probably wouldn't have been so popular if it had been named more honestly as 'anybody's anything'.

As I have mentioned before, there is a considerable cachet in 'specialist' conditions such as 'tennis elbow', 'golfer's knee', 'polo neck', 'Finian's rainbow' etc, and there are many people who have an entirely sedentary life-style who are quite proud to have contracted something to do with athletics, albeit the only thing they have in common with athletes is the smell of their socks.

Anyway, the thing about athlete's foot is that it is simply an infection with a particular species of fungus called a yeast. Now this is not the same kind of yeast that is used in making bread or fermenting alcohol, so don't run away with the idea that any material associated with athlete's foot can be used for making sandwiches or for home-brewing. THIS COULD CAUSE PERMANENT DAMAGE TO YOUR TASTEBUDS AND FRIENDS.

To put it simply, there are thousands of different kinds of yeasts. Some make simple Beaujolais, some make Château La Tour, some make bread and some just rot your toes. And of course, the same applies to the French people. Actually, yeasts are even more specialised than the French (and a lot less bureaucratic, too) and there are some yeasts that will only infect certain areas of the body, to whit, the embarrassing areas that we sometimes call 'the groins' although everyone knows that we mean the sensitive equipment which is stored nearby. The yeast that specialises in this infection is called *Tinea cruris*, but it hasn't got a popular name, simply because the medical profession couldn't decide between 'gigolo's groin' and 'brothel-creeper's crutch'. They tried a compromise eponym ('sexual athlete's foot only higher up') but it was rejected because doctors couldn't fit it in the space on the sick certificate.

BUNIONS

Bunions are completely different. Mainly because they mostly affect women. Bunions are a deformity of the joint at the base of the big toe, caused by wearing pointy shoes in an attempt to pretend that the feet are pointy. I have never understood who first had the idea that pointy toes were sexy, perhaps it was someone who fell feet-first into a pencil-sharpener. In fact, a recent survey of adult males in Atlantic City showed that in the list of things that they thought looked sexy when pointy, toes came 23rd, while the gall-bladder, curiously enough, came 19th, which must mean something.

Anyway, the wearing of tight shoes angulates the first metatarso-phalyngeal joint, causing the bunions, which are named from the Spanish *bogniones*, which were a kind of heavy sugary wheatcake which caused serious pain and deformity if dropped on the big toe.

The treatment of bunions is predominantly surgical and the greatest advances have come, oddly enough, from Japan. The most promising approach was proposed by a group of orthopaedic surgeons from Kyoto in a recent publication (*Bunions – a step in the right direction*: Itchikahula, Michigabula, Bippiti, Bobbittee and Bu). In that part of Japan, the worst bunion problems are caused by patent-leather slingbacks in the 1950s style e.g. Audrey Hepburn. The Japanese surgeons have perfected a prosthetic counter-tension operation in which, under general anaesthetic, a proximal incision is made which is then widened distally and medially, the defect then being repaired with a graft of matching patent-leather. This effectively enlarges the shoe by two sizes at the toe end, and the surgical team claim that they can do a heel and re-sole under the same anaesthetic.

If it is unsuccessful, the surgeons may then have to amputate the entire shoe and replace it with a prosthetic device which they call a 'hakaramatzo' or 'new shoe'. If it catches on, the surgeons have proposed a similar approach to other common orthopaedic problems, including gloves and underpants, and they intend setting up an inter-disciplinary multi-centre surgical department store incorporating an out-patient heel-bar.

In the United Kingdom, this approach is unlikely to be successful, because we have had centuries of surgical experience and training in the health service and are literally dozens of years ahead of the Japanese in many important respects, particularly waiting-lists.

Looking into the future, I think advances in orthopaedic surgery will have a significant impact within 20 or 25 years. In fact, I would go so far as to guess that by the year 2000, many of the people awaiting bunion surgery will have had their operations. But I could be wrong.

THE DOCTOR ANSWERS YOUR QUESTIONS

Q: I have this recurring nightmare in which I imagine that I am married to the Prime Minister of Great Britain. Then, when I wake up covered in sweat and trembling, I find that it's true. What should I do?

A: Stay asleep.

MEDICAL SUPPLIES

The idea of a whole shop just for doctors may strike you as somewhat unnecessary. After all, once a doctor's acquired a black bag, a stethoscope, a few bits of wood for sticking down people's throats and a white coat, what more does he need? Well, that may be all he needs if he's a doctor in Norwich, Newcastle or Northampton but if you aspire to, say, Harley Street then you'll have to do better with the accoutrements.

Near the south end of Harley Street is John Bell & Croyden, a shop where there are as many brands of doctor's bag as Safeways has tea. The Webley, the Wigmore and the Shamrock jostle with the Shearline, the New Invincible and the Albert Major (grained). And if those aren't quite what you want they'll show you the Captain, the Classic, the Continental with outsize pocket (or without extras) and the Lynmouth. These are obviously no ordinary doctors' bags. At £128–£179, the New Invincible, the most expensive, obviously contains design features that will cure the richest and illest patient within minutes of the doctor clicking open its smooth Eezi-spring locks and reaching into its capacious interior. If you can only afford the Classic (£61.21), you're going to have to work a lot harder at the doctor-patient relationship.

When I visited John Bell & Croyden the place was deserted apart from a man in a mackintosh eyeing 'vaginal specula, all sizes – large, medium, small, virg.' No salesperson disturbed my browsing amongst Harpenden Skin Fold Calipers, Wart Scoops, Bone Props and St Marks Dilators. There is a strangely Victorian feeling about the stock-in-trade. The modern thrusting approach to marketing has passed them by. Things appear to be named either after people who sound as if they've long passed on (De Wecker Scissors, Franks Blood Lancet, Keynes Radium Knife) or places you only ever pass through (examination couches are called Kingston, Croydon, Purley, Heysham).

But, of course, this is the secret fascination for all shop watchers – a glimpse into an unknown world where nothing is what it seems. We each carry such a world around with us and it's only *other people's* worlds which we enjoy exploring. Who would have thought that you could buy *accessories* for stethoscopes? Ear tips, small, medium or large, 58p, and Non-Chill Sleeves (for that *caring* doctor). What exclusive design features could make a doctor choose Majorca Cabinet instead of a Minorca? How much Emergency Eyewash does the average surgery need?

Although, as patients, we must come in contact with many of these necessary objects, we are never really aware of them. The finer points elude us since we are usually eager to spend as little time as possible in the surgery. As we turn our heads away from the field of action we never learn enough to tell the difference between a Noott's Ear Trough, a Walton's Eye Spud and Needle, or a Jobson Horne Aural Probe. Eponymy is rampant on the shelves as shiny steel instruments gleam out the names of men and women whose long efforts to make a better aural probe now have doctors from all over the world beating a path to their doors, or to John Bell & Croyden's anyway.

I suppose in the days when reputation and income went hand in hand, it impressed the patients of Dr Jobson Horne to know that their ears would be probed by his very own invention. But what rivalries underlie the two types of Uterine Sound stocked by John Bell & Croyden – Uterine Sound Horrocks (tally-ho?) and Uterine Sound Galabins?

What is most disturbing about a shop like this is the constant reminder, if you're not used to them, of bodily distress, infirmity and pain. To see three types of electroconvulsive therapy devices, for example, sitting on a shelf as calmly as if they were toasters or irons, pulls you up with a start. (Now which one shall I buy? The £379 model, the £414 or the £517? Do you get more volts for your money? Or less amnesia? Or just a prettier pair of electrodes to go on the patient's head?)

A half-dissected foot in realistic plastic is presumably either a paperweight or a revision aid while waiting for the next patient. Such aids are commonplace in America, where I recently saw a plastic rectum for doctors to improve their tumour-hunting technique with finger or fibroscope. There was also a life-size rubber new-born baby for practising lumbar puncture technique. Rather like those dolls that weep real tears, this one gave forth imitation spinal fluid if the doctor hit the target with his needle.

From medical school onwards, the extraordinary becomes commonplace, the distressing becomes routine and medical progress demands that doctors go about their business of cutting, probing, dilating and shocking our frail bodies in the most efficient way man can devise. At shops like John Bell & Croyden's the search must never stop for bigger and better doctors' bags, aural probes, eye spuds, ear troughs, blood lancets and examination couches. As we head for the twenty-first century the backroom boys must even now be scouring the gazetteers of the United Kingdom for a name for the first microchip-operated, all synthetic-fibre-covered, floor-hovering examination couch. The Penge? The Luton? The Milton Keynes?

Karl Sabbagh 5.11.1980

Do-It-Yourself Sickness Benefit Claim Form

Name of Employee .... Name of Employer ....

Address .... Address ....

1. Give date on which you deemed yourself to be unfit for work ....

2. State briefly why you deem yourself to be unfit (*First read Notes below*) ....
Do **not** say "poorly", "groggy", "under the weather", "indisposed", "knackered", "a touch of the mange".
Do **not** use over-colourful descriptions: e.g. Montezuma's Revenge, Inca Quickstep, Delhi Belly, Turkey Trots, Churchyard Cough, Black Death.
Do **not** list advertisers' diseases: e.g. Sinking Feeling, Ashtray Breath, Dishpan Hands, The Greasies.
Avoid use of "martyr", as in "martyr to rheumatism".
If you suffer from an anti-social complaint, avoid invidious references to other nations: e.g. The French Disease, The Italian Disease. But Maltese Fever and Hapsburg Lip are acceptable.

3. How sick are you? ....
If you are not as sick as a parrot, what are you as sick as? ....

4. Did you have to receive the kiss of life before you were able to collect this form?
Yes (   ) No (   ).

5. Do you regard your own conduct as in any way contributable to your condition? (*Think carefully*) ....
Were you engaged in
(   ) a domestic brawl
(   ) a pie-eating contest
(   ) resisting a mugger
(   ) jogging
(   ) glue sniffing
(   ) a rugby celebration?

6. In addition to your illness entered at (2), do you suffer from any of the following?
(   ) delayed shell-shock (do not list battles before 1914)
(   ) agoraphobia (*see Note 1*)
(   ) asthenia (*see Note 2*)
(   ) worry about the Bomb (*see Note 3*)

(   ) advanced torpor (*see Note 4*)
Note 1: Could you advance into the middle of a 50-acre field to collect £100, if it was waiting for you? If you could, you do not suffer from agoraphobia.
Note 2: There is no such thing as asthenia.
Note 3: The Bomb is not a legitimate reason for absence from work, unless it is actually dropped.
Note 4: If, when you are lying on your back, a brimful tumbler of water placed on your chest does not overflow, you need not complete this form, as you will no longer require State aid.

7. During your self-certificated absence from work, have you
(   ) operated your car as a minicab
(   ) served behind a bar
(   ) given video exhibitions to a male audience for gain
(   ) gone shopping with your family to Boulogne
(   ) taken a holiday of more than three days overseas?

8. Have you ever certified yourself as ill before or after
(   ) a Bank Holiday
(   ) a Christmas Fortnight
(   ) a Cup Final
(   ) a Test Match
(   ) a Papal visit
(   ) a Royal Wedding

9. Give the date on which you propose to return to work, if you can see no other course ....

10. Would you be willing to have your condition investigated by a panel of six faceless medical experts answerable only to the State?
Yes (   ) No (   ).

Declaration
I understand that any false statement in the foregoing may bring upon my head the Utmost Rigour of the Law.
I claim whatever benefit is going.
I wish to forget the whole thing.
(*Strike out whichever line is inapplicable*)

Signature of applicant ....

'Congratulations, Mrs Wilcox! You
are the first person in medical history
to fall victim to Ambrose
T. Pendleton's Disease.'

'You're not really a hypochondriac. You only think
you're a hypochondriac.'

'I've been shrugging an awful lot of this aside.'

'I can't afford both so I've decided on cirrhosis.'

'. . . and the doctors all said they'd never seen
one like it.'

'No, not a sex change. I want to be a
Sagittarian.'

'I must say you're in pretty poor shape even for one in the upper-income
bracket.'

'Best cigarette of the day, I always
think . . .'

THE GOOD FLU GUIDE

A.2/HONG KONG/82

An outstandingly robust little virus with a fine pink eye and full-bodied lung accumulations which has been causing quite a pandemic of interest throughout the Far East where attempts continue to bottle it.

Newly-shipped into Britain last month by a sweating passenger from Rangoon, A.2/Hong Kong/82 is essentially an amusing antigenic shift on last year's very popular A.2/Hong Kong/81 but offers a shade more debilitating lassitude and is distinguished by a striking pharyngeal chill and a very full nose.

EPIZOOTIC CATARRHAL FEVER B3/82 OR HOGS' CROUP

Earlier reports suggested this sturdy bacillus might prove to be one of the all-time classic strains of *Influentia Coeli* – or heavenly infliction – first described by Umberto Pfeiffer when his legs collapsed from under him and he was carried off from the 1767 Leghorn Swine Fair complaining of rawness in the nasopharynx.

So far as is known, however, Pfeiffer's tonsils were largely unaffected which has led to speculation that Epizootic Catarrhal Fever B3/82, where a thickly furred tongue and a short, hacking, unproductive bark are typical, may prove to be this year's most exciting viral coryza.

A.1/TAIWAN/ RHINOPNEUMONITIS/82

'Delirious prostration' and 'Absolutely knackering' were typical of our testers' descriptions of this stunning paranasal sinusitis served up with a temperature of 104°F and a selection of aches and pains compared by some to the legendary equine fever.

Certainly this would seem to be one of the most persistent epipharyngeal inflammations currently to be sampled anywhere in the UK with effects that can last weeks rather than days.

After a double dose *and* streptomycin by the bucket, one tester reported dropping a teaspoon and bursting into tears.

B.2/PURULENT PNEUMOCOCCI/ BARCELONA/82

With not even the suggestion of any effect from sulfonamides or Night Nurse, B.2/Purulent Pneumococci/Barcelona/82 looks set to be with us for many years to come and offers chilliness, swooning, dejection, nausea and streaming from the nose on a grand scale. Indeed, this particular virus has been held to represent an antigenicity and pharmaceutical resistance second to none and with its rip-roaring throat, deep-seated wheeze and magnificently debilitating fever has been compared with the finest cases of consumption or the matchless bronchitis of '47.

All our testers went down like flies within 24 hours of making the first acquaintance with this noble strain and as many as 80 per cent reported they had never felt more dejected.

A.9/SIBERIA/FERRET POX/81

Now well established as a bacterium of truly exceptional virulence with a shivering febrile malaise, giddyness, pyrexia and strength of irritation to the fauces singled out for particular mention, A.9/Siberia, known affectionately throughout the Russias as Ferret Pox because of the apparent similarity between the symptoms in humans and a ferret with the pox, is still worthy of mention for the continuing outstanding eruptions of Rhonchi and scattered râles in the base of the lungs, but never *too* consolidated. Perfectly complements Lucozade.

C.1/GREATER LONDON/82

Currently all the rage in the West End and throughout Southern Region, this latest little outbreak shows all the signs of maturing into a full-blown epidemic. At least 200 testers reported sensations 'as if being borne on a stretcher into a world full of throbbing cascades, discharging into a sea of sodden cotton wool and camphorated corpses' though a further 800 were unable to speak at all. Wins our only award of a 2-hankies rosette as a perfect everyday flu, ready to strike at a moment's notice.

DOC BRIEF

Robert Buckman on
SOCIALLY TRANSMITTED DISEASES

SOCIALLY TRANSMITTED DISEASES

The subject of socially transmitted diseases is on everyone's lips these days. And very unpleasant it is, too. I am often consulted in my capacity as a doctor and pompous oaf by some poor, terrified and ignorant young man – these days perhaps a schoolboy, or 'rock musician', or equally uneducated person such as a Cabinet Minister.

'What could I have caught?' is the usual question, and, 'Is it too late?' (to treat it, that is, not to catch it. It is never too late to catch anything. Except a train).

Well, of course many unpleasant conditions can be transmitted at the festive season. Some are transmitted by kissing and some by more intimate contact, but virtually all of these conditions can be transmitted by publication (*vide* Ms Keays, or rather don't).

So when it comes down to it (or preferably before), the vital question is what can a chap catch under the mistletoe? Well, the answer is that to begin with mistletoe is itself an infectious disease (as I mentioned at this season last year), but only of oak-trees. As far as I know no human has ever actually caught mistletoe in the sense of having the stuff grow from the armpits or groins, although even if that did occur it would certainly be more decorative than herpes.

Pathologically, the major transmissible diseases can be divided into the emotional and the physical. Though they usually aren't.

TRANSMISSION BY PHYSICAL MEANS

The main danger areas for transmitting infection are the mucous membranes, including for example the mouth, the nostrils, the back of the throat and the back of the car.

The second most important areas are the so-called erogenous zones which include the down-belows, the ear-lobes and Fulham. What is more, these danger areas are summative in their effect and health-risk. Thus kissing someone's nostrils in the back of a car in Fulham is almost equivalent to a typhoid outbreak just by itself. Though I suppose it depends a bit on the car. Although I once knew a consultant in infectious diseases who said he'd rather have typhoid than a Renault any day. (As a matter of bizarre and morbid coincidence he was later summoned by the WHO to investigate a typhoid outbreak in Ulan Bator, and died there – run over by a Renault.)

Anyway, diseases transmitted in this way include the common cold, pharyngitis, gingivitis, infectious mononucleosis and, if we believe the prosecution, coded signals from Cyprus.

Another question I am often asked at Christmas (apart from 'will you kiss me?' or 'doctor, have you met my daughter?') is whether or not kissing can transmit dental decay, or caries. Well, indirectly the answer is no, though it's still a good idea to make sure none of your teeth is very loose before commencing kissing activities. Particularly if you want to avoid loss of self-esteem, body-image, poise and of course teeth.

However, if I may take a moment to look at the wider issues. Kissing and licking as behaviour patterns are not limited to human beings. Particularly not in San Francisco (where they *really* know how to have a party. And epidemic).

In fact, both kissing and salivation are actually primitive biological signals with an interpersonal, species-specific function roughly the equivalent of 'hi!'. This applies even among the lower orders of mammals such as lobsters, which often kiss and salivate. Though it's damn difficult to tell when they are underwater. Or in soup for that matter.

This then means that kissing is, as it were, 'designed' to initiate an affectionate response in the kissee. This then means that kissing, as a sort of prelude or initiator, may easily lead to the transmission of many other things, including your genetic material, phone number, resignation and inheritance.

That having been said, please don't take any

notice of grouchy old me and try and have some real fun at the office party this Christmas. While you can.

EMOTIONAL CONDITIONS

There is an extremely virulent kind of socially transmitted epidemic that descends on people at this time of year. It is called 'relatives'.

Many cures are claimed, but sadly few are proven. The problem is that no one knows the precise cause of relatives, though the mistletoe has certainly got something to answer for, and the Tia Maria is probably responsible for most of the rest. Relatives are best defined as 'kith' which is what it sounds like when they try to say 'kiss' with loose teeth and caries. The most peculiar thing about relatives is that they are often emotionally quite close to you, which means that all kinds of signals of special significance can be transmitted throughout close-knit families, e.g. vendettas.

Thus it is that at Christmas time, certain families, particularly religious ones, find a deep solace and mutual support in sharing certain kinds of fundamental behaviour patterns, e.g. getting drunk. What is even more interesting is that other primates, including baboons and gibbons, exhibit the same visible behaviour as us, induced by enforced propinquity with aunts and uncles, i.e. hatred and loathing. In fact, we had the baboons round last Christmas and they hated my uncle Frank even more than I did. What's more they ate more tidily, helped with the clearing up, understood the mottoes in the crackers and beat me at Pacman.

Still, at least this Christmas things will be different. I'm going round to their place. Though they probably only invited me to show their friends how liberal they were. That's the whole trouble with the season of peace and goodwill to all mankind – you just don't know where you are any more.

THE DOCTOR ANSWERS YOUR QUESTIONS

Q: I have a terrible personal crisis which I hardly dare discuss with anybody. I have a problem with obesity, and am also rather extroverted and enjoy going ho-ho-ho a lot. In my more manic phases, I give away most of what I possess, but what I'm really worried about is the amount of time I seem to be spending in children's bedrooms. Can you help me?

A: Only if you bring me an electric train set and a BMX bike with a pennant on the back. Like you promised last year.

3

The Best Medicine

'He firmly believes laughter is the best medicine.'

'He's celebrating his third liver transplant.'

'Can't grumble really – I tried to jump the varicose veins queue.'

THE SHRIMP CURE

(By *Pegwell Bey*)

Sir, – My title is Oriental; but I am a British subject. I address you as an expert. This is the time of Cures – you have the Grape Cure, the Whey Cure, the Water Cure, the Bath Cures, the Cures by German waters – another and a shorter Whey Cure – and the Cure by French watering-places. You have the Homburg Cure, the Wiesbaden Cure, the Royat Cure; indeed, every kind of Cure, except the only Perfect Cure, which I assert to be the 'Shrimp Cure!'

I know that the pages of *Punch* are read by all, and, for the benefit of all mankind, I give these notes from my note-book, which is that of a physician who has had great experience all over the world, and especially in the East End of Europe, in order that rich and poor, prince and peasant, may read, and happily find that true balsam, which will so far purge his complaints, that he may become whole and well, and a comfort to his family circle, and the pride of his country. Yes, Sir, come to Pegwell Bey for a

cure, and P. B. exclaims, 'In the name of the Profit! Shrimps!'

A few explanatory words about my installation in the locality. I wanted a Sanatorium. An unfinished row of villas about a mile-and-a-half distant that had long been on the hands of a local speculative builder struck me as the very thing. I took the whole terrace forthwith, speedily instituted a bathing machine fitted up as an ambulance to meet the down-train, and here I am in three months literally turning patients away. I may as well add that to enable me to procure a fresh and constant supply of shrimps for the necessities of my establishment, I have managed to secure the services of a Retired Smuggler, who says he knows the coast, and thinks with a lawn tennis net cut up into pieces, and the assistance of one or two donkey-boys, or even patients, he can undertake to keep me supplied. But to revert to my experiences.

No. 1. I commence with one of my first cases. I wish to be truthful. It was not a successful one at first. A.B., æt. 45, of nervo-bilious temperament, complained that his nights were fearful; no sleep, pains everywhere, an uneasy sensation as of billiard-balls being poured down his back, a horror of society, and distaste for pastry. I had him placed in the establishment, and began by giving him three pints of shrimps every four hours. For the first twenty-four hours he improved wonderfully, he increased in weight and strength, and his appetite was greater – no other food than shrimps is allowed; but on the second day I found him with a temperature of 205° Fahrenheit, a pulse of 270, respirations 76 in the minute, and in fact in a critical state. I remained with the patient, I sent for my electric lamp and other instruments. I made an examination – a careful scientific examination – and I found that he had eaten the *heads* and *tails*. What was to be done? I called in the Retired Smuggler, and asked his advice. He immediately suggested warm greengage jam. After many anxious hours, this had the effect of completely soothing the system, and my patient breathed again. What relief! Having learnt by experience, I sat with that patient days and days, saw each shrimp carefully peeled and dipped in weak solution of carbolic acid – the result was wonderful. All his hair came off, he looked twenty years older, and completely lost the use of his legs, but he is now able to pursue the laborious occupation of an Art Critic with pleasure to himself and gratification and edification to his numerous readers.

No. 2.   The case of a woman in an active stage of consumption is also remarkable. She consumed everything, from a periwinkle to a Perigord pie. In other respects appetite normal. Received her into the establishment – fed her on shrimp-sauce, in quart pots. She came back like the rebound of a watch-spring. She only remained three days – said she was quite well, and suddenly left, unfortunately without giving her address, and so her account remains unpaid. I do not think she will return. The Retired Smuggler is of the same opinion.

No. 3.   My next case presents singular features of interest. My patient in this instance was an aged Duke, whose symptoms were unique and peculiar. He had deafening noises in his head, like the explosion of heavy foot artillery, coupled with a continual sensation of descending rapidly, as in a diving-bell out of order, accompanied by sudden and unexpected seizures in the spine, as if he were violently run into in the back by an omnibus-pole. His sight was also affected, magnificent displays of fireworks taking place between him and his morning paper whenever he attempted to look at the leader. I saw at a glance that there was congestion in the case, and at once ordered a *massage* bath of hot potted shrimps. This was followed at first by the exhibition of some feverish symptoms, but, by a persistent recourse to it uninterruptedly for six consecutive months, they gradually disappeared, and I consider him now in a much improved condition. It is true that his faculties appear to have left him, and that he addresses me as 'King of the Coloboo Islands,' and, whenever he gets a chance, puts things on the sly across the railway lines to upset the trains, and eats his newspaper; but I fancy the noises in his head have disappeared. I have lately sent him out in charge of the Retired Smuggler, who assures me that, beyond bonneting a middle-aged lady on a donkey with the shrimping-net, beginning a war-dance in a neighbouring public-house, and pushing a short-sighted naturalist who was collecting zoophytes at the end of the pier into the water, there has been nothing at all to distinguish his behaviour from that of any ordinary nobleman making a short stay at the sea-side. I have him now watched, for I think it as well, by six attendants night and day, but I consider him quite my showcase. The more I look at him the more it is brought home to me what wonders the shrimps have done for him.

I could, of course, continue my extracts, but my space is limited, and I must stop here. I think, however, I have revealed enough of the new treatment to induce any waverer to no longer hesitate, but to get it at once, and put himself or herself unreservedly under the careful charge of your highly scientific and circumspect correspondent,   PEGWELL BEY.

Francis Burnand 19.11.1887

AIDS AND COMFORTS

Even now that ingenious medical engineering has allowed the disabled to play polo and climb mountains and eat boiled eggs, there are still gaps to be filled. Take baths. There may be steps, back-rests, taps within reach of wrinkled toes and hands and overhead hoists; but take-off is still not altogether perfect. After all, even the fairly well preserved can be grateful for a rubber mat, held to the bottom of the bath by suction cups; but this is only passively helpful. What is needed is an Ejector Rubber Mat.

One of the difficulties which come with age is a tendency to find that listeners are thinking their own thoughts. Of course, the old don't want visitors to join in the conversation, just listen. Visitors feel that they have to talk; but monologue to a receptive ear is the thing.

Designing receptive ears should not be past the appliance industry. A small, plastic ear could be pinned to the pillow. It should be lifelike, not completely without charm and, if male, slightly hirsute. It should not remain completely passive but flap a little from time to time and interject occasional laughs, mutters of assent and low whistles.

From mouths and ears to eyes. Sometimes nurses wear badges with their names. Unfortunately dim eyes can find the letters a bit small and close peering at girls' bosoms could easily arouse sisters of the thrawner sort. The answer to the difficulty is a miniature camera which, rapidly and unobtrusively, photographs torsos and blows up images so that the badge looks like a street name-plate. I am not suggesting that inventing this device would be easy – but how well worth doing!

An important element in the disabled life is sympathy-selection.

When I was a dear little cripple child and the most ruthless family exploiter since Tiny Tim, I found that it was essential, not merely to arouse sympathy, but to make good use of it once aroused. Otherwise people tended to give me things which they thought that a besplinted waif should want, rather than things that I actually did want.

What I liked was, not games where you stuck coloured pins in holes and made the kind of patterns that orientals weave for tourists, but additions to the collection which I kept in an old shoe-box. It included door-knobs, bent cigarette-tins, skewers past their best and heavy bits of metal of unimaginable origin. With these I made happy clangs and wove many fantasies. This, I would say to my Mother, banging a detached hammer-head, is my submarine that can go through walls. I did not demand any visual correspondence between an article and its role. I had a doll dressed in the uniform of one of the Women's Services. To me it was a clergyman called 'Jack' who lived *underneath* the vicarage.

Sympathy puzzled me. When I was lying in my spinal carriage, while my Mother queued in shops, I would be telling myself stories about Lionel, a rather repulsive toothbrush. Passing ladies would beam down at me and say things like, 'What a brave little chap!' This inexplicable remark never led to anything desirable, like a small headless statue or the works of a clock. Only once did it lead anywhere and then, as World War I was on and there was a Scare, I rebuffed the gift, saying politely, 'Thank you, but my Mother does not let me take sweets from strangers in case they've been poisoned by the Germans.'

As other children were having to go to kindergartens and, I supposed, being birched by large, wild schoolmasters, I felt very well off. I wondered why the ladies did not sympathise with me over the real low-spots of my life, like having my ears washed and cod.

Well intentioned benefactors, whether cooing at children or visiting adults in hospital, need direction. I am imagining a device not unlike those small black boxes which produce maniacal laughter and, carefully used, can wreck family life. Speaking as the visitor, it would use a silly voice and say things like, 'We'll soon have you up and running races. I do envy you your stylish plaster ruff and your leg-pulley and all those exciting tubes, ha-ha! I've brought you some grapes and a jigsaw puzzle – I can't remember whether you do them – and a wild-life magazine.'

Then a sensible voice would say, 'Is the food filthy? I didn't much like the look of the sister. The little, perky nurse with the splendid bottom looks possible. Does it hurt worse when you breathe in or breathe out? I've brought you some Scotch, an avocado, *Playboy*, the *Times Literary Supplement* and the new Muriel Spark.'

This gadget would offend the kind of visitors whom one would wish offended and train the rest.

When memories begin to fade, social unease arises. The old do not like having to keep asking people sitting beside the bed who they are. What they need is a whispering pillow, which would repeat at minute intervals simple messages like, 'This is your niece Maud. She is a teacher. Ask after Tom. Don't mention Sid.' One of the Voluntary Services might programme pillows, in cooperation with the family. The scheme, I frankly admit, would need careful organising.

Most mechanical aids assist the disabled to perform worthy tasks, like cutting up meat, reading newspapers or, in the tough, athletic world of Stoke Mandeville, winning obstacle-races. But, if the object of medical gadgetry is to render possible the whole range of human activities, there are gaps, though, of course, one does not *know*.

The subject of unworthy prosthetics is not one for airing in a family magazine – what kind of family have journalists who use the phrase known? – but I will mention one mild example of ingenuity.

When Malcolm Muggeridge was Editor he felt

that he ought to visit the dying Milne, one of the major *Punch* contributors in its whole history. He didn't relish the prospect, thinking of Milne primarily as a children's writer. What was his delight to find a cynical man, who said he hated the little ones, except as a source of income, and had a long pair of lazy-tongs with which he lifted the nurses' skirts.

R. G. G. Price 19.8.1981

DOC BRIEF

Robert Buckman on
DRUGS FROM PLANTS

DIGITALIS

Perhaps the most famous of all drugs obtained from plants is the heart drug *digitalis*. On the other hand, since very few people have actually heard of it, perhaps it isn't as famous as its press agent says.

Either way, digitalis was originally extracted from the flowers of the foxglove plant and it was given its present name in memory of the great physician Dr Harvey Foxglove, the inventor of heart-attacks.

The foxglove itself is a tall, purple plant with long, bell-shaped flowers whereas by contrast, as all botanists know, digitalis is a little white pill. I've always wondered about that, and how digitalis was discovered and why it's white – maybe the pills grow naturally inside the flower. After all, you get red cherries on trees with white flowers, don't you?

Anyway, digitalis is an interesting drug and is sometimes called a Type II positive inotrope, particularly by doctors who don't know what that means but want to impress their private patients. Digitalis causes the heart to beat more strongly and thus resembles many other cardio-stimulant substances, e.g. *Playboy*. It also restores the normal rhythm of the heartbeat. This may not seem much, but sometimes the heart goes into an irregular rhythm called *atrial fibrillation* which, when heard through a stetho-scope, sounds like Max Roach on an off day. Whereas, after digitalis, it sounds as ordinary as Abba on a good day.

CURARE

Curare is a muscle relaxant drug used in anaesthetics, and was originally discovered in Borneo, where it was used as an arrow-tip poison. I think it was obtained from the juice of crushed pygmies and, once smeared on to an arrow, would cause instant paralysis, which is why to this day there are so many paralysed arrows in Borneo. No, that can't be right; it must have been the pygmies who discovered it and used it on boar and game as a cure for running away. Hence its name, which in the local Borneo language means 'muscle relaxant drug useful for anaesthetics'.

It was discovered by naturalists in the early twentieth century who realised at once what a boon such a drug would be to anaesthetists, neurologists and psychopathic killers. However, when it was first introduced into anaesthetic practice, many patients objected strongly – although what upset them most, apparently, was the presence of the pygmies sharpening their arrows in the anaesthetic room.

Curare acts at the neuro-muscular junction, where nerve impulses go from the neurone to the muscle. It blocks that transmission and is thus the neurological equivalent of secondary picketing. When the drug is given, it causes every muscle in the body to become paralysed so that no voluntary movement, or even facial expression, is possible. The patient thus immediately requires either ventilatory support or the offer of a Cabinet post.

OPIUM

Opium, laudanum, morphine and heroin are all members of a family of drugs called *alkaloids* (meaning 'like alka-' as in Alka-Seltzer, Alka-Pone, Alka-Traz, etc).

Interestingly, the opiate alkaloids are all derived from distillates of the poppy flower. This led to the fascinating case-precedent of *Regina vs McNutt*, in which McNutt pleaded that he thought he was allowed to carry four ounces of opium because he was labouring under the delusion that he was a five-acre field of poppies. The most amazing thing is that he got away with it, but a year later the Government struck back by building the Melton Mowbray by-pass over his head.

Opium has been the inspiration of many great poets and writers, e.g. Coleridge, De Quincey, William Burroughs, Hunter S. Thompson and Jean Cocteau, who is now known by us *cognoscenti* not to have been a woman but to have been French, which is another excuse for writing unintelligible mystical drivel.

Also a critical appraisal of the works of Chaucer has led me to the conclusion that he must have done a lot of dope and was probably bombed out of his skull most of the time, to judge by his spelling and grammar. Anyway, the opiates produce their effects on the brain by binding or locking on to special receptors and they prevent the brain from receiving stimuli of pain, unpleasantness or unhappiness, or, in the case of William Burroughs, any coherent thoughts whatsoever.

ASPIRIN

Yes, that's right, *aspirin*. The commonplace aspirin tablet is, as I have told you before, derived from the bark of the willow tree. The willow was known to Hippocrates as a cure for hangovers when one fell on his head, rendering him unconscious. Since that day, modern pharmaceuticals have progressed and it is now possible to render someone unconscious by hitting them on the head with a bottle of aspirin.

I can't remember exactly how many willow trees that is equivalent to, but if you're having trouble you can always use a cricket bat, which is equivalent to less than one, and can be used again. In fact, you can use a cricket bat for most of the conditions that require aspirin now I come to think about it – but of course the reverse is not true, i.e. you can't play cricket with an aspirin (although the way we've been playing against the West Indies until recently, we might just as well have been).

QUININE

Quinine is an interesting drug and also the tastiest constituent of tonic water. It is derived from the bark of the cinchona tree, which is a handy thing to remember if you're stuck with a gin and no tonic – except that no one knows what a cinchona tree looks like. So if you drop

willow bark into your drink by mistake, you'll end up with a gin-and-aspirin.

Other barks will give you gin-and-cork, gin-and-wormwood and maybe even gin-and-bracket-fungus. All of which may cause less of a hangover but will lack a certain *je ne sais quoi* – in this case, tonic.

However, quinine is known as a treatment for malaria and, to this day, many old 'India hands' still drink three gin-and-tonics every sundown as malaria-prophylaxis, which has certainly reduced the incidence of malaria in the Home Counties.

THE DOCTOR ANSWERS YOUR QUESTIONS

Q: Hello doctor, I have two questions: firstly, where's the money and, secondly, do you like your kneecaps the shape they are?

A: This is a fascinating area in which we doctors are becoming increasingly involved and I think that I can best answer the first query by saying Friday. There'll be no problem Friday, right? I've got a cheque from *Punch* coming in soon, they won't let me down, it'll all be all right. And secondly, yes I do, but nobody else does haha. Friday.

'You're a hypochondriac, but you've come to the right man, I'm a quack.'

RATIOCINATION.

Country Doctor. 'DID YOU TAKE THAT BOTTLE OF MEDICINE TO OLD MRS. GAMBIDGE'S? – BECAUSE IT WAS VERY IMPORT——'

Surgery Boy. 'OH, YESSIR. AND I'M PRETTY SURE SHE TOOK IT, SIR!'

Country Doctor (after a pause). 'WHAT DO YOU MEAN BY THAT, SIR?'

Surgery Boy. 'WELL, I SEE THE SHUTTERS UP AT THE 'OUSE AS I PASSED THIS MORNIN', SIR!!'

GETTING IN SHAPE

An Easy-To-Follow No-Nonsense Extremely Fashionable Diet 'n' Exercise Regime That Will Shed Unsightly Pounds Just Where You Want To Lose Them Without Expensive Equipment, Hazardous Drugs, Or Very Dodgy Surgery.

BREAKFAST
1 Glass Fresh Orange Juice
1 Slice Wholewheat Toast
Black Coffee

Squeeze orange (*tones up wrist, washes out eye*), strain and rip off tie (*tones up thumb & forefinger*), drink, spit out pips (*firms flabby lips*).

Run to smoking toaster (*strengthens thighs & calves*), jab in breadknife to lever out clinker (*firms forearms*), receive major electric shock (*general livening-up to entire system*), scream (*tones up throat*).

Percolator now goes bubble, bubble, wheeze, stop, since main kitchen fuse blown by toaster. Crawl into fuse-cupboard under stairs (*tautens lower lumbar region, toughens palms & knees*), turn off mains, plunging fuse-cupboard into blackness (*tones up eyes*), knock fuses off shelf, listen keenly for exact spot fuses rolling to (*tones up ears*), fit fuse, straighten up, bang head on shelf (*tones up brain*).

Now no time to drink coffee (*saves 40 calories*).

Hi! Well, how did you get on with breakfast? Can you feel those stomach acids beginning to gnaw at your viscera? That's what we in dietetics call the Prometheus Syndrome, and it can be a truly terrific boon, believe me! Busy-busy people like you often have no time to count calories or consult some dinky cut-out-'n'-keep chart from their favourite Fleet Street cat-litter, and that's where heartburn can really help. With any luck, you won't feel like eating anything else for hours! So instead of nibbling away at all those naughty fat-forming inch-creeping health-threatening elevenses, why not try a little dry-retching instead? Not only will it tauten those

old tummy muscles we haven't seen too much of this past year or so, it will also drive sweat out through those clogged pores, stopping unsightly blackheads before they have the chance to form, and cleansing our entire system in **Mother Nature's own way!**

But first things first: there's a whole morning's vitalising exercise before we come to *that*. Tingling all over from our fused toaster, Elastoplasted forehead, and self-eating stomach, it's time to rush out of the house, bang the door, run to the car, realise that we have left all our keys on the bedside table, run back even more frantically and healthily, and bang on the door again. Can't you just *feel* all that fresh warm blood racing up to firm those flabby temples? Don't you just *know* that that tired old muscle we call Mister Heart is getting tougher and tougher all the time?

Now it's time to crouch down, toning up sagging bottoms, and shout through the letter box to somebody to let you in. Perhaps a small child, say, may be persuaded to run up and stick a felt-tipped pen in your eye, allowing you to release all that pent-up tension which science tells us it's so important to let out. Yell long enough, and with a little luck the alsatian next door will drop by to see what all the fuss is about! Flailing away at a crazed dog once in a while has been shown by experts to be up to five times as effective as even the most expensive rowing-machine!

So now you're in your car, and you're driving to work. Too often, busy-busy people like you make that an excuse for letting up on the exercise, but, believe me, opportunities abound for working out that lazy old body of yours! Why not keep an eye open for mad bastards? These will often be prepared to overtake you on the inside, shoot across you on the red light, or cut in without signalling: so jam on the brakes, firming up ankles, grip the wheel until your fingers go white (shedding grammes of unnecessary and unsightly knuckle-fat), and bang your head on the windscreen. Nosebleeds clear the head wonderfully, especially in summer.

Arriving at work, why not park some way from the office, remove your folding bicycle from the boot, and attempt to put it together? Throwing a partly assembled folding bicycle into the road and shouting at it *gets the whole body working* – especially if a mad bastard comes around the corner and runs over it.

Jog to the office, feeling the wind caress your oil-damp hands and face, and when you get there, do remember to take the lift NOT the stairs.

It's a mistake so many keep-fit fanatics make. Stairs will only firm up flabby legs and hips, but a lift brokendown between floors will enable you to jump up and down, wave your arms about, bang your fists on the doors, fall to your knees, and, perhaps most important, get those lazy old lungs and heart of yours working overtime!

Until you're ready for

LUNCH

1 Large Gin & Tonic + Ice & Lemon
1 Round Rare Roast Beef
1 Round Mature English Cheddar
1 Large Brandy

Walk into Rat & Cockle, shove through crowd (*strengthens shoulders, knees, teeth*), stand four-deep at bar for 20 minutes, make spasmodic attempts to leap above mob (*firms toes*), shout order 18 times (*tones up flabby larynx*). Eventually receive large gin & tonic (*no ice or lemon in it; saves 20 calories*).

Shove back through mob towards sandwich counter, stand four-deep at counter, struggle to raise gin & tonic to lips (*tones up biceps, lengthens neck muscles, builds lower jaw*). Glass tips, drink soaks into jacket (*no calories*). After 20 minutes of further firming of toes and toning up flabby larynx, receive 1 round roast fat plus roast string garnish. Let drop to floor (*no calories*).

Continue firming toes and toning up flabby larynx for 20 more minutes, finally receive 1 round processed cheesoleum, still in plastic envelope. Sniff (*tones up nose*). Eat plastic envelope (*no calories*).

Shove back through mob towards exit. Grow aware (*tones up short hairs on back of neck*) of being followed by large tattooed citizen with 1 round roast fat in trouser turn-up. Buy him large brandy (*no calories*).

Hi! How was lunch? Isn't it *great* to be able to take in Mister Belt a couple of notches? I know you're feeling pretty tired by now, but that's the way it is when you suddenly start exercising seriously: I promise you that your new body will soon accustom itself to your summer regime; any day now, you'll be able to leave out the plastic envelope altogether.

Of course, you may be looking a little green, but this can instantly be turned to your advantage: someone will suggest that you ought to take the afternoon off, and this is the opportunity you must grasp to go shopping for *an exercise bicycle*. Some experts maintain that it is better to go shopping for a real bicycle, but since you are not even doing real shopping, the point seems to me to be academic and irrelevant. You can get just as much exercise pretending to shop for a non-real bicycle!

Go to any large store, preferably one which has been advertising exercise bicycles, and ask them where you will find one. They will direct you to the enquiry desk on the top floor, who will direct you to the sports department in the basement, where everyone will be either at lunch or off sick, with the sole exception of a Finn brought up in Taiwan. You will run around together for a while, pulling out badminton sets and shotguns, until his colleague returns from lunch and summoning all the English you would expect from a Chinese brought up in Finland, directs you to the seventh floor, which will turn out to be Ye Old Copper Kettle Burgerbar and Staff Infirmary.

A fist-faced matron will then send you back to the enquiry desk on the top floor. However, since you have now run some four or five miles through the store, shedding POUNDS POUNDS POUNDS and firming up everything (including intention to strangle), you may now pause and drop into Ye Olde Copper Kettle Burgerbar to reward yourself with

TEA

1 Pot Lapsang Soochong
1 Toasted Stoneground Tea Cake
2 Bath Olivers (no butter)

Sit down on counter-stool, wrapping legs around chromium monopod to stay mounted (*tones up hips, buttocks, insteps*), put sleeves down in ketchup rings, whip sleeves up again (*firms elbows*), order tea as recommended above.

Return waitress's stare for 5 minutes (*tones up jaw muscles, makes blood race*).

After 30 minutes (*manufactures adrenalin, grinds unsightly edges off teeth*), tea arrives. It is a Charlie Chomper Champion Cheeseggfish-beefburger Fourpounder Plus Charliechips, accompanied by a mug of something so iridescent that it clearly has a Zippo lighter at the bottom of it.

Gaze at this for a while, and leave (*no calories*).

Hi! So how was tea? Isn't it fantastic to be *lean*? Think how much fitter you are to run back to your car, especially as it has now been towed to Waterloo Car Pound! Feel those feet hit the pavement! Feel those knees jerk! Any day now we're going to be in shape to catch one of those waving bus conductors!

Leap that road island, dodge that motorbike, vault that shopping-cart, pump those muscles, burst those lungs, tone up that

DINNER
1 Saline drip
1 Cylinder oxygen

Alan Coren 2.6.1982

'Acupuncture may work for a while Mr Tidworth. Any quack treatment may work for a while. But only true scientific medical practice can keep a person alive forever.'

TO SUFFERERS FROM NERVOUS DEPRESSION.

IT'S VERY WELL TO GO DOWN FOR SIX WEEKS INTO THE COUNTRY BY YOURSELF, TO GIVE UP TOBACCO AND STIMULANTS, AND TO LIVE THE WHOLE DAY, SO TO SPEAK, IN THE OPEN AIR; BUT ALL THIS WILL DO YOU NO GOOD, UNLESS YOU CULTIVATE A CHEERFUL FRAME OF MIND, AND TAKE A LIVELY VIEW OF THINGS.

*'Plenty of exercise and one high protein morsel daily –
that's our method!'*

THE SURGEON TO HIS HENCHMAN

What ho! my staunch Assistant, there is work to do anon,
So gird thee with thine apron true, and put thy stout sleeves on.
Prepare to pound; drugs must be ground; the brazen mortar ring,
And the pestle roll in the marble bowl, and the scales will have to swing.

It is the merry Christmas-tide, when worthy people eat
Five times as much as is good for them, drink ten times more than meet.
The fields lie bare in the winter air, or yield beneath the plough.
Though fallow be they, we make our hay; 'tis the doctor's harvest now.

The boys are home for the holidays, and they feed unchecked by rule
Of dietetic discipline, and economy at school;
Roast beef they cram, and turkey and ham, or sausages tuck in,
And pudding of plum, till they become filled nearly to the chin.

But oh! the vast capacity which the juveniles evince!
Each urchin still some room can find within for the pie of mince.
Or tart of jam and blanc-mange they cram and their skins with jelly stuff,
And custard and cream, and yet they deem that they have not had enough.

Dessert succeeds; new appetite its delicacies wake,
And they gobble up apples, oranges, nuts, almonds, raisins, cake;
Besides a deal of candied peel, and dates, French plums, and figs;
Whence business to us shall accrue, so please the little pigs.

The revel is not ended yet – for pastime they stand up,
And that restores their appetite, and heartily they sup.
They gorge a mash of rich sweet trash – at midnight seek their beds.
The sun will smile, next morn, on bile, and no end of aching heads.

There will be pills for thee to grind, and draughts for thee to pour,
And powders thou wilt have to weigh; provided be, therefore.
And mingle and make, all ready to take, each remedy and cure,
For feeling queer, of Christmas cheer to come which will be sure.

Mix plenty of the dose of black, roll many a pill of blue,
And also compound colocynth, and compound aloes too;
And the powder grey in doses weigh; likewise the Pulv: Jalap:
And the Pulv: Rhei – they'll be wanted by right many a little chap.

To remedy too much mince-pie put up Vin: Antim: Tart:
And Ipecacuan: which will like benefit impart,
And to distress from fond excess in pudding give relief,
And the system clear of the wine and beer together with the beef.

Of Senna good provision make, and Scammony as well.
Divide in doses manifold a lot of Calomel.
Cheeks will grow pale, on beef and ale if maidens dance and romp.
Quinine at hand have, therefore, and Mistura Ferri Comp:

See that our lancets all are sharp; our cupping-glasses sound;
Scarificators springing well, and well, if need be, ground:
Our leeches all right, and inclined to bite: for blood must needs be shed,
In case it should, through too much food, be determined to the head.

See that Unguent: Cantharidis is at thine elbow nigh:
For blisters it may also be our duty to apply;
And since we're afraid that so many our aid this Christmas will require,
The red-lamp clean – that it may be seen – and look to the night-bell wire!

Anon 3.1.1857

*'I want you to meet Miss Hepworth – she too is on decoagulants
and diuretics.'*

*'You're a mess, Mr Bulstrode. It would be cheaper to knock you
down and start again.'*

DOC BRIEF

Robert Buckman on
MODERN DRUGS

ANTIBIOTICS

You may not know this, but one of the most
extraordinary episodes in modern pharmaceutical history occurred nearly ten years before the
invention of penicillin in the tiny laboratory of
the Swedish bacteriologist Ajax Venders. He
was growing some dangerous bacteria (*poxinella
nastii*), isolated from the groin of a London dray-
horse. Always a meticulous observer, Venders
noted a tiny fleck of white powder had fallen on
to one of the dishes, and when he rubbed it, the
bacteria came off! Excitedly, he gathered more
small particles of powdered stone and rubbed
them all over the bacterial plate – and in that
moment, Ajax Venders became the inventor
and father of . . . scouring powder! He soon
realised its potential in fighting mankind's
greatest enemy, ground-in dirt, and, as everyone
knows, he named his invention after his son

Vim and ten years later Alexander Fleming Bell
stumbled across penicillin while trying to discover the secret recipe of Kentucky Fried
Chicken.

Anyway, nowadays there are dozens of different antibiotics produced for different
purposes. Here's a consumer's guide to what's
what in today's infections:

Penicillin – the first and, for many, the classic
antibiotic. Unmatched in its class, it kills
streptococcal organisms at an astonishing rate
(from 0 to 60 in 7 seconds). Named by Alexander Fleming Bell after 'Penny', his wife's daily
housekeeping allowance, it is one of the few
things that make one proud to be an infected
Briton and says more about you than
septicaemia ever can.

Ampicillin – the Pepsi-cola of penicillins. Named
after Alexander Fleming Bell's second son
Ampony (Alexander had bad hand-writing as
well as being mean), it has a broader spectrum
than its parent Penicillin, its brother Willycillin
and its cousin Norman StJohncillin. It is active
against some gram-negative bacilli, most encap-
sulated cocci, all Welsh nationalists and selected branches of Tesco's.

Gentamicin – the connoisseur's antibiotic.
Strong without being brash, distinctive without
being expensive, it is very forward on the palate
(which is why it's given by injection) and goes
well with infections of flesh, fish or bowel.
Never leave the Intensive Care Unit without it.

Tetracycline – a subtle, mysterious, elusive compound, at its best treating infections of skin,
genitals and Sagittarians. There may well be an
unexpected change in your travel plans and
financial arrangements on Thursday, and you
will be visited by a tall, dark woman. Take the
tetracycline for a week afterwards.

TRANQUILLISERS

We tend to think of stress as something that is
exclusive to man and the Primates, but this is
simply not so. Not in the least bit so, in fact. It
has been shown by a group of Norwegian zool-
ogists that the most stressed animals in the
world, or at least Norway, are the gold-crested

newts. The main experiments were published in 1979 by Jensen, Svensen, Rasmussen and Cnut-face in the *International Journal of Behavioural Investigations Into Things Newts Do*. They observed the newts for many years, using very sophisticated monitoring equipment, including telemetric blood-pressure cuffs, and bugged their phones. Eventually they learned to recognise the characteristics of newt-stress, which included outbursts of aggression, arguments and stopping kids' pocket-money for no reason. Interestingly, newts procreate by fertilising the eggs outside their body after the female has laid them, so as often as not, it was the male that got the headache on Saturday night. After literally thousands of observations on these colonies, the Norwegian group knew so much about newt stress patterns that they were able to sell the newts nearly half a million dollars' worth of Librium and retire. I guess the only moral of the tale is that tranquillisers can work for more than one species at a time.

Here are some of the common tranquillisers:

Librium and Valium – The Castor and Pollux of the benzodiazepine firmament, only not so far away and easier to swallow. They are both immensely active tranquillisers, and in a huge multi-centre double-blind trial were placed third in the list of the most powerful sedating and soporific substances. The two ahead of them were hymns and Richard Baker.

Herculaneum – This is not so much a tranquilliser as an Italian city buried by lava when Vesuvius did its number in the fourth century BC. However, as the contemporary historian, Pliny the Slightly Elder, recorded at the time, 'This is certainly one way of dealing with insomnia, but I'll bet it won't catch on.'

Tritium – This is not much of a tranquilliser either. In fact, it's the radioactive isotope of hydrogen that is found in heavy water. Perhaps the nicest thing one can say about heavy water is that, contrary to popular supposition, it isn't fattening. It is, however, the starting material for nuclear bombs, so in a curious way is one of the main causes of all the things we use Librium and Valium to deal with.

WATER-BEDS

Water-beds are not really members of our modern pharmacopoeia either (I'm sorry, I don't seem to be able to stick to the subject very well this week, but I have got a doctor's note excusing me from coherence on Wednesday). Anyway, the point about water-beds is that they have many properties of addictive drugs – people get acclimatised to them and feel peculiar if deprived of them. Water-beds are found in many parts of the Western world, e.g. bedrooms. It is said that the warmth and the rocking to-and-fro motion triggers subliminal memories of pre-natal life in the womb. That may or may not be true but it's a good line and my friend Derek said he's never failed with it. Mind you, like many water-bed users, he is an incorrigible liar, and became so fluent and skilled in deceit that eventually he was forced to leave university and go to medical school.

THE DOCTOR ANSWERS YOUR QUESTIONS

Q: I seem to be obsessed with ladies' knickers. I think of very little else and in an average week, I handle thousands of pairs in all colours and sizes and styles. Is this normal? Marks and Spencer, London.

A: I don't think you should worry unduly. You sound to me like a perfectly healthy, if slightly immature, department store, and this may be just a phase you are going through. Try and develop an interest in other things – socks and quiches, for instance. Get out and about a bit, open a few branches in the country or abroad. If you find that the knicker problem is really destroying your peace of mind, perhaps this is something you should discuss with your stock-room manager.

'Actually, that's the beauty of a placebo. It just gives the illusion of an overdose.'

'Look, he's raised you from the dead – don't you think it's coming it a bit to start pestering him to do something about your receding hairline?'

'I *SAY*, OLD MAN, WHO'S YOUR CHEMIST?'

NOT A LOT OF IT ABOUT

Free sex will soon be available on the National Health Service, it was claimed yesterday. Dr Martin Cole predicted that substitute lovers will be prescribed for patients with bedroom hang-ups. He believes that other doctors are now coming round to the view that making love with a stand-in husband or wife does help cure problems.

The Sun

Mr Kevin Dunmoe limped heavily into the waiting-room, eased himself onto one of the wormy bentwood chairs with a heroically muted groan, stretched his right leg out in front of him with both hands, and smiled the smile of the damaged brave.

There was, of course, nothing wrong with his leg. But, in his frequent visits to his GP down the long arches of the years with his myriad minor malfunctions, the head colds, the whitlows, the aches, the corns, the alopecia, the passing quirks of ear and sphincter, Mr Dunmoe had invariably chosen a waiting-room persona which suggested that his right leg had come off at the hip, but that his upper lip was taking this in its stride. Once, when a small boil beneath his left arm had refused to come to a head, he had turned up in crutches and a rudimentary neck-brace fashioned from a raspberry cloche.

Today, in particular, his ailment required subterfuge of a high order. The leg would ward off risky solicitude. Even so, a pre-emptive strike might be wise. He turned, wincing, to the large middle-aged woman beside him.

'I see,' he said, 'that your little boy has got his head stuck in a saucepan.' He tapped the utensil with his knuckle. 'Who's been a silly little fellow, then?'

'NYONG!' cried the saucepan. 'BOYNG!'

'What did the little lad say?' enquired Dunmoe.

'He said *Sod off*,' replied the woman.

'Dear, dear!' said Dunmoe. 'How old is he?'

'Forty-three,' said the woman.

Dunmoe stared at her.

'But he's got shorts on!' he exclaimed. 'He has got two badges for woodcraft. He has got a jack-knife and a woggle.'

'That,' said the woman, 'is part of his treatment. You nosey bastard,' she added.

'Are you his mum?'

'I am his wife. As you're here, would you like your other leg broken?'

The waiting-room door opened.

'Mr Dunmoe?' enquired the receptionist.

Dunmoe got up, with dramatic difficulty, and followed her into the dark green corridor. She stared at his stiff leg.

'Bit of cramp,' said Dunmoe, straightening up.

She led him into the doctor's surgery. The doctor glanced up from baggy eyes, and down again.

'Mr Dunmoe,' he said.

'There's a bloke out there with his head in a saucepan,' said Dunmoe. 'Also, he is a boy scout from the neck down.'

'I have a number of sexual cases, Mr Dunmoe,' murmured the doctor, 'now, if you'll just go behind . . .'

'Oh,' said Dunmoe. 'Ah. Got you. He, er, he likes something a . . .'

'I do not discuss my patients,' said the doctor. He wound his propelling-pencil lead up, and then down again, slowly. 'What is it this time, Mr Dunmoe? Colic? Chaps? A terminal blackhead?'

'As a matter of fact,' said the patient, drawing his chair an inch or two closer to the desk, 'it is the other. Not, I hasten to add, anything involving saucepans, nothing of that order, it is a fairly straightforward case of, er, thing.'

'Thing?'

'Basically, what I am suffering from might be described as not enough.'

'I see.'

'It is now May, practically June, and if I tell you Boxing Day, and a possible near miss on February 11, if my memory serves me right, I assume I do not have to draw pictures? Also, Boxing Day she was knitting throughout.'

'Knitting?'

'A bed jacket for the cat. You see where the priorities lie, I take it?'

'What do you expect me to do, Mr Dunmoe?'

Dunmoe cleared his throat.

'I pay my stamp regular,' he said. 'I expect to get a prescription. Also a certificate for off work, due to where I shall need to be in bed, I assume, unless it is matter of doing it on the premises at Boot's, which I should definitely not prefer, what with people coming in for Gee's linctus etcetera all the time, also staring at you from the weighing machine.'

The doctor sighed, and pushed his prescription pad around his desk.

'I take it you have discussed this with Mrs Dunmoe?'

'I hardly see her. She is up cat obedience classes all day. The bugger will not get into his bedjacket. That is possibly what is giving her all these nocturnal migraines, wouldn't you say?'

'I really have no idea.'

Dunmoe sniffed.

'Makes no odds, anyway. I have definitely gone off her. It really come home to me when I got a lift up here on his truck from my mate Brian and I realised how unattractive my old woman was by comparison.'

The doctor glanced up, a small gleam of professional interest lighting his eye for the first time.

'You mean,' he said, 'that you find Mrs Dunmoe less attractive than your friend Brian?'

'No,' said Dunmoe, 'I find her less attractive than his truck.'

The doctor stared at Dunmoe for a while, chewing his lip. It had been a long day, and it wasn't over yet. There was old Mrs Rapaport and her insatiable need for lollipop men to sort out, there was the not inconsiderable diagnostic hurdle of Detective Inspector Wimbley and his parrot Russell, there was the postmistress whose husband had taken to hanging upside down from the shower-rail and who was now insisting on her right to a free NHS wooden stake and mallet, to say nothing of the man in the saucepan. So he sighed, and he scribbled on his pad, and he ripped the prescription off, and he handed it to Dunmoe, who took it and ran, in his haste almost knocking over the incoming patient; who appeared, to his fleeting eye, to be a Merino sheep in a gymslip and pith helmet.

'Yes?' enquired the pebble-eyed girl at the chemist's prescription counter.

Dunmoe pushed his crumpled paper across, awkwardly.

'I was, er, I was rather hoping for a man,' he muttered.

'That's not what it says here,' said the girl, scrutinising the scrawl. 'Your doctor is doubtless trying to wean you off 'em.'

'I didn't mean that,' whispered Dunmoe.

'It says here,' said the girl doggedly, 'small rat-head with – God almighty, some of them have appalling writing! What's that say?'

'I'm not sure, I –'

'Give us it!' cried a large woman beside Dunmoe, who was waiting to pay for an elastic stocking and a pelican bib. She put on her glasses. 'Small red-head, that is. Small red-head with lard bust.'

'Large bust,' hissed Dunmoe, gripping the counter. 'Large bust.'

The salesgirl turned, slid back a ribbed glass partition, and shouted:

'Mr Dennison, we got any of them big-busted little redheads in stock?'

Most of the customers looked round. Dunmoe closed his eyes. When he opened them again, the pharmacist's head was poking through the hatch.

'No, Doreen,' he said. 'I'll have to get one made up.'

'You'll have to wait,' said Doreen to Dunmoe.

'I'll take anything!' cried Dunmoe, his neck reddening. 'Blonde, brunette, you name it. I do not wish to hang about all day, narmean?'

The pharmacist stared at him, and back at Doreen.

'Some people!' he cried. Several customers nodded. 'Take anything, he says! He does not appreciate that mine is a skilled profession, Doreen.'

'Could kill him, a blonde,' said Doreen. 'Some people!'

'Took me three bloody years to qualify!' shouted the pharmacist at Dunmoe. He hurled the partition shut. The ribbed glass cracked.

Dunmoe, hotfaced, walked away, accentuating his limp, feigning interest in a display of

trusses. Customers whispered. After some fifteen minutes, his name was called, very loudly, and he looked up.

The pharmacist was approaching with a short dumpy woman in a bright red wig and an asymmetrical bosom.

'Bloody hell!' cried Dunmoe. 'Can I have it in a bag?'

'You shut your face!' shrieked the prescription. 'You are bloody lucky to get me.'

'She can go like a bomb, under the right conditions,' said the pharmacist.

The prescription stared at Kevin Dunmoe.

'Fat chance,' she said.

'Once a night,' said the pharmacist, 'with a glass of water. It is dangerous to exceed the stated dose.'

'Dangerous?' cried Dunmoe. 'It is bloody impossible!'

'Come on,' said the prescription, 'you got to get my dinner ready.'

'What?'

The prescription passed Dunmoe a green voucher.

'That,' she said, 'is a DHSS chitty entitling me to a hot dinner, to include soup and a choice of pudding. You tear off your half and claim it

'I've been looking at the tests, and I can find nothing wrong with you, except that you are slightly old hat.'

back via Swansea. I do not eat pork, by the way, it gives me wind.'

Dunmoe thrust his way through the chemist's, limping appallingly, biting his lip, the prescription clacketing after him on her broken heels, and pushed out into the street.

At the bus stop, an idea suddenly occurred to him.

'Here,' he said, 'funny thing, I suddenly feel a lot better! I could very well have undergone a miraculous cure. Well, well! My, my! I'll be saying goodbye, then.'

'I should cocoa,' said the prescription. 'I do not get mucked about, sunshine. There's laws. You could get done for malingering, false declaration, wasting public time and money, all that. You could also get a kick in the slats. You do not slide out of your hot dinner commitments that easy, son, also roof over my head for seven nights, catch my drift?'

Bitterly, Dunmoe limped aboard the bus. The prescription followed him upstairs. They sat down together, behind another couple. Dunmoe gasped.

It was the man with the saucepan over his head. Beside him sat a tall, lissome, Chanel-wafting natural blonde, clinging to the patient's arm. Dunmoe leaned forward, and peered. She had the best legs he had ever seen in his life, the dimpled knees just visible beyond the gleamingly cream *balcon* of her decolletage.

Dunmoe banged on the saucepan.

'How?' he cried. 'How?'

'UNGYUNG!' replied the saucepan. 'MYO-ING! CLANG!'

'What did he say?' shrieked Dunmoe.

'He said,' murmured the blonde, her voice like molten gold, 'that he decided to go private.'

Alan Coren 31.3.1982

'I think it's those pep-pills he's been taking.'

Richard Gordon
DREAMS OF IDEAL MEDICINE

Britain's top growth industry of the Seventies is sickness. In 1970, the National Health Service takings were a miserable £2000m of taxpayers' money. Today, it rakes in a healthy £6000m. It provides interesting work for Britons of all levels of intelligence, from BMA through NALGO down to NUPE. Employment has leapt in our hospitals by 30 per cent – by 20 per cent in 1973–76 alone, during their reorganization for greater efficiency.

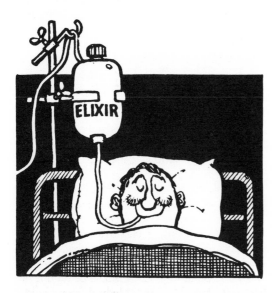

Like the leisure industry, the illness business has spin-offs creating millions for pharmaceutical companies, health farms and health shops, and the constructors of hospitals for Arabs, body scanners and joggers' track-suits. Freddie Laker had nothing on David Ennals.

Now axewoman Thatcher, mad as Lizzie Borden, gives our country's biggest, booming conglomerate forty whacks. Things could be worse. If homo behaved sapiently, it would go bankrupt.

Who in their right mind would smoke?

Tobacco would disappear like the smallpox virus, except for samples kept in research laboratories under stringent security. This would be the death of cricket, but would cheer up the 10,000 Britons a year who now die to keep it alive. What sensible man would drink alcohol more readily than drain disinfectant? Our disused pubs could be refurbished as Social Security offices, for the glorious but necessarily unemployed undead. Nor would he eat much. As every serious weight-watcher knows, baked jam roll with hot custard is but another slippery path to the grave.

With a 10 mph speed limit, road accidents would be as sensationally reported as nuclear ones. It would clearly not increase journey-times in towns, and anyway most people drive not to arrive, but to ventilate their aggressions and express their personality, both of which are flattened by modern governments like bluebottles under the swat.

The British people should ideally approach sex with the same responsibility as they fill their pools coupons. Abortion would be abolished and contraception a redundancy, with the incidental benefit of eradicating VD, pleasing the Pope and extinguishing the Festival of Light.

'Christ, Linda! The perfume of your naked flesh is driving me mad!'

'Oh, Cyril! Squeeze me tighter – can't you feel I'm trembling like a trampoline?'

'Linda, love . . . shall we . . . have a baby in nine months' time?'

'Yes, yes! I want you, Cyril! Like an aching tooth the dentist.'

'It's a serious business, you know. We'll have to miss going to Benidorm.'

'I don't care, I don't care . . .'

'Okay, darling. We'll get married on Monday morning, then we can go ahead.'

An ideal world is self-expanding. Without sexual hang-ups, smoker's hypochondria, dyspepsia and the traffic, tranquillisers would be our caviar and psychiatrists obliged to open booths as fortune-tellers.

As our medical resources are as limited as the oil, and the old gulp the biggest doses, euthanasia should be an incident accepted as casually as childbirth. This is a respectable medical idea. Edwardian clinical biggie Sir

William Osler wanted everyone permanently chloroformed at 60, though he grew less enthusiastic over the notion as he himself approached retiring age from life.

Our imperfect world is fastidious about involuntary redundancies from the human race, which should not be in the slightest unpleasant. Euthanasia Hiltons can be opened in such agreeable resorts as St Tropez or Great Yarmouth, to follow Thomas Mann's suggestion that 'The dying are to be treated as though in enjoyment of a permanent birthday.'

Six months of subsidised gambling, free bar and grill, free wenching (if capable), should produce a jolly 'end of term' atmosphere. Christmas would be held twice a year. The merry moribund would scribble their comic cards (post free) depicting vulgar undertaker jokes, 'Having wonderful time, before it is up.' So sybaritic a regimen would in many cases render unnecessary the eventual gassing, performed with infinite discretion in the basement. The same principle inspired Ancient Rome, when caged Christians at the Colosseum were obliged to dance and sing before the wooden floor was whisked away for the hungry lions in the layer below.

If five-star genocide were unacceptable to a world ideal but still cost-conscious, the alternative is sick rationing.

All would be issued with books like the familiar hand-prop of every TV show about World War II. The commonest fatal diseases – cancer, coronaries, strokes, bronchitis – would have its page of tiny coupons, to be snipped by the doctor at each consultation. Other complaints would be obtainable on the 'points system', used by Churchill's government for tinned food and biscuits. The patient's points may be surrendered for any diseases fancied. A neurosis would be valued at 2 points, tonsillitis only 1, fractured leg 12, perforated peptic ulcer 20, blindness 50, eczema 3, schizophrenia 6. Constipation and the Common Cold are off the ration. Pregnant women are issued with a special book entitling them to free vomiting and a Caesarian. When the coupons run out the book is burnt, and so is the patient.

Rationing inevitably throws the shadow of a Black Market. Doctors would be finding their best patients cases of gallstones or dysmenorrhea under the counter, slipping them heart or hair

transplants. Fond mothers would sacrifice their own points, so their little ones might enjoy the polio, measles and whooping cough which they would otherwise never know. Spivs at street corners would offer coupons for everything from acne to zoster. This would be countered by a vigorous Government advertising campaign, with the slogan ILLNESS CAN SERIOUSLY DAMAGE YOUR HEALTH.

Our geriatric hospitals, being mostly in pleasant open countryside, can be reopened as cheap motels for the healthy and lustful young. Unused general hospitals found conveniently in the middle of cities – Bart's, Guy's, the Edinburgh Royal – need only slight alteration to become multi-storey car parks. The NHS could sell off mountains of tablets, lakes of potions and scrapyards of instruments through stores handling army surplus. A disposable scalpel is exactly the instrument for a British steak. Syringes are excellent on the greenfly, home X-rays so much more interesting than home movies, and the experience of a steel band on bedpans unforgettable.

As hospital waiting-lists become as outdated as the Dead Sea Scrolls, consultants would be permitted to tout. This would boost the economy by millions through the ingenuity of Mayfair advertising agencies.

Schsssss ... prostatectomy will restore that youthful stream.

Agoraphobia. Don't leave home without it.

Quins? Well, they said anything could happen.

Don't be vague, ask for a lobotomy.

The Department of Health's residual functions could be conveniently absorbed by the Environment, alongside clean air, anti-noise and water pollution. There would be no one at home in Her Majesty's Medical Household, though as a Government concession the Foreign Office would be allowed unlimited diplomatic illness, tennis could retain its elbow, housemaids their knees and athletes their feet.

But if nobody was ill, what should we talk about after the weather?

Richard Gordon 14.11.1979

PARSONS AND DOCTORS

Many surgeons, doubtless, remarked an absurd letter from a clergyman which appeared the other day in *The Times*, recommending charcoal – in combination with brandy and opium – as a cure for cholera. One of them, dating his letter from Bloomsbury Square, has fortunately written an answer to that communication, pointing out that the quantity of the last-named drug prescribed by the parson would amount to 10 or 12 grains every half-hour; and of course destroy the patient. This clergyman, no doubt, is a well-meaning person, but he should confine himself to pointing the way to Heaven, recollecting that the opposite place is paved with good intentions. Possibly he overstated the quantity of opium, by what may be called a clerical error; a proper dose of it is well known to be beneficial in the complaint in question: brandy is also found useful: and to these two ingredients of the mixture we should be disposed to ascribe any favourable result of its administration. The third is probably inert; otherwise it would be a convenient medicine, as anybody, in case of need, might munch cinders.

Clergymen, in their anxiety to do good, are too often accustomed to add the treatment of bodies to the cure of souls. In order to minister to patients as well as penitents, they ought to possess the gift of healing, and that having ceased to be supernaturally imparted, they had better acquire it in the ordinary manner, by attending the hospitals. Some add homœopathy to what the rubric prescribes in the Visitation of the Sick, and by so doing do the least harm that it is possible to do by empiricism; as the swallowers of their globules at least die of their diseases: but we would advise even the homœopathic divines to stick to theological mysticism, and not deal in 'riddles' which will generally be 'affairs of death'.

Percival Leigh 22.10.1853.

FASHIONS IN PHYSIC

[The President of the British Pharmaceutical Conference lately drew attention to the prevalence of fashion in medicine.]

A fashion in physic, like fashions in frills:
The doctors at one time are mad upon pills;
And crystalline principles now have their day,
Where alkaloids once held an absolute sway.
The drugs of old times might be good, but it's true,
We discard them in favour of those that are new.

The salts and the senna have vanished, we fear,
As the poet has said, like the snows of last year;
And where is the mixture in boyhood we quaff'd,
That was known by the ominous name of Black Draught?
While Gregory's Powder has gone, we are told,
To the limbo of drugs that are worn out and old.

New fads and new fancies are reigning supreme,
And calomel one day will be but a dream;
While folks have asserted a chemist might toil
Through his shelves, and find out he had no castor oil;

While as to Infusions, they've long taken wings,
And they'd think you quite mad for prescribing such things.

The fashion to-day is a tincture so strong,
That, if dosing yourself, you are sure to go wrong.
What men learnt in the past they say brings them no pelf,
And the well-tried old remedies rest on the shelf.
But the patient may haply exclaim, 'Don't be rash,
Lest your new-fangled physic should settle my hash!'

Mr Clarke 4. 10. 1890

ADVICE GRATIS TO THE POOR.

Doctor. 'YES, MRS BROWN! YOU MUST GIVE HER PLENTY OF NICE PUDDINGS, SOME CALVES' FOOT JELLY – A LITTLE WINE – A FOWL OR TWO – TAKE HER TO THE SEASIDE, AND, IF POSSIBLE, GO WITH HER TO BADEN-BADEN.'

'He's **much** better. Receiving the last rites seems to have been just what he needed.'

'. . . so in the interests of national economy, I thought I'd wait until my face was full up then have it lifted all at once.'

'What we propose to do is remove your head, have a look inside
your neck, and then close you up again. It is a brand new
technique and it would be less than candid of me to pretend that
it does not involve certain dangers. The question is: How badly
do you want to get rid of that cough?'

Heart Specialist (meeting patient whose case he had
pronounced hopeless a year ago). 'YOU STILL ALIVE!
WHAT CONFOUNDED QUACK HAS BEEN TINKER-
ING WITH YOU?'

'You urgently need a holiday, Mr Abthorpe –
Might I suggest Lourdes?'

'We **treat** illness here, Miss Rothbart. If you insist on being
cured, you'll have to go to some quack.'

WHICH SPRING TONIC?

A consumer's guide to seasonal pick-me-ups

NURSE BETTY'S BLOOD-CLEANSING VERNAL PURGATIVE AND SLUG DESTROYER

Based on the root-extract of an Indonesian holy turnip and used for over 3,000 years to alleviate bovine constipation, this aromatic syrup makes a useful top-dressing for orchids as well as a bracing basis for admixture with almond gin and brine to make a general-purpose spring tonic and upper-cylinder lubricant.

First popularised during the Crimea as a treatment for herpes or badly-rusted cannon hubs, the mixture later became known to thousands of sufferers from athlete's foot, alopecia and gunpowder scorching when it was administered by Nurse Betty, or Betty of Breganza, a war photographer at Guernica who had used it for developing films. Nurse Betty was the first to attempt to bottle the stuff on any scale but was asphyxiated by the fumes when accidental spillage caused a reaction with an iron bedstead.

The purgative is harmless to fish at room temperatures but it is best to avoid contact with polished veneers, certain fleshy fruits, brightwork trim or aspirin.

BOLSOVER'S CAMPHORATED EMOLLIENT SLUICE, THROAT BALM AND LAWN REVIVER

Available as a gargle, ointment, suppository, aerosol spray or lozenge, Bolsover's is claimed to clear out sinuses, drains, blocked livers, impacted topsoil, sumps, waxy ears, wormy cats, gutters or seized hinges in a matter of moments. As little as half a teaspoon in 1 gallon of tap-water is sufficient to kill most aphids or will shift really stubborn stains on washday. It also promotes strong bones.

Primarily intended as a treatment for rheumatism or a hangover, the sluice is also ideal for reviving badly-tarnished brass or can be used to smear a length of oakum string to make a waterproof caulk. In normal use, the lozenges are not caustic.

Many homeopathic practitioners use Bolsover's, together with vetch, dandelion and extract of toad's spleen, to flavour a restorative yogurt, whilst the smoke is said to be efficacious against arthritis, ox-bite and witches.

Must not be used near inflammable upholstery or to glue flexible plastics. Store out of reach of children or small birds and do not allow to come into contact with nylon surfaces, dry-cleaning fluids, nail-varnish remover or badly-inflamed tonsils.

DOCTOR HORACE JUVENAL'S ABSTERSIVE SPRING LINIMENT AND GREENHOUSE FUMIGANT

Millions throughout Greenland swear by this traditional remedy for frostbite, chilblains, cuts, stings, grazes, stains on the bath and unsightly blubber rashes. Dr Horace Juvenal is believed to be the name used by a number of Gilyak or Nivkhi pharmacists who, in 1701, pooled their resources to try and come up with an effective poison to use against visiting missionaries. It was when one of their number chanced upon the discovery that the resultant prototype venomous liniment cleared up any mucopurulent discharge from the pharyngeal passages of moose that he wrote up his findings in *The Roederer's Dyjèst Bøk of Wintrie Woenderes* and word spread amongst the local goatherds.

Modern laboratory analysis of the liniment has shown that it is highly effective against moss and can be used as a refollicating poultice to treat influenza in sheep. When warmed, the preparation is a useful bark oil against boring insects on the eucalyptus and the salts are believed by some to work wonders on the feelings of general lassitude which sometimes accompany an attack of malaria.

Not suitable for negative-earth batteries or as a tortoise polish.

SYRUP OF CROCUS DEPURATORY CORDIAL AND RADIATOR SEALANT

Equally effective as a nasal decongestant, hardwood oil, bath gel, kettle fur remover, corn

remover, lip salve or expectorant, syrup of cro-
cus is believed to have been first synthesised in
1106 by the Abbot of Rheims who sold it as an
alexipharmic herbal rub and ointment for repel-
ling gnats. During the Civil War in America, a
similar preparation was widely used to control
gophers and there is sketchy evidence that it
formed the basis of the famous 'Little Phoenix'
all-purpose remedial paste and alcohol-rich
elixir which all but wiped out the Sioux.

Later refined by the addition of tin, Bavarian
hog spittle and powders derived from the
daffodil, the cordial is now highly-prized
throughout the Kalahari as a mulch and for
dipping the tips of arrows used for hunting
warthogs, which it sends into a deep sleep.

Must be kept in a cool place, preferably in a
sealed lead container, and should not be introduced undiluted into the inner ear. Makes a
refreshing tea.   *17.3.1972*

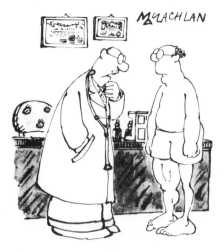

*'My advice would be to go back to a
manual gearbox, Mr Abthorpe.'*

EPISODE IN HIGH LIFE.
(From Our Jeames's Sketch-book.)

The Lady Kerosine de Colza. 'I CANNOT TELL YOU HOW PLEASED I AM TO MEET YOU HERE, DR BLENKINSOP, AND ESPECIALLY
TO GO DOWN TO DINNER WITH YOU.'
Dr Blenkinsop (an eminent Physician, much pleased). 'YOU FLATTER ME, I'M SURE, LADY KEROSINE!'
Lady Kerosine. 'OH NO! IT'S SO NICE TO SIT BY SOMEBODY WHO CAN TELL YOU WHAT TO EAT, DRINK, AND AVOID, YOU
KNOW!'

FATSTOCK TRIALS

It's just coming up to the seventeenth month since I quit smoking. I had a real, oil-burning habit. Eighty cigarettes a day. To people who pointed out that I couldn't have smoked that many even if I smoked one every five minutes, the answer was: what do you mean, every five? I could annihilate a full-sized filter cigarette every *three* minutes, yielding a fire-cone slimmer than a red-hot wire. Tallulah Bankhead went through 150 cigarettes a day. Some people have professed their incredulity at this. But considering that she rarely slept, and had a mouth wide enough to smoke four at a time like guns in a turret, there's no mystery. She had the dual psychology of the ideal heavy-duty smoker: i.e., the constitution of a water buffalo and the death-wish of a Zulu regiment. So, in my small way, had I, and still have. But I no longer have a nicotine habit, and what follows is an account of what happened when I kicked it. It is a story less about tobacco than about blubber.

I started smoking on a regular basis when I was about nine years old, although it was not until my early teens that I climbed above 20 a day. At school and at Sydney university I worked my way towards the forty a day mark without suffering notably in health. My intake of impurities was delicately balanced, the beer which should have made me fat being offset by the tobacco that should have made me thin. As it was, I was the complete surfing hero, with a waist nipped like a bee's and buttocks firm enough to break a needle. As I strode squeakily onto the hot sand of Newport or Avalon (ritzy northern beaches to which the young culturati raced on weekends to rub barn-door shoulders with the bourgeois girls they despised and would one day marry) I was a miracle of finely tempered poise, with nothing to conceal my unearthly beauty except a pair of shades and a weightless pair of blue nylon trunks with a ten-pack of cigarettes and a lighter crammed sexily into the waist band.

When I got to Britain the eco-balance of my body started to come apart in a big way. First of all, I averaged nine quid a week for nearly four years, and needed fags and booze not just as decorations to life but to make life worth living

at all. The beer, as Barry Mackenzie so rightly howled when first encountering it, was piss. The cigarettes were Players Weights bought in packets of five. Bumming pennies from my fellow factory-hands in order to score another packet of this archetypal pleb snout still haunts me as one of the most indulgent episodes in a life that has never been exactly rich in forbearance. A diet consisting almost exclusively of starch completed the job of tilting my system over the edge of the slide, and from there on it was downhill all the way for ten long years, until, seventeen months ago, I was thirteen and a half stone – two stone up on the fighting weight that my tanned plates once wafted airily over the fine white sand – had been more than two years at the aforesaid 80 *per diem*, and had a cough like a polar bear with a dum-dum through the throat. I used to wake up with collapsed lungs (it feels like a combination of jactitation – that sudden fall when you're half-sleeping – and choking on a marshmallow) and would have to start my own breathing artificially. Years of bad diet had done for sixteen of my teeth and 90% of my hair: my clobbered frame was wallowing like the *Scharnhorst* after the British battleships had ceased shelling. The only question was whether I was going to let the cigarette companies box me in and finish me off with torpedoes.

Suddenly, afraid, and with a nod of relieved assent from my brilliantly tolerant wife, who had never nagged but must long since have been worried ill, I got a grip. I quit cigarettes cold turkey. Celebrated for my capacity to get addicted to anything, I was smart enough not to try switching the affection to any substitutes – except food and drink, which I planned to acquire a taste for. Anyway, my motivation was as strong as it could possibly be: stop smoking or get dead. And I had a good idea for a system of rewards: spend *all* the money (which at 80 a day is practically enough to run a Rolls) on something you like – don't try to save it. What I spent it on ensured that I had something to show, every week, for my miracle of self-control: music. I started buying two or three cheap-label records every weekend, and by the end of the first year possessed practically everything in the Turnabout catalogue that Brendel, Frankl and Klien had ever played on. It was good, at the end of six months, to be able to ponder the image of an inspiring line-up of Beethoven sonatas played by Alfred Brendel, instead of an enormous pile of cigarette butts smoked by Clive James. For years I had used the hub-cap off a Bedford van as an ash-tray. I threw it away.

The pang of want never stopped, and probably never will. I still wake up at two o'clock every morning and reach automatically for the cigarettes. To find them missing remains a shock. But on the whole the urge was fairly easily contained – principally, I suppose, because life was on the whole running my way. (It seems to be almost impossible to kick an orally-centred habit when you're on a downer.) It was lucky this part of the job was manageable, because one of the side-effects turned out to be a terror. I mean the weight. Up it went. Two stone overweight already, I thought I would have at the most only half a stone more to contend with before any further increase levelled out. Wrong, baby.

I got unhappy about being heavy and when you're unhappy you eat, thereby getting heavier. I couldn't pass the kitchen without taking a snack. A typical meal on Saturdays was a pound of minced beef divided into 16 mini-burgers fried in butter and eaten between slices of fried bread, the whole deal topped off with two differently flavoured packets of crisps. I would then go to sleep. As my weight edged up past fourteen and a half stone, I bought bigger and bigger pairs of jeans without finding a pair loose enough not to chafe me when I walked: sweating lard onto the central seam of the trouser is an unbeatable way of slicing your upper thighs to bleeding ribbons, resulting in a walk that looks exactly like piles. I asked a doctor friend why everything I wore smelled like Brie. His answer was, fat stinks.

I had been working on the theory that only a year's indulgence in as much food and booze as I wanted would tide me over the first wave of terror at quitting fags. By the time the year was up, I was $15\frac{1}{2}$ stone and needed a quack. My doctor was a lady who put me on the National Health diet, which at first glance looks like a warrant sequestering everything you have ever loved: it's a bitch. There are two ways to stay on it. The first is to remember that it allows three times as many calories as the ordinary diet in the Soviet Labour camps, and should therefore sustain life, even when it feels like it's going to kill you. The second is faithfully to ingest the accompanying drug, a variety of amphetamine which would drive you crazy with irritable depression if it were not so evident, within the very first week, that the diet *works*.

It really does. I lost a stone and a half in three

'. . . and to think if I hadn't have given up smoking I'd have had to miss out on all this.'

weeks – call it a pound a day – another stone in the next six weeks, and am now levelling out at a few pounds above twelve stone, which is my medically advisable minimum. And it was all so easy. As with ditching the cigarettes, all I needed to trim the weight was to be afraid. Men, it can be done.

You know the rest: all your old clothes come back to you as a brand new wardrobe, people mistake you for your younger brother, etc. But what needs to be emphasised is that you can *eat* so much better. Steaks as big as your pocket allows, with half a pound of crisp sprouts piled on top. It's expensive – diet is a middle class luxury – but not as expensive as snacking between fatty meals. The only thing I eat between meals now is apples. Can this be the same man who used to wait until his wife wheeled her trolley into the distance of the Marks & Sparks food hall as a prelude to purchasing a packet of jelly babies at the cash-desk and furtively eating them all before she got back? Once again I walk everywhere, and my squash partner – ten years younger than I am and a fanatical athlete – has to break me at deuce in the fifth game instead of blowing me away to nothing in the third. The mirror is my friend again. Imagined sand squeaks beneath my feet. Marble-Bum returns. Time-traveller.

The secret of kicking a habit is to control the side-effects – of that I'm certain. Anti-smoking propaganda ought always to stress this fact: otherwise it's just asking people to quit for a while, get fat, and then get back on the weed, which won't make them slim – all you're doing is turning a thin sick man into a fat sick man. Nor does any man who understands the evil of this world care a damn about living longer. The thing to emphasise is that you'll live *better*. No more Pompeiian ash-clouds when you knock over the hub-cap, or dark-night-of-the-soul encounters at three in the morning with a cigarette machine that charges your last thirty pence for a look at an empty drawer. Instead, you're clean. And if you've been forewarned you can be slim, too. Which is another way of living better. Use my system, designed by an immoderate man for use by immoderate men: if you can't stop getting addicted to things, get addicted to self-control.

Clive James 9. 1. 1974

NEVER DONE ME ANY HARM

Did you see where Doctor something, some doctor, I meant to jot his name down and I think I did but I forget where – are you listening, darling? – perhaps I wrote it on the thing, the kitchen thing, he says that smoking affects the what-is-it, the you know, the memory.

I was discussing this, actually, in the – what's that pub called with a horse in it, where we saw what's his name last week with the very thick, oh hell, very thick things, spectacles, he's retired now, used to be a you know, took people's teeth out, Dawson, Tarrant, some name like that, it doesn't matter, Horrocks, something like Cosgrave. Nag's Head. I was discussing it with Jack Gibbs in there, Dobbs, the chap who had the house on the corner of the street where your language woman lived, linguist, Connie, Naomi, you were going to have thingumajig lessons, Greek. Down where the buses stop at the place-thing, bus-stop.

Yes, you do. You always say he reminds you of that actor in the Nixon, the Washington, the Watergate Behind Closed – No, because we saw it at Leicester in a proper how-d'ye-do, cinema, All the President's Men not on TV, begins with D, Jason Roberts, the weekend we went up to your Uncle Frank's – what? – Uncle Fred's, and coming back we had to stop overnight at Rugby, I don't know why I said Leicester, and you said then he reminded you of Jason Robards, I mean, or the other way round, Robards reminded you of him, Dick Dobbs. Gibson. Want a cigarette?

Well, I will. Could you shove the thing across – thank you. If it works. I think it wants a new what-is-it, they knap them in Norfolk, flint-knappers, wants a new flint. No, it's OK. I'm thinking of the one on the dressing-table in the, on the sideboard, in the, you know, darling, through there, where we've just had supper, in the dining-room. Dick Dobson's got one of those with a, with an electric, with a little, what do you have in cars, batteries, a little battery. He was showing it to me in the Horse's Groom, in the where they serve the drinks, the place with the, in the drinks place, the bar, you just press the doodah and up comes the doofer, the flame. Bought it at Grant's what used to be Grant's, no messing about filling it with, used to be Graham's, don't have to keep filling it with stuff. Used to be Bennett's, did it? Where Mrs Fenwick did part time, Mrs Harris? Used to do mornings for you when we lived in you know, the other house.

Dick had read about this new smoking scare as well, said if anyone had lost their memory because of cigarettes it certainly wasn't him. He'd been on cigarettes as long as he could remember. Forgot exactly when he'd started, must have been before the, what's the word, the business with who-is-it, Adolf what's-his-name, before the war. Or just after. But he said there might be something in it, because he'd been talking to someone, couldn't remember who, and they were on thirty a day and said they kept forgetting their wife's name, even – stub that out for me, Ethel, this ashtray's full, I mean Edith, sorry, thanks – because according to this doctor names are the first to go. I told him it was me he'd been talking to, and he said, 'You're right, Trevor, it was,' and I said, 'Ralph, actually', and he said, 'Have another drink,' and I said, 'Same as last time,' and he asked me what I'd had last time.

He smokes thingummies now, with the end things, what are they called, filters, not for health reasons, the what-is-it content, the you know, melts when roads get hot, the tar content, just that the plain ends stick to his where the mouth opens, lips. Could you pass the cigarette box, darling? No, it isn't. It's not full, but it's not empty, there are five in there, you can't tell me I ever forget how many cigarettes I've got, there you are, one, two, three, four, five. Five. Four now. Well, I do pride myself, I admit it. You can't tell me I ever forget – have I just said that, sorry. Names and faces, yes, the office phone number, what tie I'm wearing, but that isn't smoking, it's age. No, well, you're younger, aren't you. Still got a few what-have-you's, brain cells.

Harry says it's age, and he's only on those long thin, those dark brown, those long brown, you cough when you inhale, dark thin cigars. He says – what? – yes, you do, the gardener, Harry, surely you know our own gardener? Walter,

then. How old do you suppose he is, Walter Sharp, fifty-five, Walter Smart? And can't name anyone he odd-jobs for. It's 'them up the road', 'him across the way', 'her down the roundabout'. Everybody knows that him across the way is Crabtree the vet, he's got it on his front where you go in, the thing you go through, front gate, a brass sort of, you see Mrs Crabtree polishing it, what Americans call a – what if I do mean Mrs Appleyard? – something to do with beaches, a shingle, they call it, brass plate.

God knows what he calls you and me, when he's talking about us up the road or down the roundabout, probably 'the Patersons'. Oh, are we? Yes. Well, I mean, if anything. Probably just 'them at The Larches'. All right, Laurels. No, you're quite right, I don't want another. I thought I'd put this one out. It's perfectly natural with advancing things, years, to get a bit, what's the word when you can't remember, to get a bit forgetful about things that don't matter, and nothing to do with the number of thingummybobs you get through, cigarettes, if you ask me. Anyway, I'm all right on essentials. I can remember when they were twenty for elevenpence-halfpenny, with a halfpenny change slipped in the thing, the cardboard what-d'you-call-it with a sailor framed in a lifebelt, the packet, when you got them out of the, put your money in the, got them in all the

'Well, I'll give the placebo a try if it'll make you feel any better.'

pubs now, slot-machines, got them out of the machine with this halfpenny in, and none of your Government thing warnings that nobody takes any, you know, attention, pays any attention, takes any notice.

Yes, I know it's the last, darling. Only in the whatsit, though, the box. I've got three upstairs in the case you gave me, but cases have gone out except at, what did I go to with Peter Coote last Autumn at the, in Park Lane, the big place where they have them. Dinners. With Peter you know. Something like Coote. Armstrong. Yes, you do, darling. Incidentally, he smokes like a funnel, not funnel, on the tops of houses, chimney.

So that's three, and in the glove-compartment of the, cubbyhole in the, out in the garage, there's what looks like an empty packet but there's one right down inside lying flat.

How about supper when I've finished this? Sorry, so we have, yes. I forgot. I suppose there's nothing worth watching on the?

Basil Boothroyd 30.1.1980

SLIM CHANCE

Twenty years at the Olivetti, five million words, many of them different, and I never wrote about smoking or diet.

What is this sentence?

A testimonial to be handed in at the Pearly Gates, while I hop from one foot to the other and wait with a chewed lip (if they have feet and lips There) for the committee to decide between harps and tridents?

An attempt to wheedle the Sun Alliance quack into turning a kindly ophthalmoscope upon my mortgage extension request? ('The applicant is a humorist who has never written about smoking or diet, ergo he neither smokes nor eats, throw the bugger another fiver.')

An oleaginous bid to charm Olivetti into kicking in with a replacement, given that after five million words the platen is as graven as a Mosaic tablet and the £ flies across the room

when struck in anger ('SIR, THIS RIDICU-LOUS GAS BILL FOR *PING!* . . .')?

No.

This sentence (i.e. *that* sentence, a foot or so of words having now elapsed) is the first sentence of an article about diet. The other sentences (i.e. between *that* and *this*) are to cover the embarrassment of writing it.

I do so only as a public service. You will have seen, of course, that every other major newspaper and magazine (with, as I recall, the exception of *The Embalmer*) has in recent weeks given over much of its columnage to diet advice. There are two main reasons for this: it is summer, when people wish to look their best in raincoats and balaclavas; and second, it is not possible for anyone to do anything about anything any more, viz. remove the Russians from Afghanistan, remove the hostages from Iran, remove the Government to somewhere with rubber walls, and so on. Faced with a world which has rendered us impotent—we cannot even stop Graham Gooch flashing at rising balls outside the off stump—man has increasingly turned to those areas over which he does retain control, i.e. cutting down to five a day and losing half a stone. Several have bought cycling machines.

When the Russians take out Molesworth, we shall simply turn our faces from the flash and, lung-clean and skinny, pedal motionlessly away.

Leading the file of jogging lard as it gasps up Fleet Street is *The Sunday Times*: not only have they come up with their own diet sheets, not only have they thereto appended recipes and other kitchenhold hints, not only have they coerced four eminent fatties, including the world's largest peer, into volunteering as guinea-pigs, they have also leaned on a number of restaurants to join a mutual promotion stunt wherein the restaurateurs now offer a Sunday Times Menu, although this may be nothing more than a timely sop to the NGA, since a glance at the restaurants mentioned suggests that only compositors could afford to eat there.

Clearly, *Punch*, ever in the vogue vanguard, could not be caught with its trousers down; or, rather, with its trousers swelling at the seams. And since I myself have, in the past four weeks, slimmed astonishingly down from an unhealthy thirteen stone three to a totally debilitated twelve stones, I felt it my duty to pass on the fruits, unsweetened, of this wonderful experience. There will also be diet sheets, kitchen hints, advice on exercise, and a free extra bonus on cigarette-reduction. There will, however, be no list of Punch-linked restaurants, but anyone writing to this office and including a stamped addressed envelope will receive a list of cheap stonemasons.

THE PUNCH DIET: SOME PRELIMINARY NOTES

I have been on a low-carbohydrate, low-cholesterol, low-protein, low-liquid diet; since nutritional experts appear to disagree on everything, it seemed best to cut out food. I have designated it the low-spirit diet, or, because it is slimmer, LSD. As it is also unnervingly expensive, we have a happy coincidence there. It is the only happy thing we have. I get no butter, eggs, milk, sugar, fried items, cheese, bread, potatoes . . . I am starting from the wrong end. The senescent Olivetti will not cope with the list of what I don't get. What I get is Swedish ceiling-board, a little sunflower oil, and water. Sometimes there are tiny fragments of fish in the water. Birthdays, I get a slice of lemon in it. Every Coronation Day, I am allowed a stick of celery.

The fact that I have lost seventeen pounds in four weeks, though, is not, I am certain, entirely attributable to this appalling regimen; mainly, it is to do with converting the fat I already had into energy, and this cranking up of the metabolic engineering was achieved, and I stress this urgently, as a direct result of *attempting* to diet.

PRE-BREAKFAST

Most diet sheets start with breakfast. That is their error. Slimming begins the moment you wake. Pre-breakfast, on the *Punch* diet, you weigh yourself. This involves, since the bedroom carpet is an unreliable base, standing the weighing-machine on the (closed) lavatory, and climbing on it, using a deep breath, a small heave, and the handle of the cistern. As you grow slimmer, you may be able to dispense with the handle. Simply dragging your adipose ruins aboard the scales, do you see, has already expended invaluable milligrams; early on in your diet, you will find that the scales frequently

slide off the lid while you are dragging yourself onto it, thereby forcing you to repeat the exercise, often losing many more grams in sponging forehead blood off the bidet, etc. Once on the scales, remove heavy items like wedding rings, yesterday's forehead Elastoplast, navel-lint, and so forth: individually, they may look little, but collectively could add up to several more grams, especially if your wedding-ring, as you fall from the slid scales, rolls under the bath. Crawling after it on nothing more than yesterday's Ryvita could expend anything up to an ounce.

This I usually follow with a little screaming. Feel the heart race! Pump, pump, pump goes the little fellow as you get those nasty waste thoughts out of your system, burning fat as you go.

Clean the teeth vigorously. The weight of plaque is often under-estimated. Shave close. Doesn't that pile of heavy bristles in the basin look *good?*

BREAKFAST

Half a cup of black coffee, no sugar

Watch the children eat four rashers, two eggs, porridge, and six slices of toast. Look at their happy, full faces! Don't you want to reach out and clout them? Well, that's a *good* feeling, on the *Punch* diet: rage is even better than screaming for metabolising fat.

Don't forget skimmed fat-free milk. The milkman always does. Running after his dwindling float and shouting 'What about my bloody skimmed milk?' is a wonderful way to slimness and health.

ELEVENSES

What! I hear you cry. *Elevenses?* Well, not as fatties know them. At eleven o'clock, talk to the people in your office, school, chambers, hospital, pit-face, or wherever, about your diet. Tell them how many milligrams you lost last night, tell them how many stairs you can run up now without gasping, tell them how many old suits now fit you again. They will run away from you. Run after them, shouting as you run. Shout about Perrier water or Flora. It is marvellous exercise, toning up calves, thighs, and jaws.

LUNCH
Half a cup of black coffee, no sugar
Slice of crispbread
Radish

Drink the black coffee. Eat the crispbread. Sticks in the throat, doesn't it? Don't you wish you'd saved some of the coffee, now? Throw the radish.

After lunch, it is time for your first cigarette of the day. Take it out of the packet. Stare at it. Put it back in the packet. If you have been on thirty a day heretofore, you will find yourself biting your knuckles, a wonderful toner-up of flabby chins and neglected forearms. The rest of your lunch hour could profitably be spent in running after all the colleagues you didn't see at eleven o'clock and trying to tell them about giving up cigarettes.

Alternatively, why not visit a health food shop? Do not buy anything; just because it is full of nourishing mouse-droppings and organic bacteria does not make the stuff slimming. But get into an argument with an assistant. You will find that the skinny young swine is all too happy to explain to you about the presence of the godhead in yak yogurt, and may pursue you for miles, ringing his little bell. This is called Reverse Elevenses.

TEA TIME
Yes, it's true. Around four o'clock, you will almost certainly, if the *Punch* diet has been assiduously followed, feel as though a man has come to dismantle your head with a coke-hammer. Now is the time to take a high tea of four aspirin in a bouillon of lightly poured water. Aspirin contains no calories, and taken regularly on an empty stomach, will rot holes in your alimentary canal, allowing any food inadvertently taken to fall through. You might also be fortunate enough to end up on a surgical ward, where the food is utterly inedible.

DINNER
Shredded white cabbage
Two slices crispbread
Large tumbler neat water
Sultana (or raisin)
Half a cup of black coffee, no sugar

In the *Punch* diet, an electric vegetable shredder is invaluable. Try to find one where the nut securing the drive shaft falls out. Then walk or run to the nearest stockist. In my own case, this was Stuttgart, so I had to compromise by running to a place that *looked* as though it might stock it, since it stocked every other bloody piece of electric rubbish. Then bang on the door. Then look at your watch. Then run home again. A wonderful exercise for legs and fatty fists and lungs. As soon as your fists are less fatty, you can begin, on your way home, punching fools daring to stare at you for talking to yourself.

Shredding the cabbage by hand, it is simplicity itself to lose a thumb weighing anything up to four ounces. Remember, for your health's sake, to use fresh coffee, ground at home. A tin of Blue Mountain, slipping from your cabbage-slimy and enfeebled fingers, will bring hundreds of little beans bouncing all over the kitchen floor, a wonderful exercise for flattening those podgy knees!

SLEEP
Needless to say, it is very important to get as little sleep as possible. Asleep, our metabolic rate goes down, there is nobody to shriek at, no way of burning nervous energy, and no means of crossing half bloody London trying to buy a cycling machine only to find they have just sold the one you reserved over the phone.

On the *Punch* diet, you lie awake wondering whether you're going crazy. Sometimes you worry whether a burglar has just torn through a partition wall or whether it was only your stomach grinding in its endless poignant hunt for an errant crumb. Sometimes you see fat lamb chops walking across the ceiling explaining to jacket potatoes that they now smoke forty a day.

The only cure for this is to get up and weigh yourself. Trying to find a wedding-ring under the bath in the dark, you could be well on the way to living forever.

Alan Coren 16.7.1980

4

A Sick Business

'To be frank, the operation will be touch-and-go – it could make me or break me.'

THE MEDICAL STUDENT

Son of the scalpel! from whatever class
You grind instruction just enough to pass
St George's, Guy's, North London, or King's College –
Thirsting alike for half-and-half and knowledge –
Thou who must know so well, (all jibes apart,)
The true internal structure of the heart –
This heart – which you 'a hollow muscle' call,
I offer thee – aorta, valves, and all.

   Though to cheap hats and boots thy funds incline,
And light rough Chesterfields at one pound nine;
Though on the virtues of all plants thou'rt dumb
Save the *Nicotiana Tabacum*,
(*Pentandria Digynia!* – Lindley – mum!)

Though thou eschewest the hospital's dull gloom,
Except to chat in the house-surgeon's room,
And practically practise, in addition,

The 'Physiology of Deglutition.'
Yet much I love thee, and devoutly swear,
With lips that move controll'd by 'the fifth pair,'
That I will ne'er know peace until our hands
Shall form a 'ganglion' with Hymen's bands.
  Then haste, my love, and let me call thee mine,
Precious and dear as sulphate of quinine,
Sparkling and bright as antimonial wine,
Sharp as the angles of a new trephine,
My reckless, noisy, fearnought VALENTINE!

Anon 12.2.1842

1846.   OUR MEDICAL STUDENTS.   1886.

COLLEGE OF GENERAL PRACTITIONERS

A scheme, it appears, has been set on foot for the establishment of a 'College of General Practitioners.' Now, since diseases, very generally, are either imaginary, or such as would get well of themselves if let alone, one highly important branch of General Practice is the treatment of cases which do not require it. The General Practitioner, though not a Consulting Physician, must consult his own interest. *Verb. sat. sap.;* but if the College Examiners are not saps, they may take a hint from *Punch.* Teachers must first be taught; and here, for the benefit of those whom it may concern, is a little

Appropriate Examination Paper: with Answers.

Q. What should be the medical treatment of a common cold, which, in fact, requires only white-wine-whey and a footpan.

A. *Pulv: Antim:* grains five, to be taken at bed-time; and *Mistura Feb:* three table-spoonfuls every three hours, with *Emplast: Picis* to the region of the chest.

Q. If you asked a patient to put out his tongue, and found it perfectly clean, what would you do?

A. Shake my head, and say, 'Ah!' or 'Hum!'

Q. What is the meaning of 'Hum,' Sir?

A. It means, '*I* see what is the matter with you.'

Q. How would you look on feeling a pulse which proved natural and regular?

A. Very serious; and I would pretend to be calculating.

Q. A lady, slightly indisposed, asks whether you don't think her very ill – Your answer?

A. I should say that she would have been so if she hadn't sent for me in time.

Q. Suppose a patient, in perfect health, demands what you think of his case?

A. I should tell him, very mysteriously, that he ought to take care of himself.

Q. An anxious mother, Sir, sends for you to see her darling child – What would you first do?

A. Begin by admiring it.

Q. How long, in a given case, would you send in medicine?

A. As long as the patient believed himself ill.

Q. That belief being erroneous, what would you send, pray?

A. I think, *Tinct: Card: Comp:* with either *Aqua Menthæ Pip:* or *Mist: Camph:*

Q. Be so good, Sir, as to translate the word 'Iter.'

A. Five shillings.

Percival Leigh 18.1.1845

Anxious Patient. 'When I wake in the morning I feel just terrible.'
Festive Physician. 'Not worse than I do, I'll wager.'

['Most of the better-class doctors have accepted Mr LLOYD GEORGE's
proposals.' – *Radical Press*.]
Butler. 'LADY JULIA GODOLPHIN WISHES TO SEE YOU, SIR, VERY
URGENT.'   *Doctor.* 'PUT HER IN THE QUEUE!'

She. 'AND WERE YOU SUCCESSFUL WITH YOUR FIRST
CASE, DOCTOR?'
He. 'Y-YE-ES. THE – ER – WIDOW PAID THE BILL!'

'Do you wish to see Dr Livingstone privately or on the National Health?'

OFFICIOUSNESS OF POOR-LAW MEDICAL OFFICERS

The following statement, which, with a voucher
for its authenticity, appears in a letter addressed
to the *Salisbury and Winchester Journal*, is quoted
by the writer from one of the medical period-
icals. The Poor-Law Guardians throughout the
country, who are so strenuously opposing MR
PIGOTT's Bill for the monstrous purpose of effect-
ing 'the better regulation of medical relief to the
poorer classes in England and Wales', are doubt-
lessly able, out of their own experience, to relate
many cases of equally gross excess of duty on the
part of medical officers:–

'A workhouse, which contained during the last year
an average of more than 25 patients on the sick list,

was visited by the medical officer 212 times, and who was knocked up twice a night. There must, therefore, have been about 5406 personal visits made, the aggregate number of miles travelled was about 105. Estimating each patient to have taken two doses daily, 18,200 were taken within the year. About 500 external applications were supplied, one broken arm and one out of joint were treated; upwards of 150 separate examinations of persons on admission were made, and 52 long weekly reports were written out. Many slight cases, as tooth-extracting, are not recorded. Many incidental duties are not mentioned. For all this about sixteen guineas are paid!!'

The fallacy of the whole of the foregoing paragraph is comprised in the last sentence – 'For all this about sixteen guineas are paid.' Sixteen guineas, in such a case, are supplied for furnishing paupers with proper medicine and attendance. The practitioner, whose ridiculous assiduities are above described, thought proper to give his workhouse patients the same amount of attendance and physic as he would have afforded to respectable people. The consequence doubtless was, that if his weekly reports were long, the Union obituary was short; conditions which ought to be precisely reversed in any such institution, the doctor of which is up to his business, which, at a salary of sixteen guineas, obviously consists in making quick work of his cases, and saying as little about them as possible. 'Above all things no zeal!' is a maxim that Poor Law Guardians desire to impress on the mind of every medical officer in their employment, for his official guidance. His private practice is another affair. He has no business to bestow on a pauper the time, skill, and attention which he devotes to a guardian, although, taking one patient with the other, he may be said to kill two birds with one stone.

Percival Leigh 26.5.1860

GENEROSITY OF A CORONER'S JURY

The generous indignation and uncalculating sympathy for which the verdicts of respectable coroners' juries, in reflecting on any hesitation at self-sacrifice in the interests of humanity, are remarkable, will appear to great advantage in a case of which the particulars, taken from *The Times*, are subjoined:–

'The Remuneration of Medical Men. – Yesterday, at the Fox Tavern, Paul Street, Finsbury, an inquest was held by Mr H. Raffles Walthew, the deputy Coroner, touching the death of Richard Clarke, aged two years. Mrs M. Clarke, 94, Paul Street, said that on Thursday last her son became ill. He had received a fall some time before. On Friday morning, at half-past three o'clock, she noticed the child getting stiff, and sent for Dr Buss. The doctor did not come for some time. The delay was occasioned by his getting her husband to sign a paper binding himself to pay 5s. The child was dead when he did come. The witness's husband was a mechanic.'

It is easy to understand how this simple statement so powerfully affected the benevolent gentlemen to whom it was made as to prevent them from considering the facts which it comprises with the calmness of cold-blooded reason. They naturally felt that when a medical man is informed by a poor mechanic that his child is ill and requires attendance, an instant inclination to rush to the child's bed-side should overwhelm every other idea in the mind of the medical man. At such a time, to be capable, for one moment, of thinking about so paltry an object as that of securing a five-shillings fee, of course they considered him a mean unfeeling fellow. Accordingly, perhaps, they overlooked the little circumstance that the delay of the doctor in going to see the child was somewhat increased by the time which was occupied in getting the child's own father to engage to pay the five shillings.

The facts, as above stated, were admitted by the medical man who had been summoned to attend the deceased child, Mr Henry Buss, M.R.C.S. He pleaded, however, that:–

'He was obliged to act thus to guard against imposition. He had to live by his profession. Those who could not pay ought to apply to the parish doctor. If a person asked him to go purely as an act of charity, he would attend.'

This last declaration on the part of the witness the jury appear to have entirely disregarded, in their large-hearted excitement created by the notion of a doctor not immediately jumping up and running off without question or consideration to see the mechanic's child that he was summoned to attend. Some of them might have been, perhaps, mechanics themselves; who knows? Be that as it may, when the coroner had summed up, and told them that the course pursued by DR BUSS was not peculiar to that gentleman, they returned the following special verdict casting censure on the mercenary medical man, and evincing fellow feeling with the poor mechanic:–

'That the deceased died from effusion of serum on the brain, and the jury desire to express their regret that medical men should refuse to attend the poor without guaranteed payment. The jury consider that as such refusals are frequent, the parish authorities should take it upon themselves to pay the fees for first visits of medical men to poor persons in urgent cases, and the jury are of opinion that such a provision would be the means of saving lives.'

The jury cannot be suspected of having had any conception of what effusion of serum on the brain meant. Had they known that, their minds might have been composed by the assurance that no promptitude of attendance would have availed the patient. Perhaps, if they had considered their verdict less under the disturbing influence of their higher feelings, they would have a little enlarged the expression of their regret, above quoted. They might have expressed their regret that any medical men should have to depend upon their profession for their living, and should be obliged to refuse to attend the poor without guaranteed payment, in order to guard against imposition. The majority of these liberal and enlightened jurors are probably tradesmen. Perhaps there is a baker among them; perhaps there is a cheesemonger. If so, we may be sure that the baker is in the habit of supplying bread to the hungry without stipulating for payment, and the cheesemonger is always ready to contribute more than his mite, and add a bit of gratuitous double Gloucester to the eleemosynary loaf. Likewise, if those gentlemen of the coroner's jury comprise a tailor, he is doubtless accustomed to clothe the naked on the same unselfish terms.

Percival Leigh 15.11.1862

BARNSFATHER'S SYNDROME
A Short Story

Paris was a disappointment. Young Mr Edgar Barnsfather FRCS had expected to find himself in the Champs Elysées, jammed between the Arc de Triomphe and the Eiffel Tower, with the Folies-Bergères opposite. The medical conference was in an angular, concrete hotel like a hospital, a five-minute bus-ride from the airport terminal. He had never been to France before. He arrived in late afternoon, and queued for his conference documents in the hotel foyer behind a fat, ruddy, gingery, rustic-looking practitioner in tweeds.

'Awful bore, these conferences,' said the fat doctor genially.

'I wouldn't know,' Edgar replied meekly. 'I've never attended one.'

'I'm only here for the beer. Exactly like everyone else. Dreadful rackets, all scientific meetings. A most damning reflection on the way we have to live. The doctors go along for a jolly, which they can set against their income-tax. Some sinister drug company subsidises it all for the publicity. As for the hotel, at this time of the year they'd entertain a convention of cannibals to let their empty bedrooms.'

Edgar could not help feeling shocked. 'I think myself privileged to be delivering a paper.'

'Really? What about?'

'Barnsfather's Syndrome. Pseudoperforation in young adults.'

'Ah! You're a surgeon?'

Edgar nodded. 'I'm a registrar at the Percival Pott.'

'An excellent London hospital.' The tweedy doctor smiled over half-moon glasses. 'And what *is* Barnsfather's Syndrome?'

'I've a paper about it in the latest *BMJ*.' Edgar's voice was twisted painfully between pride and modesty. 'The first I've published, actually. I collected a series of young persons admitted with the signs and symptoms of acute perforated peptic ulcer. Abdominal pain, rigidity, vomiting, that sort of thing, but nothing physically wrong. All psychological.

Stress, you know. Very interesting. Some were even operated upon. But perhaps this is not in your line?' he apologised.

'Not really.'

'And what do you do in the profession?'

'Oh, I just go on being President of the Royal College of Therapeutics.'

A pretty French girl in a thin white blouse stood behind a long table with piles of plastic-covered folders, each emblazoned in gold with the name of the drug company and the products it hoped the assembly would go home to pre-scribe. When Edgar introduced himself, she smiled delightedly and pinned to his lapel a card saying E BARNSFARTER.

'Have a nice time,' she said.

He stared at the lace edging her bra. He was full of unsurgical thoughts. It was his first night in two years of marriage away from his wife. The girl had given him such a lovely smile. 'Is there anything to do in the evenings?'

'There are excursions by autobus to the Opéra and Comédie-Française.'

'I mean of a more . . . er, intimate nature.'

'You like the *boxe*? There is a tournament just near the hotel.' She smiled delightedly at the next doctor. 'Have a nice time.'

Edgar bought a postcard of Napoleon's tomb, addressed it to his wife in Putney, but could find nowhere to post it. He slipped it in the pocket of his John Collier suit. He would take it home to put on the mantelpiece. It would save postage. He went up to his cuboid bedroom. It was getting dark. He gazed through the double-glazing at the wintry fields, the brightly lit motorway, the ugly anonymous buildings which fringe all airports. Apart from seeing people drive on the right, he could have stayed at home.

He sat down with *Le Canard Enchaîné*, which he had extravagantly bought at Heathrow, to get in the mood. He had been irritated at hardly understanding a word, having imagined that anyone with his intelligence and O-levels could read French. In the plane, he had thrown back his head and laughed loudly over the pages, just to show that he could, until the other passengers started staring at him oddly. So he had read through all the leaders in the *British Medical Journal*, his pale, domed forehead stamped with critical furrows.

He went carefully through the printed con-ference programme, received from the girl downstairs. He would be speaking the following afternoon to the psychosomatic section, between a surgeon from Chicago on the diges-tive processes of confused rats and a professor from Milan on phantom tapeworms in nuns.

He drew the *BMJ* from his briefcase, its han-dle secured at one end with a surgical suture. The learned pages fell open at the paper on Barnsfather's Syndrome. He read it again all the way through, as though returning to the oft-folded sheets of a love-letter.

He sighed, staring through the window at the cars flicking along the motorway. This would be the first conference in a lifetime full of them. He might be a mere surgical registrar, but one day he would ease himself into a professorial chair. Everyone in the hospital told him that he was far more use in a lab than an operating theatre. He looked at his watch. It was dinner-time. He could savour the famed French cuisine.

Edgar crossed the foyer towards a notice saying:

INTERNATIONAL
GASTROENTEROLOGISTS
AND CHOLECYSTOLOGISTS
OFFICIAL DINNER.

'Monsieur?' icily demanded a man in striped trousers at the door.

'Dinner,' Edgar explained. '*Dîner. Com-prenez?*'

'Monsieur has an invitation? This is the din-ner for the officials of the Congress. I assure monsieur that he will find an excellent dinner in the hotel restaurant.'

The restaurant was a long room hung with brown plastic curtains, so dim nobody could see the food or read the menu. He ordered *cervelle au beurre noir*, because he was fond of kidneys. He chose half a bottle of Beaujolais, because it was the only name he recognised. When the dish appeared, he realised that he had made an error in anatomy. The wine tasted peculiar, but he was too timid to complain. He ventured after-wards into the bar, but it was jammed with doctors drinking free brandy and noisier than students. He went to his room, undressed and read *Recent Advances in Surgery* until he fell asleep.

He woke. The curtains were drawn, the room pitch. He felt terrible.

He groaned, clasping his stomach. It was the brains, the wine. Some vile, explosive chemical reaction had occurred between the two. Brains always solidified in alcohol. That was how pathologists kept them, in pots.

He gasped. Colic tore at him with tiger's claws. He lay back on his pillow, breathing quickly. He was ill. He was also a doctor. He must decide what was wrong with him.

Intestinal obstruction? Appendicitis? Meckel's diverticulitis? Acute pancreatitis? Alarming diagnoses leapt through his mind, like questions fired at students over the bedside. The referred pain of coronary thrombosis, perhaps? Or of acute meningitis? Bellyache could be anything.

The tiger leapt again. He sensed sweat on his brow. He groped in the darkness. His watch said it was barely midnight. He fumbled for the telephone.

'*Allo?*' said a woman's voice.

'*Je suis malade.*'

'*Vous êtes Monsieur qui?*'

'*Malade.* Ill. Kaput. OK?'

'Monsieur wants room service?'

'No, I want a doctor.'

'*Oui*, monsieur. Which doctor?'

'Any doctor.'

'But monsieur! The hotel tonight is full of doctors.'

Edgar bit his thumb-nail. It was like having a riot at the police ball and dialling 999 for the squad cars. 'Has the hotel a doctor? One who comes when the guests are taken *malade?*'

'*Mais bien sûr*, monsieur. But he is in Paris.'

'Get him,' commanded Edgar, as another pang exploded in his stomach. An hour passed. The pains were worse. He was dying.

He picked up the telephone again.

'*Allo?*' said a man.

'*Je suis presque mort.*'

'*Ah! Monsieur desire quelque chose à boire?*'

Edgar put down the telephone. He rose, reaching for the red-spotted dressing-gown his wife had given him for Christmas. He staggered to the lift, descending with his forehead resting on the cool metal side. The foyer was empty. Edgar knew his materialisation was alarming, but desperate diseases needed desperate remedies.

'Why, there's the surgeon,' exclaimed the ruddy-faced President of the Royal College of Therapeutics. 'Sleepwalking, eh? Or astray on your way to some nice lady's bedroom? You surgical registrars, all guts and gonads. Or is there a fire?'

The official dinner was breaking up. From the door earlier barred to him, drifted twenty or so doctors in dinner-jackets, all chattering noisily and slapping each other on the back.

'I'm ill,' said Edgar shortly.

'*Ill?*' The President was amazed. 'But you can't be ill here. We're all off duty. Enjoying ourselves at some crooked drug company's expense. Excellent dinner, Harry, don't you think?' he enquired of a tall man swaying beside him. 'I'm so fond of *cailles à la gourmande*. But of course, I should never dream of paying for them.'

'The wine was fine, Sir Marmaduke,' said the tall doctor, an American.

'I'm *so* glad you liked it. I chose it myself,' disclosed the President smugly. 'I must confess a favouritism towards claret rather than burgundy, and the Château Figeac '72 *is* very good. On the other hand, the champagne they gave us—I say,' he added irritably, as Edgar groaned loudly. 'Can't you do all that sort of thing in your room?'

'I'm in agony,' Edgar doubled up. 'I've got an acute abdomen.'

'Really? Well, I suppose you should know. I'm only a physician. I never feel at home below the umbilicus.'

'Sir, Sir Marmaduke—' Edgar staggered towards him imploringly. 'Can't you help me? I think I'm dying.'

'My dear fellow, of course, if *that's* the case,' said Sir Marmaduke more amiably, blowing into Edgar's strained face billows of brandy. 'One has one's Hippocratic tradition, and all that, eh? Human life must be preserved, however unworthy. Better have a dekko at your belly. Just jump up there.' He indicated the table previously supervised by the girl with the see-through blouse. He pulled up Edgar's mauve pyjama-top and pulled down his pyjama trousers. The other doctors crowded round. It was an unexpected after-dinner entertainment.

'Where does it hurt?' asked Sir Marmaduke, staggering steeply forward and pressing hard.

'*Ouch!*' screamed Edgar.

'Jolly interesting. You've got a retroperitoneal abscess.'

'Can anyone have a feel?' murmured Harry.

'My dear fellow, help yourself.'

'You're wrong, Sir Marmaduke,' Harry disagreed. 'It's a case of haemoperitoneum.'

'Don't really think so, my dear old boy.' Sir Marmaduke had his eyes closed. 'Patient would be more collapsed.'

'Ah! But they collapse and die suddenly. Like that.' Harry tried to snap his fingers, but missed.

'Excuse, please.' A Japanese doctor wriggled to the front, grinning. 'Please?' he asked, hand poised over Edgar's goosepimples.

'Dear Saki-san, do plunge in. I'm sure we can all benefit from your oriental wisdom.'

'Please,' decided the Japanese. 'Clear case, hernia foramen of Winslow.'

'Now *that's* a jolly good diagnosis,' agreed Sir Marmaduke warmly. 'Any improvement on a herniated foramen of Winslow, gentlemen?' he invited, looking round.

'*Ja so*, we haf the jaundice?' asked another doctor, pulling down Edgar's eyelid.

'*Mon cher confrère*,' suggested another. 'This case reminds me of one I saw some years ago in Algeria. Ruptured amoebic cyst of the liver. Has your patient lived abroad?' Edgar shook his head violently. 'Well, that is not necessary to get amoeba,' the French doctor consoled himself. 'My case was fatal by the way. They nearly always are.'

'How about Legionnaires' pneumonia?' remarked another brightly. 'It's very popular just now.'

'Lassa Fever can present like this,' came a voice from the back. 'Though of course I've never seen a case, nor even done a post-mortem on one. They whisk the bodies away so quickly in metal coffins.'

'Well, I must be toddling off to bed,' said Sir Marmaduke. 'Delightful evening. Delightful chaps. Don't forget the golf tomorrow, Harry. Anything to avoid the bloody papers.'

'What about me?' cried Edgar, sitting up.

Sir Marmaduke seemed to have forgotten him. 'I should get a glass of hot water from room service. Do you the world of good. Old remedies are best. If you're not better in the morning, toddle along to my suite and we'll have another prod.'

The doctors disappeared, yawning. Edgar crawled to the lift. He fell into his bedroom. He dialled Putney.

There was a long wait. 'Who's that?' began his wife suspiciously.

'Edgar.'

She gasped. 'Did you miss your plane? God knows, you insisted on getting there early enough.'

'I'm in Paris—'

'What do you mean, phoning?' she demanded crossly. 'It's dreadfully expensive. And at this hour, too. You scared me to death. Or perhaps you imagined I was out for the night,' she added cuttingly, 'and were just checking up on me?'

'I'm ill.'

'There're plenty of doctors to look after you.'

'They're all drunk.'

'What's the matter?' she asked with more concern.

'I've some sort of abdominal catastrophe. I'm

Nurse (*who has been many hours on duty – to patient's mother*) 'WHEN DO YOU THINK I SHALL BE ABLE TO GO TO BED?'
Patient's Mother. 'GO TO BED? I THOUGHT YOU WERE A TRAINED NURSE!'

coming home. There's a plane at five a.m. I'll try and get on it.'

'But what about your paper?'

'It'll be printed in the Congress proceedings. I should have liked to read it, but . . . what's the point, if I'm dead by tonight?'

'Oh, Edgar!' she cried. 'I'd no idea you were as bad as that.'

'I am. I must see a sober English doctor as soon as possible.'

'Oh, Edgar!' she said again, bursting into tears.

Groaning, gurgling, gagging, Edgar collected his luggage, ordered a taxi, staggered into the airport, changed his ticket, relaxed in his seat of the half-empty plane. He slept, exhausted.

He woke with the stewardess gently shaking him. 'Where am I?' he cried in panic.

'We've just landed at Heathrow. Don't worry, sir,' she said caringly. 'The captain had a radio message about you. You're in good hands.'

She tenderly helped him to the aircraft door. He found himself sitting on a fork-lift truck. Two uniformed men were waiting below with a stretcher. They slid him into an ambulance, which instantly raced across the tarmac with light flashing and horn blaring. A young man with glasses was leaning over him.

'I'm a doctor,' said Edgar.

'Are you? Well, so am I. Your wife alerted the airport. An acute abdomen, isn't it? I'd better take a look at it.'

He felt Edgar's tummy in silence. 'H'm.'

'What's the diagnosis?' Edgar asked anxiously.

'Without doubt, I'd say a clear case of Barnsfather's Syndrome. There was a lot of guffle about it in this week's *BMJ*.'

Richard Gordon 5.7.1978

AT HOME

THE SUCCESSFUL DOCTOR

DOCTOR ON THE BOTTLE

HONEYSETT drinks to the news that alcoholism is rife in the medical profession . . .

'Let me through, I'm a doctor.'

'There's no need for that, nurse – just let Dr Jimpson breathe over him for a few minutes.'

'I much preferred it when he used to use the village hall.'

'Here comes our doctor now.
He'll give you the blood test.'

'I'm afraid we're going to
have to operate again, Mr Grubly.
I think I may have left my
bottle of gin inside you.'

'I demand a twenty-third opinion.'

'Doctor can only see foot
disorders today, I'm afraid.'

DOCTOR SPARERIB'S SURGERY

'There has been a discernible increase in the complexity of complaints against the NHS, according to the Health Service Commissioner's Annual Report.'

The Times

'Good morning, Doctor Sparerib.'

'Good morning, Mrs Brone, and what brings you to us all bright and fresh today?'

'I am so very tired, Doctor Sparerib.'

'So am I, Mrs Brone, so am I. And I can tell you why we are both so tired.'

'Why is that, Doctor Sparerib?'

'This morning, Mrs Brone, at 4 a.m., when I was returning from Mrs O'Halloran's ninth confinement – a fine little chap, Liam Padraig – I was passing Chico's Room when I caught a glimpse of you emerging assisted by the resident reggae singer. This makes for tiredness.'

'But I must have some small relaxation, Doctor Sparerib. I have also a monumental headache and my sight is blurred.'

'Me too, and again I can help. I diagnose lack of sleep. You and I have, so to speak, come straight to the surgery from our night-chores on just a cup of Nescafé. Frontal headache and visual spectra may be expected.'

'Doctor Sparerib, you are less than fair with me. It is not as though I were a National Health patient. I bring you excellent symptoms – lassitude, headache, disturbed vision – and you simply will not diagnose a thing out of which I can get any conversational mileage. When Cynthia Crouche gave you similar symptoms you diagnosed a multiplicity of most interesting bodily malfunctions which make her the centre of attraction at the Bridge Club and the Golf Club. For me – nothing.'

'Now it is you who are being less than fair to me, Mrs Brone. Your friend Mrs Crouche is assisted, as you must be well aware, by the fact that she has one metal arm ending in a motorised hook. This cannot fail to make her the centre of conversation pieces at the Bridge Club and the Golf Club. Six no trumps and a handicap of twelve are for her the tours de force.'

'Then what am I to do, Doctor Sparerib, stay forever in the shadows?'

'I am thinking. Let me see, two lines open up. I could do for you what I did for General Sir Angus MacFie who was in charge of the searchlight defences of Lytham St Annes during the Korean War. In a long and distinguished career he had unfortunately sustained no visible or disfiguring wounds and thus little military conversation was stimulated by his appearance or movements. However, by prescribing inactivity and a diet largely consisting of port and marmalade pudding I successfully produced the most violent and painful gout I have ever seen. The resulting limp and anguish enabled him – I have the figures here somewhere – to increase his share in the conversation in the bar of the Army and Navy Club to forty-one percent. This from an occasional Harrumph!'

'What a clever idea – when do I start, Doctor Sparerib?'

'Before you do, it would be unprofessional of me not to tell you that we did go on to produce deep-vein clotting, a thrombo-phlebitic condition which has resulted in amputation of the left leg.'

'I am not mad about that – it would impair my activities at the De Mille Dancing Academy.'

'Then another thought, Mrs Brone. Develop aggressive tendencies. Have a fight in a couple of public bars. Park the Rolls on a zebra crossing and hit the traffic warden with your handbag. Eventually I could send you to a shrink and if you attacked him he would refer you with a bit of luck to a neurosurgeon. He would strap you in a chair and clamp your head in a metal ring. Then he would bore two holes in your skull, give or take three inches apart, into which he would insert two instruments like knitting needles but with diathermic capacity at their ends – that is to say you can heat the tips. These he would stir around until he got the right reaction or your gag burst and he would then superheat the points to burn out your aggressive tendencies. Nobody knows why it works but on your return who could fail to ask what had happened and how you were – particularly with your shaved head.'

'Do you recommend it, Doctor Sparerib?'

'Again, as your physician I have to outline the possible flaw, which is that if the brain mechanic lights his lamp as you might say at the wrong spot you could go clean off your rocker. This may well stimulate conversation when Mr Brone leads you into the Golf Club Bar – the only thing is that you would not be taking any part in it. What do you think?'

'On balance, no, Doctor Sparerib. Yet I am becoming desperate. I had to pretend pregnancy to get five minutes uninterrupted speech at the W.I. last week and as you know my husband just shows no sign of having another coronary. What is more the girls foil my every attempt now by saying how well I look the moment I walk in.'

'There we have it, Mrs Brone, there we have it. A good diagnostician must learn from his patient. You look TOO well.'

'I am not following you, Doctor Sparerib.'

'You will, Mrs Brone, you will. First of all I shall prescribe for you a powerful emetic, a primitive and rapid purgative and a maximum dose of diuretic daily. Dark sunglasses . . .'

'Dark sunglasses, Doctor Sparerib?'

'Very dark and very large. These will heighten the ghostly whiteness of your haggard face after a fortnight of the above treatment. What size shoes do you take, Mrs Brone?'

'Shoes, what on earth have shoes . . . size six, why?'

'Then I shall also prescribe for you a pair of size four surgical boots. The wearing of these will produce in you a stumbling and agonised gait which must provoke enquiry and sympathetic conversation. I daresay that at Crowe Martin Golf Club the term for you will soon be ". . . that brave little lady . . ." as you hobble whitely from tee to tee.'

'Write the scrips, Doctor Sparerib, write the scrips. You are a genius, Doctor Sparerib, a genius.'

'Why thank you, Mrs Brone. Now if I may without offence remind you . . .'

'Of course, how do you want the cheque made out?'

'As usual, Mrs Brone. Horace Sparerib M.D. and if you would kindly on this occasion just cross it Holidays and Wine Account! That is

indeed very generous of you, Mrs Brone.'

'Here we are, Doctor Sparerib. And a very good morning to you.'

'Good morning to you, Mrs Brone, a pleasure to do medicine with you.'

Paddy McKiernan 31.5.1978

MATERIA MEDICA.

American Physician (to English Ditto). 'Now in Vienna they're first-rate at Diagnosis; but then, you see, they always make a point of confirming it by a Post-Mortem!'

REFORM YOUR DOCTORS' BILLS

How to pay honestly and fairly for medical advice may have been a problem to a few of our readers, most of whom, being entirely constitutional, have had few dealings with the doctor. A help towards the solution thereof has been

furnished in an extract from a letter in the
Morning Herald, the writer of which, speaking of
Californian practice, says that 'for three
"ahems!" and a "ha!" he paid in August last
twenty-seven dollars.' Hence may be derived a
scheme for the reformation of doctors' bills. To
charge a shilling or eighteenpence for a draught,
consisting of an infusion of rose holding a
neutral salt in solution, value one penny, would
be a monstrosity, did we not know that the
practitioner's education, knowledge, and abilities, are supposed to be dissolved along with the
Magnes. Sulph. in the *Infus. Rosæ.* But this is
merely a supposition. You can't dissolve medical
science and skill, either in *Infus. Rosæ*, or *Mist.
Camphoræ*, or *Aqua Pura*, or *Aqua Pump*. Why,
then, should not medical practitioners follow
out the Californian notion, and charge for their
opinions, as expressed in their interjections? As,
for instance –

		s.	d.
Humph!		2	6
Ha!		1	6
Oho!		3	0
Indeed!		4	6
Well, well!		5	0

The idea might be extended, so that the scale
of fees should rise proportionably with the
elongation of the professional utterances: as
thus:–

		s.	d.
Put out your Tongue		6	8
Let me feel your Pulse		13	6

But here we forbear; considering that our
recommendation to charge – addressed to doctors – must appear to patients rather like the
exhortation, 'Up, guards, and at them!'

Percival Leigh 15.1.1853

'THE EARLY BIRD CATCHES THE WORM.'

*Struggling Young Physician (who, after listening with rapt attention to the symptoms of his first patient, strikes a hand-bell, and
summons his faithful Attendant).* 'O – ER – ROBERTS!'   *Roberts.* 'YES, SIR.'
    Physician. 'WHEN MR GLADSTONE COMES, TAKE HIM INTO THE BREAKFAST-ROOM, AND ASK HIM TO BE SO KIND AS TO WAIT
A LITTLE WHILE.' (*To Patient.*) 'NOW, MADAM!'

DOC BRIEF

Robert Buckman
A USER'S GUIDE TO THE RANKS OF THE NHS

THE HOUSEMAN

The houseman is the bottom of a heap which is composed entirely of people who remember exactly what it was like when they were at the bottom, but who have put on a lot of weight as they've clambered upwards. It's actually very difficult for me as a doctor, albeit an exalted and renowned one, to explain to my lay readers (albethey exalted and renowned ones, grovel, lick, toady, slurp-slurp) what it once felt like to be a houseman. But I'll try.

Mostly, it was like being a galley-slave in *Ben Hur* in the bottom row of a trireme. Or rather, it was like being the bloke that washes the underwear of the galley-slaves in ditto ditto ditto. As a houseman, you feel as if you know nothing except what your superiors tell you, which is mostly that you know nothing. You have power over nothing and responsibility for everything, like the Minister in Charge of Earthquakes, or Denis Howell, in the days when we had one of those.

You have to know everything about your patients e.g. allergies, fads, blood pressure, size of liver, war record, innermost unfulfilled fantasies, sock size etc. And as if that wasn't bad enough, you're in servitude to your consultant (see below, but look up while doing so) who is probably an autocratic old bastard and you're expected to know everything about *him*, e.g. fads, allergies, size of liver, wife's birthday, mistress's birthday, war record, mistress's war record etc.

As regards rank, status and dignity, you have none. Your place in the scheme of things is such that even the hospital cockroaches will get their own personal space in the staff car-park before you do. In the great ceremonial parade into Christmas dinner you walk in behind the matron's cat. The only people in the world that you can look down on are drug reps. And psychiatrists. Oh, and the patients of course.

Without going into boring 'when I was a houseman' stories, I'd just like to say that when I was a houseman I was on call one night in two and paid £108 a month (half my hourly rate as a baby-sitter). And why did I do it? Why did I persevere and slave in the service of medicine and mankind? Well, because like all young doctors, deep in my heart I had a burning desire to be the leader of the Social Democrats, of course.

But it certainly wasn't all misery. There was camaraderie; there were girls and there were women and sometimes there were nurses, too (this was before Griffiths); there were parties and minor short-lived bacchanalia, gasps of passion, desperate mouths seeking another, and hurried intimate fumblings – and all that just to get a cup of tea at the League of Friends cake-stall.

Recently, a young student listening at my knee (we can't afford chairs in my teaching hospital) asked me, as I recalled these vivid scenes, whether I'd do it again if I had the chance. With a twinkle in my wise old eye, I chuckled and said that I'd rather do the splits on a barbed-wire trampoline.

THE SENIOR HOUSE OFFICER

If the medical hierarchy can be compared to a tribe (and believe me it can – with cannibalism, massacres, blood feuds and the whole schmeer), then the Senior House Officer (SHO) is like the pubertal man-child.

The name is a misnomer and part of the outdated military flavour of the profession – like calling the common room the 'Doctor's Mess', which is admittedly less of a misnomer. Anyway, the SHO is what you become after your houseman year. It's like a sort of purgatory in that it still scares the blazes out of you, but it's better than hell. You're still pig ignorant, but you have one factor in your favour that endears you to the older, more desperate members of the nursing profession, i.e. you're still alive and might make it to a marriageable age.

As time passes, you know a fact and then another. You learn a third fact, and then realise in a flash of insight that you've forgotten the first two. A week of burning the midnight oil and you re-learn the first two, of which one is now outdated. You try looking after cases (or people if their diseases aren't interesting). You make a mistake and feel embarrassed. You make the same mistake twice and now you call it experience. You repeat it three times and now you can say, 'in case after case after case . . .'

All the time you are growing older. Soon it will be time to spin yourself a cocoon, to become a pupa, to dissolve your old self, thaw and resolve into your new form. Soon you will emerge from your chrysalis into the bright new dawn as the multi-coloured and fully-fledged maggot we call . . .

THE REGISTRAR

The registrar is the wonderfully wise young man who knows all the answers, but hasn't yet learned which are the important questions. (All this pseudo-philosophising of mine is utter and total cobblers by the way – my doctor says it's all a side-effect of my hay-fever tablets. Sorry.)

The registrar stands on the threshold of Learning, with his hand on the doorknob of Knowledge, his eye on the physiotherapist of Temptation, his lips on the backside of the Establishment and his signature on the . . . on the mortgage of . . . erm . . . His New House. Yes, well. For this is the Age of the Getting of Wisdom, when he shall become no stranger to research, and shall be found amidst dusty old tomes or else consulting the sayings of ancient sages as they clarify the mysteries of the occult, e.g. the 3.30 at Kempton Park.

At this stage of your career, you can begin to show an interest in some form of specialising. With luck, you can suck up to some consultant in some rarefied speciality and think of some immensely useful question that needs to be answered, e.g. the relationship between long-sightedness and the colour of your left parathyroid, or the chance of successful hernia surgery if your brother-in-law is an MP etc.

And then you take some extra exams to get more qualifications and half the alphabet traipsing after your name. And the future looks bright and you want to discover the cure for something – the common cold maybe, or perhaps

halitosis, or even boredom. Then, just as you're zooming down the runway and approaching V2 and take-off, along come the economic cutbacks and suddenly your only chance is if you want to specialise in diseases of Channel Tunnel workers. At the end of which the light appears very dim indeed, and the only fate awaiting you is that of being a consultant, which is what I shall tell you about next week, if the tablets wear off in time.

NURSES

I recently conducted a poll in which 17,000 members of the public (or friends of ditto) were asked to arrange the 100 most difficult jobs in the world in order of difficulty. Amazingly, the job of nursing came equal third – lagging behind the jobs of diving for natural pearls in New Bond Street and stalking roebuck on the M40, and tying for third place with Enriques Ramon, who is Baby Doc Duvalier's estate agent.

For all practical purposes, nurses have the hardest, the most wearing and the most exhausting job in the NHS, with the possible exception of the patients. The point is that the entire focus of a nurse's life is looking after sick, demanding, frightened people with a wide range of mental or physical problems, i.e. doctors. Nurses get trained in biology, physics, practical electronics and psychology; are ready at any moment to defibrillate an arrested heart; compress a severed artery; wipe a bottom; brush away a tear; or make a cup of tea (the last three tasks usually performed for a houseman).

And for these Herculean tasks their pay and standards of living have almost always been so rotten that marrying a doctor seemed almost attractive by comparison. In the days when I was a Junior Registrar (way back in the dawn of 1980), nurses were paid roughly the same as the daily take of a parking-meter in the West End. Now things are different – parking-meters do much better.

I honestly don't know what the Griffiths report will actually do for the future of nursing – perhaps, what the British Navy did for the future of the dodo. But, in my opinion, nurses are, on the whole, the most dedicated, successful and outstanding group of professionals anywhere in the United Kingdom. And will therefore probably be sold to the Americans next week.

CARDIOLOGISTS

Cardiologists are heart doctors. Unlike nurses they do not have to wear frilly hats and armbands. They wear a different kind of uniform – usually a subtle, thin-stripe, grey suit and matching facial expression. They are not the same as heart surgeons in that nobody showed them how to do surgery. This means they have to pretend that they could do it if they wanted to, but don't want to, because it's soppy, so there.

Cardiologists use a thing called a stethoscope through which they listen to the heart – an activity that is called 'auscultation' in order to make the patients think that the doctor is doing more than just listening to the heart. By listening to the sounds that the heart makes, a cardiologist can detect all kinds of problems, such as stenosis of the mitral valve, calcification of a bicuspid aortic valve, deposits of carbon on the plugs or bent tappets. It takes nearly nine years to train and believe me you need six of those just to work out which of the heart sounds is 'lub' and which one's 'dub'. Come to think of it, I'm not sure why you need to know, unless it's to ask a surgeon to cut one of them out. My best friend Dave wanted to be a cardiologist and turned up for his first day on the coronary care unit to look after a Very Important Cabinet Minister who'd had a heart attack, and the consultant said, 'How good are you at listening to soft muffled sounds and making sense of what you hear?' Dave replied very good, and the consultant said, 'Then you can ring for the Minister's taxi.'

But that experience didn't put Dave off at all; he slaved and studied for another eleven years and trained under the best doctors in the field, and now he's Shadow Minister for Transport in the SDP and gets taxis for everyone.

CARDIAC SURGEONS

Cardiac surgeons are unutterably glamorous and brave and wonderful and specialise in dashing around and buckling their swashes, like a medical equivalent of Indiana Jones (with the thoracic cavity playing the part of the Temple of Doom).

Generally speaking, they do not lack self-esteem or pride in their work, and one of them said that if the human body was like a motor-car, his job was changing the spark-plugs with the engine still running. Not to be outdone, a cardiologist (i.e. non-surgeon type, see above) said that *his* job was even worse because he wasn't allowed to lift the bonnet, and could only listen to the engine, sniff the exhaust fumes, check the ash-trays and then add digoxin to the petrol.

Cardiac surgeons have at least three options open to them. They can perform open heart surgery, closed heart surgery or (on Thursday afternoons) early closing heart surgery. In open heart surgery, the patient's circulation is kept going by a pump (probably an American one, dash it all) and the heart flops about like a twitching, palpitating fish, just like when you're in love for the first time, only this time someone's holding it. And slicing it open, come to think of it.

Open heart surgery is altogether a very upmarket, yuppy, A1-B1 kind of surgery, performed on people who have big BMWs by people who have bigger BMWs. You've probably seen this kind of surgery on the telly. The patient is anaesthetised after being checked for cardiac function, ventilatory capacity and credit status. Then he (usually a he, because heart disease only partly participates in Equal Opportunities Programmes) is connected to a ventilator and the by-pass pump-and-oxygenator, which are complex machines that go FWTHUMPP-P'TISSSS, and cardiac output monitors, which go FNEEP-FNEEP-FNERRRP-BIP if all is well, or MNEEEEEEEEEN if they are broken or the patient is dead. Then a whole lot of things happen under the drapes to do with bits of gristly stuff and slippery mushy substances (this is just to get the patient's pyjamas off, mind you). Next, the surgeon opens the heart, removes the bit that isn't working, or is broken, and replaces whatever he has to. Then he wakes the patient up and gives him a receipt for the bit he's taken out.

It's a highly thrilling, demanding and exciting business (particularly for the doctors, less so for the patients) and I think that if you asked most cardiac surgeons why they did it, they'd say it was for the betterment of mankind, the alleviation of suffering and the thrill of using

machines that go FWTHUMPP-P'TISSSS.
And who can blame them?

THE DOCTOR ANSWERS YOUR QUESTIONS

Q: I used to suffer from megalomania, but I
cured myself by sheer will-power and concentra-
tion. In fact, I think I've done an amazingly
brilliant and stunningly clever job in controlling
the tendency. Don't you agree?

A. Yes, you're the most famous cured mega-
lomaniac in the whole world. Now, could you
get out of my light please, I'm trying to write an
article?

Q. Will you mention me in the article?

A. No.

*'I wasn't satisfied with
the blandness of my
first doctor's
reassurance.'*

*'I'll be with you in a moment, Mr Willard, which will give you a
chance to quickly check out my diplomas.'*

'According to the bank, Mrs Barton, your last cheque was a placebo.'

'IN MEDIO TUTISSIMUS.'

Country Practitioner (about to go up to London on Business). 'I SHAN'T BE MORE THAN TEN DAYS AT THE FURTHEST, MR FAWCEPS. YOU'LL VISIT THE PATIENTS REGULARLY, AND TAKE CARE THAT NONE OF 'EM SLIP THROUGH YOUR FINGERS – OR GET WELL – DURING MY ABSENCE!!'

'I'm afraid there's absolutely nothing I can do for you, Mr Maynard. I only handle operations over £2,500.'

'We'll be wantin' a doctor soon.'
'That's all right – I am one.'

The Patients' Association has made a report of callousness and unconcern by GPs. LARRY went down to his local surgery to check the story out . . .

HARD TIMES FOR DOCTORS.

NOT A POLICE TRAP, BUT ONLY UNEMPLOYED MEDICAL MEN WAITING ALONG THE
BRIGHTON ROAD ON THE OFF-CHANCE OF A MOTOR-CAR ACCIDENT.

LOVE LETTERS TO A DOCTOR

'A "passion file" containing letters and gifts from love-sick patients to their doctors is being kept by the Medical Defence Union in London. The letters are mainly written by middle-class women with a crush on their doctors ... "When a doctor gets something of this sort he treats it like a hot potato," Dr Wall said. "He always gets rid of the patient on to someone else's list" ...'

Daily Telegraph

Dear Dr Grant,

You must help me. I can hardly sleep at nights. I lie awake in a sort of fever, tossing and turning, just thinking of you. I have lost my appetite and seem no longer able to concentrate on anything. You are the only person I can tell about this.

yours
Elizabeth Jones

Dear Mrs Jones,

I am transferring you immediately to Dr Horslock's list. I hope you will understand that there can never be anything between us and that it is better if we do not see each other again. I trust you will recover soon; Dr Horslock is an excellent practitioner and I recommend her wholeheartedly.

yours sincerely
Arthur Grant

Dear Dr Grant,

I thought you might like to know that Dr Horslock diagnosed my trouble as influenza and that I am now in excellent health.

As for the other matter to which you refer, I had no idea you felt like that about me and I can only admire the way you have always hidden these feelings. It was entirely honourable of you to transfer me to Dr Horslock. Rest assured your secret is safe with me.

yours
Elizabeth Jones

Union Comment
Dr Grant has sent us thirty other similar correspondences. We have urged him to be less suspicious.

Dear Dr Anstruther,

I want you to examine me all over.

yours
Fiona Standing

Dear Mrs Standing,
   How do you mean?
                Dr Anstruther

Dear Dr Anstruther,
   What I say. I want you to take a look at my body. Please.
          yours
          Fiona Standing

Dear Mrs Standing,
   Yes, but is there any particular reason? I mean, what do you have in mind? I would appreciate a detailed answer before I can make an appointment.
          yours
          Dr Anstruther

Dear Dr Anstruther
   Yes, there is something special I want you to see.
          yours
          Fiona Standing

Dear Mrs Standing,
   I hope you will understand if I tell you there is now a special questionnaire I am sending to female patients who wish to be examined. Please fill it in and return.
   1. What are your feelings about your doctor?
   2. Do you undertake to behave as I ask you during any physical examination?
   3. Are you happily married?
   4. If necessary, would you consent to have someone else present during the examination?
          yours
          Dr Anstruther

Dear Dr Anstruther,
   I find your veiled proposals nauseating. If I cannot request my doctor for a straightforward chest check-up without being invited to an orgy, whom can one trust? Thank God I found out in time.
          yours
          Fiona Standing

Union Comment
Mrs Standing was transferred to Dr Horslock's list, at her own request.

To Dr Carstairs
My darling,
   I cannot wait to see you again. I love you so terribly it hurts. I think of you night and day. But it won't be long now.
          all my love
          Kate

Union Comment
Dr Carstairs has requested the return of this letter, which he now realises is from his wife.

Dear Dr Hastings,
   I have been recommended to come to you for treatment of my complaint. Briefly, my symptoms are that I blush very easily, twist my hands, stammer, cry without warning and tend to swoon. I would like to see you as soon as possible.
          yours sincerely
          Virginia Maltby (Mrs)

Dear Mrs Maltby,
   Before I make an appointment to study your ailment, it would help me to know who had recommended you to me for treatment.
          yours sincerely
          Dr Hastings

Dear Dr Hastings,
   I have been passed on to you by, in chronological order, Drs Grant, Anstruther, Campbell, Woodleigh, Simpson (père et fils), Hay, Mendoza, Wilcox, Bentinck and Carstairs.
          Virginia Maltby (Mrs)

Dear Mrs Maltby,
   I am referring you to a Dr Horslock, who will probably be able to help you more than I can.
          yours sincerely
          Dr Hastings

Union Comment
Thank God for Horslock.

Dear Dr Woodleigh,
   Just a hasty note to tell you that I have eaten too many oysters and fear this has led to my present strange condition. May I come and see you?
          yours
          Margaret Price

Dear Mrs Price,

It is, ah, possible that oysters may, as it were, have an effect on you, but I would not worry. Why not pop in, in, well, a few weeks' time and let me see. But meanwhile *for God's sake* don't take any more oysters, or shellfish, or rhino horn, or Spanish fly, or champagne, or lampreys. Promise? If you don't feel any better meanwhile, I'd get in touch with Dr Horslock, who's very good on these things.

yours
Dr Woodleigh, er, Jim

Union Comment
Surprised he didn't warn her off love filtres.

Dear Dr Hay,

Just a note to say thank you for the pills, which did the trick. Really, to be honest, I wanted to know how *you* were feeling. I couldn't help noticing, when I came in for my check-up, that you were obviously under the weather. I mean, the way you were sweating, and hid hunched up behind your desk, and retreated with a great start every time I came near you – it seems obvious to me you've been overworking and that you won't admit you're ill. Is it something to do with your eyes? I say that because, between you and me, I *did* notice that when you were examining me you actually had your eyes fixed on the far end of the room. I told Jim about it (in all secrecy) and he's worried about it too. You must look after your-self. Love to Sarah.

yours
Betty Pike

Union Comment
Man's a fool.

Dear Dr Mendoza,

Nothing personal, but I am getting a bit tired of your examinations. For the last few years you have only viewed me through bin-oculars from the far end of your surgery. I would understand if I were highly infectious, but even that would not explain the dark glasses, the trilby pulled down over the fore-head and the loaded gun on the desk. Can you please recommend me another practitioner?

yours
Violet Ponsonby

Dear Lady Ponsonby,
Dr Horslock.

yours
X

Union Comment
Hmm.

Dear Dr Horslock,
I love you.

yours
Desperate

Dear Desperate,
There's a lot of it going around. Have you tried aspirin?

yours
Sensible

Union Comment
God give us more Horslocks.

Miles Kington 25.7.1973

'*The trouble with parties is that as soon as people hear I'm a doctor, they insist on describing their private health insurance schemes to me.*'

DOCTOR PATEL'S DIARY

March

Sometimes I wonder why I ever came to this backward country from India. I am not discouraged in my mission to bring health and enlightenment to the British – it is merely that they seem so slow to shake off their old superstitions and barbaric ways. I often think back to my Indian college days where all was so neat and clinical, and then I think with a sigh of my patients. There was a man this morning. He said his leg was playing him up.

'I beg your pardon,' I said.

'Me leg. It's playing me up.'

'Could you be a little more precise?'

'Ah. Well, to be dead honest, doc, it's giving me merry hell.'

I asked him to explain it in correct English.

'I've got pains in my leg.'

I chided him for not having said so before and asked him if it was the first time.

'No, doc. I always get it when there's rain about.'

They are like children. How can a civilised man believe that his arthritis is caused by the weather? I do not think he actually believes in a rain god – they are all godless savages – but I would not be surprised. I explained to him patiently, in correct English, the cause of his ailment.

'Thanks,' he said. 'I'll tell you another thing causes it. A north wind. Think there's anything in these copper bracelets they talk about?'

April

Mrs Wardrop has been three times this month. She is trying to shake off 'flu, or, in correct English, influenza. But she insists there is a bug going round. She is the fifteenth person who insists that there is a bug going round. Twelve said they don't feel well in themselves. Another five claimed to be under the weather. (The weather again!) None of them can describe their symptoms without a great deal of urging and prodding. They have no conception of scientific medicine. Or of English, come to that.

May

Of course, the big trouble is that they are used to their own quack doctors, as they call them. These are British GPs who work on the old tribal methods, believing that a patient can be cured by faith. I had a new patient yesterday, a Mrs Partington, and my goodness she is one of the worst, I am telling you.

'I got a right dickey throat, doc,' she said.

After ten minutes patient conversation, I have managed to elicit a description of her symptoms from her, without any of these unintelligible dialect words like dickey, lousy, rough, gammy, rotten or 'orrible. (I once had a New Zealand patient who claimed to be 'real crook'. I had sent for the police before he explained what it meant.) I diagnosed her ailment as pharyngitis, and prescribed a new drug which I find very efficacious.

'That can't be right,' she said. 'Dr McIntyre always gave me red and yellow pills. They did the trick.'

'Madam,' I said. 'I am telling you that this is the cure for your discomfiture.'

'I wouldn't know about that,' she said, 'but Dr McIntyre gave me red and yellow pills. They worked a treat.'

A curse on all these primitive Dr McIntyres and their primitive juju.

June

I wrote earlier that my patients are godless savages. I was wrong. Today a female patient claimed to be suffering under a curse. After twenty minutes careful interrogation it emerged that she thought of her menstruation as a curse! I think she wanted an incantation.

July

A curious man in my surgery on Monday. At first I thought he was subject to delirium but it turned out that that is how they speak in the region from which he comes, called Scotland. It is a fascinating dialect. I gathered he was suffering from pink eye, which is indeed a painful affliction, oh yes. But I could find nothing wrong with his eyes.

'Your eyes are quite all right,' I said. 'There is nothing wrong with you.'

'Eyes? Whit ye're havering aboot, mon?' he said. (The transcription is approximate.) 'It's ma hand!'

He poked his little finger at me.

'Your little finger?' I said.

'Aye,' he said. 'Ma pinkie, ye ken.'

I made a note in the essay I am preparing on British dialects: the Scots refer to the little finger as a pinkie. How he managed to get it stuck in a whisky bottle and dislocated it is a mystery which we never elucidated.

August

We doctors are not the only Indians attempting to convert the population of Britain. The missionaries have, as usual, got here first. Why is it that the spread of civilisation is spearheaded by the myths and creeds of the priests? Anyway, I was approached today by a Mrs Firkin who is a firm devotee of our Indian beliefs.

'I am absolutely crazy about Yoga, Doctor,' she said. 'It is absolutely divine. You can't imagine what bliss it has brought me. I am a new woman. These super exercises have done me a power of good.'

To cut a long recitation quite short, she had been carrying out some of the harmless ideas of our Indian gurus as if she really believed in them, and had sprained an ankle. I told her how to treat it and gave her a short warning.

'Do not imagine that you British have a monopoly of superstition,' I said. 'If you wish to adopt Indian wisdom, come to a doctor first.'

September

Today, for the first time, I met one of the most primitive of English tribesmen. I have made full notes elsewhere, but let me just say that he was a country-dweller, living on his own patch of land, tending his own flock of deer and goats. I have never seen such an unspoilt fellow even in England. His name was the Earl of Godalming. His dialect was almost completely bereft of meaning . . .

'Well, look, the trouble, don't you know, is that, as it were, I get this funny feeling, damned hard to describe, sort of, odd twinge, get me? That sort of thing.'

I really must start writing a book. *My Life Among the Stone Age British? An Indian In Outer Europe?* In any case, I cannot continue much longer in this back-breaking effort to convert the natives. They are charming folk but quite impossible.

His trouble, by the way, was a simple case of gout, caused by the local fermented spirit.

Miles Kington 2.10.1974

'Let me through – I've been struck off!'

'How's it going since we cut out the Valium?'

'I see this as something of a challenge because at the moment nothing is going round.'

DOCTOR NO

Doctors are increasingly travelling incognito when on holiday because of fears that they will be called to help in a medical emergency.

Daily Telegraph

Beneath the brass sky, stepping gingerly from patch to scorching patch of gritty sand between the supine and motionless ranks of simmering mahogany flesh, the white English couple picked their serpentine way across the Riviera beach, the only moving things, like stricken relatives come to identify victims of some unimaginable act of arson.

A few yards from the shore at which the poisonous Mediterranean licked, they found a tiny space, hemmed by two other couples less blackened than the rest, but darkening, it seemed, with every passing second. The newcomer raised his sun-hat, wincing as the noonday pounced on his thinning scalp.

'Excusez-moi,' he said, haltingly, 'mais je – that is – wondered if this, er, space was . . .?'

The couple on his left sat up.

'It's all right,' replied the man, 'we're English.'

'Not doctors, though,' said his wife quickly.

'Oh no, definitely not doctors,' said her husband. 'English, but not doctors.'

'Not medical at all,' said his wife. 'I was never a nurse, even before I got married.'

'Nor was I,' said the woman on the other edge of the space, sitting up and re-fastening her top.

'I can vouch for that,' said her husband. 'Not being a doctor, I never ran into nurses. I remember thinking, down the pit, it's a good life being a miner, but it almost certainly means you won't marry anyone medical.' He squinted up at the white couple, shielding his eyes with his hand. 'You're not doctors, are you?'

'*Doctors?*' cried the newcomer, throwing back his head and laughing for some time, rocking back on his heels, slapping his ivory thigh. '*Us*, doctors? Ha-ha-ha, good God, my word, bloody hell, did you hear that, Alice?'

'Yes, Norman, how incredible, I thought, being taken for doctors when we're actually in the . . .'

'Tyre business!'

'. . . confectionery trade.'

They looked at one another. A gull flew by.

'We have a tyres and confectionery shop,' explained the man, after a time.

'How interesting,' said the woman on their left.

'Yes. They go very well together, actually,' said the white man, sitting down. His wife lowered herself beside him, removed her sun-dress, rooted for sun-oil in her beach-bag. A magazine, as she did so, fell out onto the sand.

The man beside her looked at it.

'Isn't that the *British Medical Journal?*' he said. Everyone stared at it.

'*Is* it?' said the white woman. 'I wonder how it . . .'

'Yes it is!' cried her husband. 'We got it for the weight, you know. We like to take every possible precaution when travelling. We went to our newsagent, and we said, look, we're going to the South of France, it's a terrible time of year for flies, August, what do you suggest, and he said, you cannot beat the BMJ, I think he called it, it has weight, it has a shiny surface for easy wiping off of fly remnants, and you will not mind using it to swat flies with because there is no possible way in which you would want to read it, since there is nothing in it of any interest to non-medical people, it is utter gobbledegook from start to finish, it is a completely closed book as far as shoe and confectionery people are concerned.' He licked his lips. 'So we brought it.'

'I thought you said tyres and confectionery,' said the man on his left.

'I did, yes I definitely did,' replied the white man, 'and that was, that was, that was because tyres and confectionery are our *main* trade, people come in for a bar of chocolate or a pound of those boiled things, sweets, and while they're in, we show them our wide range of tyres.'

'And vice-versa,' said his wife. 'But many of them coming in for a bar of Crunchie, for example, do not have cars, do they, Norman?'

'No.' He took off his hat again and wiped the sweat from his forehead with it. 'But . . . but they all have feet. And we can often sell them a shoe or two. We find.' He glanced quickly at the man on his right. 'It must make a nice change for you, being on the surface?'

'What?'

'Rather than down the mine.'

'Oh. Ah. Yes, yes it is, yes you're right there, old man! Yes it's not like the Riviera at all, down the pit.'

'You have a remarkably slim build, for a miner,' said the white lady, 'if I may say so.'

'Yes, I do,' said the miner. He spent some time lighting a cigarette. When he at last removed it from his lips, he was smiling. 'That is because I do not in fact do any digging or shovelling or anything of that order. I look after the canaries.'

His wife turned to gaze out to sea, and began, very slowly, to oil her shins.

'I didn't know they still took canaries down mines,' said the white man. 'I thought they had instruments for assessing the atmosphere.'

The miner took a long draw on his cigarette.

'They do, yes, you're absolutely spot-on there, they do. They, we, take the canaries down for the singing. It is an old tradition. There is no other entertainment in the pit, as you probably know.'

'Ah,' said the white man, nodding. The miner lit another cigarette from his stub. His fingers were shaking slightly. The white man tutted. 'I say, old man, you shouldn't, I mean I hope I'm not out of order here, but you really shouldn't smoke so much, as a miner, should you?'

The man on his right said:

'Why? Can smoking be bad for you?'

The white man looked at him, for a time. The others waited.

'Er,' muttered the white man, 'it's just that I seem to have read somewhere about these experiments they carried out with smoking mice.'

'He isn't smoking mice,' said the man on his right.

'No,' agreed the white man, nodding slowly, 'no, that is true. You do have a point there. But don't miners run the risk of some kind of chest complaint, anyway? Didn't I see that on the box, or in one of the confectionery papers, perhaps? Isn't it called, er, sili . . .'

'IN THE EXTREME!' shouted his wife suddenly, spilling vast gouts of Ambre Solaire. 'I remember now, it was in *Toffee News*, they pointed out that it was silly in the extreme to smoke down a coalmine, it could blow up, it was much better to suck sweets!'

'Ah,' said the man on the right. Nobody said anything else for a while. They took handfuls of sand from one side of their legs, and put them down on the other side. Sometimes they patted them flat. Then the man on the right said:

'*We* have a canary, interestingly enough. But it doesn't sing.'

'They don't always,' said the miner.

'Perhaps, when we're back home, you could come and look at it,' said the man on the right. 'It may have something wrong with it.'

'Ambrose doesn't do house calls,' said Ambrose's wife, quickly.

'What?' said the canary's owner.

'You'd have to come during pit hours,' muttered Ambrose. 'It really wouldn't be worth your while getting filthy, they don't have to sing, they're quite decorative just hopping about after a ball of wool, I find. Busy chap like you.'

Everyone looked at the man on the right.

'Yes,' he said, 'yes, that's true, we are very busy, right now.'

'Doing what?' enquired the white man.

A ball bounced among them before the canary owner could answer, and was retrieved by two apologetic Swedes.

'I make goalposts,' said the man on the right, 'yes, that's what I do.'

'How remarkable!' exclaimed the white woman. 'One had never imagined goalposts being specially made, but of course they have to be, don't they?'

'It's highly professional,' said the goalpost-maker, nodding. 'There's the angles, for one thing. It is illegal, under the rules of soccer, to have anything but a right-angled corner bit, as we call it. There's not many people know that. Furthermore . . .'

He broke off. A fearful shriek had cut through the heavy air. The crowd sprang to its feet, peering into the aching glitter of the sea whence the noise had issued. Far off, a dark blob was making pitiful ripples on the silvered calm.

'Seems to be waving at someone,' murmured the miner.

'Probably enquiring about pedalo prices,' suggested the goalpost-maker.

The white man took a pair of binoculars from his beach-bag.

'Might be a baritone,' he said, 'rehearsing for . . . *Good God!*'

'What is it?' cried the other two.

'It's an Arab!' shouted the white man.

He was two lengths up when they hit the water, but the others had only paused to pull on flippers, and from then on, it was anybody's race.

Alan Coren 5.8.1981

'*There's another rep to see you.*'

UNFINISHED BUSINESS

A Short Story

Four veiled figures gliding together in black robes like a flock of exotic ravens swooping from the long polished Mercedes and sliding noiselessly up the steps in through the door without ringing one of its eight bells, didn't even pause to consult the array of prestigious names alongside. 'This must be Harley Street,' she thought wrily and was amused and irritated to be right. It was such a cliché, like a *Punch* cartoon that would be cited by humourless academics years hence as indicating the social climate of the 1970's: Arabs in Mercedes buying up Harley Street, its services if not its buildings.

What irritated her more was that she too was heading there, and she was married to an Arab. She was part of the cliché. But not quite. She would argue hotly that she was far from it, her ardour confirming how touchy she was on the subject, and thus that there might be some truth in it. But not in her opinion. How could she, a white Christian American who had graduated at Sarah Lawrence which everyone knew was packed with Jews, belong to the joke world of Arab harems and banned alcohol? Wasn't it merely an accident of love and domicile that now linked her to the world of Arab ethics, money and customs, the wife of a Cairo antique dealer? Well, not quite love and not quite an accident. In private moments she owned to herself that Ahmed's charm for her had lain in his foreignness: his ornate Eastern wooing had intrigued her for longer than the monosyllabic sexual bouts of Harvard freshmen. She was amazed and impressed by the fervour of his pride in his country, and she admired his overt ambition to do well. And as the years passed – it was ten years now since they married – these characteristics bore fruit: an elegant if not acrobatic sex life, a position of prestige in the community, and abundant and conspicuous wealth. She frankly enjoyed all three.

But although she lived among Ahmed's people – she was resolutely not of them. She stayed American, thinking of herself as one in the long line of expatriates, an exile she fancied like Scott Fitzgerald or Peggy Guggenheim living a life of money and taste in one of the world's most cosmopolitan cities. Hadn't she come to London alone on just such a fashionable and worldly mission? Indeed she had. Kate Hashad was visiting Harley Street for an abortion.

Dr Andrew McKendrick was in his way almost a cliché himself. He had been born after his parents settled in Australia, but his name, education and briskness of manner were thoroughly Scottish. He returned there to graduate at his father's university of St Andrews and rather than return to Melbourne, he'd taken a houseman's job at Barts. Gradually it became clear to him and his disappointed parents that he would settle in London. He said it was because of the symphony concerts. They had hoped he would return triumphant and be a visible source of pride in their declining years. When they heard in which branch of medicine he had chosen to specialise, they were reconciled to his staying in London and referred to his successful career in the vaguest terms.

Thus Dr McKendrick had settled for London, symphony concerts, gynaecology and a jovial wife called Peggy. She it was who admired him as the typical Scots doctor, half way, she once proclaimed, between Dr Cameron and Dr Finlay, though of course they were actors. Dr McKendrick hadn't bothered to check on the likeness; but he was pleased that television kept his wife happy. It meant he could get on with his work. And he worked all hours, dividing his time between the needful National Health patients and a small remunerative consultancy at the best of medical addresses. His mother hadn't been vague at all when telling her Melbourne friends about that.

Despite the rigours of his Presbyterian upbringing, Dr McKendrick had no qualms about having an abortion clinic. Indeed he might claim that it was the moral absolutism of his early church-going that fortified him in his present convictions. He believed resolutely in a woman's right to control her own body. Peggy agreed with him almost as absolutely and had a part-time job in a State-run family planning clinic. Both of them were irritated by silly teenagers using abortion simply as a form of birth control, getting needlessly pregnant and returning over and over to the hospital. When that happened Dr McKendrick gave them a strict Scots lecture, before helping them out. Then he usually referred them to his wife.

And now his appointment book said Mrs Hashad. And he feared the worst – that he would have to cope with the awkward cultural inhibitions of a Moslem wife. Only in his twenties had he thrown off the sexual taboos of his own background; he found those of other cultures impenetrable. So he tried simply to get on with his job. At first he thought the appointments had been mixed.

'Mrs Hashad?'

'Yes, that *is* me. My husband's Egyptian, but I'm not. I'm American myself.'

'Oh, I see. Well, please sit down,' he said with relief.

His desk was set diagonally across the centre of his first floor consulting room which differed little from all the others in the street. Once built for elegance, the room was now too tall for the intimacy of its use, too spacious for the few pieces of furniture it contained, furniture just distinguished enough as antique to draw attention to its inappropriateness in a medical setting. They faced each other across the desk marooned on the island of an Isfahan carpet, surrounded by empty pale green walls.

While she enumerated her reasons for wanting an abortion he weighed her up. What a charming woman she was! His canny Scottish eye was not impressed by fashionable beauty: he reserved his grudging admiration for a broad brow, a strong straight nose, and a manner that was confident without being strident, personable without familiarity. She fitted the description exactly. As she explained that she had two sons already, now aged nine and seven, he imagined them, dark, dapper-suited like all expensive Mediterranean children, huge dark eyes and neat hair bisected by startling white partings. They would have a stillness and respect for her, he liked to think, that combined the best of Arab manners with the easier freedoms of her background. When their father chided them she would laugh them out of their silence, when they neglected their lessons she would sit with them and help them through. At least he imagined her like that. As she went on to explain her commitment to her husband's social

and political life he could imagine that too. He saw her approaching guests across the cool, leafy courtyard of a white home, gowned in frail silks that floated from her shoulders. A charming hostess who would take the President's arm and without guile win favours for her husband. As she leant seriously forward, touching the gold chain at the throat of her white silk shirt with slight anxiety, she explained one thing further. She had come to London on the pretext of attending a sale of porcelain at Sotheby's. Her husband had felt that such discretion was advisable. It meant that she would be returning at the weekend. Could she have the operation the next day?

It was unexpected, but Dr McKendrick was used to such urgency. The timetable of an abortion practice had certain rigours of its own and he had known women hysterical with last ditch hopes or lavish with late bribes. Mrs Hashad, quite obviously not that kind at all, was merely putting sensible pressure on his daily routine. So he conceded easily. Once agreed, their transaction was brisk. He reached to a switch, opened a file. The nurse conducted Mrs Hashad to her examination. While he waited for her to undress he mentally cancelled the Brahms concert at the Festival Hall. If she was to have the operation and to leave for Cairo on Saturday, just thirty-six hours away, he must make a second visit in the evening. Peggy would be cluckingly cross, almost as a matter of routine. A round of golf on Saturday would compensate.

Tests completed and arrangements agreed, Mrs Hashad held out her hand. 'I am truly grateful, Dr McKendrick. I shall come into the clinic, then, at 6 pm tonight.'

'That's fine. And by the following evening, if all goes well, I'm sure I shall be able to discharge you.'

'I can't express how pleased I am. And I shall be on the 8.20 flight the next morning.'

On the way out Dr McKendrick's receptionist explained one or two medical procedures, handed Mrs Hashad her appointment card, and asked how she would settle the account. 'Oh, I'll pay directly myself at the time.' In the event she didn't. She left by taxi from the clinic the moment Dr McKendrick had made his evening visit. By the time his account had reached her

London hotel the next morning, Mrs Hashad was on the plane to Cairo.

It was five years later that Andrew McKendrick and his wife Peggy went for a well-earned holiday. It's true to say that Dr McKendrick was genuinely engrossed in his work and had pioneered a number of developments in the technique of his trade. He was now highly regarded and sat on committees. He was also considerably wealthy and used that wealth to extend his interest in music. He and two fellow medical men had purchased a box at the Albert Hall; he and Peggy had favourite seats in the Grand Tier at Covent Garden. There, in the intervals, they occasionally met other medical men, other committee members. It was a small world of the medically successful. And Andrew harboured a secret suspicion that it was only the nature of his speciality that denied him an Honour.

The holiday came about because Peggy put her foot down. Andrew's long hours denied her his company. And when she did have it, it was shared with Mahler, Verdi and Shostokovitch. Andrew conceded without too much reluctance. Peggy was, after all, as sensible a wife as he could wish. Her role at the Family Planning Clinic had developed; she was now its area director. She was able to talk shop with him and he admired her practical approach to matters that excited dogmatism or irrationality in others. As her years increased her golf handicap fell. While he worked longer hours, she kept herself happy at the local golf club. He admired her for that, too. Other doctors he knew had whining wives who nagged them home to 7.30 suppers. So when Peggy said she really insisted on a holiday, he concurred. It would be their first in six years. They chose a cruise up the Nile.

He hadn't remembered the unpaid bill until they landed at Cairo airport. 'I just wish we knew somebody – just one familiar face,' said Peggy, her capable poise slackening slightly at the sight of so foreign a place. And then he remembered. And the memory made him smile. He hadn't smiled at the time, of course. Then his lips had tightened with irritation, and stayed shut. His receptionist, however, had lapsed with alarming ease into phobic phrases – 'no more than you'd expect from a wog'; 'fancy marrying a greasy Moslem anyway' ... He had glared

sharply at her, slammed his door in disapproval, and fallen into a recollection of the urbane American. He felt sure the mistake was simply an oversight on her part. He knew how traumatic an abortion could be. Some women could cope straightforwardly. Others fell into deep depression and self-hatred. Others wept. There was no knowing the tangle of deep feeling that could be detonated by the operation. But she had been lively enough, certainly medically fine and, more to the point, sincerely grateful. Her failure to substantiate her thanks was certainly a misunderstanding. Perhaps she thought she had; perhaps at home she had servants who did that for her. Perhaps – and he allowed himself a sour smile – she expected him to take American Express. Certainly the hotel assured him they had forwarded his next letter to Cairo. There had been no reply. His receptionist had wanted to pursue the matter further. But when the hotel refused to divulge the Cairo address he finally gave up. And now that he was in Cairo himself he still had no idea where she lived.

He tried to put his memory of her in a Cairo context. It was a hot, noisy and smelly city. But as in all capitals, the rich moved at a protected pace between limousine, shops, clubs, restaurants and, particularly, each other's lavish houses. He, a tourist now, was aware of their shadowy lives as they quietly conducted their affairs – financial, social, political – behind the showy surface image that traffic and crowds give to the Cairo streets.

He remembered the broad brow, the strong straight nose; how forthright she had been without the gruffness that he felt sometimes marred Peggy's directness. Kate – yes, he recalled that was her name – Kate was pliant without being ingratiating. He could imagine her – as he had always suspected – the focus in Cairo of a small but brilliant coterie of intelligent people, a credit to her husband's professional and political aspirations. Surely they must be bearing fruit by now. And the joy of her two sons, now grown gawkily tall but still deferring to her natural grace. He thought about contacting her, looking her up, phoning, sending the bill. He thought about it intermittently up the Nile and down. But he almost left it too late. Then on the final evening he decided.

He was sitting opposite his wife in the bar of

their Cairo hotel. Peggy was well settled behind a brimming whisky and soda; he had always taken his whisky neat. Suddenly he leaned across and grasped Peggy's denim-skirted knee. 'You know, I am going to do as I said. Now. I meant to all along. Why shouldn't I? The money doesn't matter that much, but it'll clear matters up. I hate unfinished business. And I don't like not knowing what to make of the whole affair. Let me just tidy things up before we leave. Settle the mystery.' He left his wife then and there in the security of a bar amply dotted with obvious tourists, went to their room and wrote out on hotel writing paper a long explanation to Mrs Hashad of what had happened . . . his quite understanding her hurry, but nonetheless . . . matter of business . . . sure she would remember and understand . . . his sincere regards . . . and, he was sure, due thanks . . . in anticipation. That sort of letter.

He went to the hotel reception intending to ask them to consult the telephone directory for the name. He would take a chance on finding one clearly indicating Antique Dealer, show-rooms, auctions or some such. He had no need. 'Hashad – Mr Ahmed Hashad – oh, yes, of course his house is well-known. It houses a gallery of paintings, very celebrated. He is a big man in the city – we know Mr Hashad here very well.' He despatched instantly a messenger boy with the letter, his own eagerness quickening at the thought of reaching her, of having her surprise in his mind's eye – and having her response in the morning to put matters right before he left. He resumed his whisky and, the business of the day now effected, fell to discussing with Peggy in which of the more exotic restaurants they should celebrate their final night.

It was as they were crossing the huge black and white tiled floor of the foyer that they became aware of the commotion. A small flurry of noise and bustle was pushing its way through the ambling desultory throng of tourists. It was topped by a huge spilling cornucopia of flowers, which, as it moved towards them, he could see was carried on the head of a small ebony-black boy in a scarlet uniform with gold buttons down the front. Behind and beside him, jostling to catch up, was the messenger he had despatched an hour earlier to Mrs Hashad. The pair were making straight towards Andrew and Peggy McKendrick. Then the small pageboy – no other word would do – held out to the doctor in his white gloved hand a gold-edged envelope. 'I think, Peggy, we'd better take this lot to our room, don't you?' They exchanged private smiles. Passers-by were stopping in curiosity and admiration for the small black child and his cascading burden. Dr McKendrick led the little procession – for the hotel messenger came too – back to their room. 'Well, now what's all this? . . .' And with the small talk of the surgery he opened the envelope. As he did so the hotel messenger brought from his pocket a small, red leather box and handed it to Peggy. 'Mrs Hashad asked me to give this to you – from her personally.' The letter explained its contents.

'Dr McKendrick, I have only this moment opened and read your letter. What it says leaves me in complete confusion and distress. I was under the impression at my departure from London subsequent to my engagement with you, that all financial matters had been left safely in the hands of my husband's financial secretary in London. Imagine the shock this is to me to find this was not so. And you with your gallant forbearance have not pressed matters. I am deeply grateful for that.

'I am most eager to make up for this error. Were you not leaving tomorrow I would have extended an invitation to dine with us. Tonight, however, I have to attend a government reception. I am sure you will understand. Otherwise I would have sent for you to come to my home this evening.

'Could I instead offer my thanks and gratitude to you now. Financial arrangements being what they are, perhaps you would accept instead from me this gift for your wife. I send my good wishes to her as to yourself. Yours sincerely, Kate Hashad.'

The letter was hand-written: the writing large, open, stylish across the linen paper. He handed Peggy the pages. She had watched him reading it, impatient that his face gave nothing away. The red leather box bobbed on her knee as she tapped her foot. 'You'd better open it.' Inside lay one of the most beautiful jewels they had ever seen.

Peggy's own collection of jewellery was meagre, not for want of a giving husband but because her taste was peculiarly fastidious. The gaudiness of most jewellers' windows appalled her. She could never understand why Aspreys expended precious skills on making ugly brooches of jewelled birds and diamond horses. Her preferences were modest for aesthetic rather than financial reasons. Among her favourites she counted a perfect piece of bluejohn mounted in silver tracery, heavily dropping earrings of the rare red amber and a large Victorian heart of quartz mounted in pinchbeck ... all antique pieces chosen to be discreetly beautiful rather than showy, yet for that reason frequently remarked on admiringly by close friends.

Now it was as if Kate Hashad had read her mind. For the jewel that lay on its cushion of suede was gorgeous without being flashy – a circling spread of bright blue stones haloing a goddess intricately carved in an unusual pink/purple stone, mounted in gold. And it differed in another way from everything else Peggy possessed. It was obviously very ancient, and it was obviously very valuable.

'Probably carries the curse of the Pharaohs, Peggy, m'dear ...' It was the voice of a leading anaesthetist, and there was general laughter in the Albert Hall box which Andrew McKendrick shared with friends. The McKendricks had been first amused, then slightly piqued by Mrs Hashad's gesture. It was really not the way to do business – but then, said Dr McKendrick, it was probably just that – exactly how they always did business. And he could understand how despite her resilient American nature, the slender western woman he had met had been drawn almost unwittingly into the modes of behaviour of her Eastern family. It was easy enough to forgive. For him, at least. He sighed and smiled, recalling the broad brow and straight nose of the elegant exile, and packed the red leather box inside his discarded sandals to avoid paying customs duty. Peggy was less pleased with Kate – but powerfully persuaded by the gift. So as she tut-tutted about her packing, she too enjoyed a private sense of outrage at such payment, and made sure the sandals were safely stowed.

At whatever occasion she wore it, the goddess jewel brought admiration. Peggy's rather austere preference for simple clothes was its perfect foil. Whether on navy silk, grey flannel or cream linen, the antique figure somehow took on a commanding and complementary tone. And Peggy – straight-backed and athletic – pinned it proudly in turn at her shoulder, her throat, her breast. Now, at the Verdi *Requiem*, Dr McKendrick's medical friends and their wives were treated to the tale. 'You know what happened to Lord Carnarvon! Mystery death hit the entire expedition ... I'd watch out!' More laughter followed with more gin. 'Well, then, isn't it a good way of paying off a doctor?'

In fact, disenchantment, when it came, had nothing mysterious about it at all. In a routine submission of their household goods for insurance Andrew McKendrick thought it wise to draw the valuer's attention to this particular jewel. But there was no need. It was routinely dismissed as a fake: a clever copy of an Egyptian tomb antique. Virtually worthless. Peggy McKendrick didn't look her husband in the eye, never mentioned it, never wore it again. She simply replaced it deliberately in its red leather box and left it, neglected from that moment on, at the back of her dressing table drawer.

Joan Bakewell 17.1.1979

'I've got a waiting room full of patients out there! What would happen if they all wanted bulletins issued?'

THE FLEEING DOCTOR

BILL TIDY follows the NHS drain

'Is this the stomach I saw
last Wednesday?'

'I see. Ask her if she's been sitting on
anything cold and hard.'

'If chief's son die, you go back National Health Service, Doncaster.'

'That's a bit of a let-down. I thought a British
doctor was the first to beat the four-minute mile?'

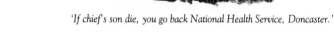

SHOWBIZ DOCTOR

Peter Permanga – born Alf Crupp – commutes between his Wilton Place penthouse, his island in the Antilles, the Victorian castle in Herefordshire he shares with his wife, Lady Linthia, and his Norman farmhouse in Essex, where he spends as much time as he can with Suzy Phuwong, the model, photographer and ex-girlfriend of Prince Colonna Orsini, the playboy ethologist. All this, of course, when he's not on location with the stars or attending rounds of parties in Hollywood.

Before he would talk about his work, I had to admire the rock-crystal panelling of his 100-foot living area and his interior decorator's scheme for the next six-monthly period – the Syrie Maugham look. I half got a question out on viruses; but he was whisking me off to see his bath, which has glass sides with tropical fish in them. Then I had to sample a new drink developed by the Society of Apothecaries research unit: $\frac{1}{4}$ vodka, $\frac{1}{4}$ tokay, 2/9 cochineal, *quant. suff.* Japanese scotch. He told me proudly that the ice was the work of his Eskimo houseboy.

Settled at last, in a chair which stroked me, I was able to ask what Liz Taylor was like as a patient.

'Fantastic!' he said. 'We're tremendous friends. She tells me everything, just like Sophia and Glenda and Barbra. I'm a real father-confessor. Liz never decides to do a film until I've read the script and advised her to. She was so grateful to me for telling her to hitch up again with Richard that she gave me a custom-built barometer. Have some caviare. It comes from Mick Jagger's own sturgeon farm.'

It was time to have another shot at getting him on to medicine. I asked him whether most stars had an outstanding physique or whether it was a matter of psychological drive. He did not seem interested in the question and replied, rather curtly, that what distinguished stars from the rest was that they were beautiful people and his close friends. A magic-eye ashtray rose to take my cigarette-ash and he dragged me into his roof garden to admire a dwarf redwood given him by Tatum O'Neal.

Back indoors, I asked him whether he had ever been tempted to join the medical brain-drain. I could not understand his answer, which was full of phrases like, 'Registered in Tristan da Cunha', 'Retainers paid in yen', 'No fees, only bonus shares' and 'Panamanian passport: practise here as a foreigner'. He then began a furious attack on coloured immigrants, calling them failed witch-doctors, fit only for the NHS and public hospitals.

Dr Permanga was very excited over a *private* hospital he and his consortium were building. Each suite would have servants' quarters, projection-unit and direct line to the principal news agencies. There would be a resident make-up team for patients' photocalls and a bulletin-drafter, who would cooperate with their own PR outfits. As he was enthusiastically describing the Pompeian murals in the Matron's swimming pool, I asked him about fees. He laughed, poured me a glass of wine from his personal vineyard – 'A pearl necklace dissolved in every bottle' – and said it was all a matter of tax-losses. They would cater mainly for beautiful people but intended to admit a few of the lighter-skinned oil sheiks, as they tended to enjoy paying in bullion.

'Will you undertake all sorts of treatment?' I asked.

'All the fashionable ones, of course. There will be a surcharge for doing rush jobs: it can cost a company thousands and thousands if a star is out of action. Of course, we shall always call in the best and quickest men.'

When I said that keeping up with research and knowing who the best men were must take up a lot of his time, he rather angrily handed me a plate of smoked salmon sandwiches from a sideboard disguised as an Art Deco harmonium and said that the leading consultants were all his close friends and stars in their own line.

Before I could get his views on the treatment of endocarditis, he was called from New York. The effusive conversation went on some time before it emerged that a jet was being sent for him. He rang off and turned to me with a delighted grin.

'Mexico. All-girl western. Saddlesores!! I have enjoyed our chat so. My book-keeper will let your office have the account. Would you be so sweet as to ask them to pay me in soiled rands? And do look at my Mycenean gold-and-ivory statuette of Aesculapius as you go. It has a rather amusing phallic caduceus.'

As a young woman dressed as a footman showed me out, the Great Healer was on the line to his accountant.

R. G. G. Price 15.10.1975

LET ME THROUGH, I'M A QUACK!

This summer, a quack – a man without any medical qualifications – was given space in the *Journal* of the Royal College of Physicians to air his heterodox views: an event ordinarily about as probable as the Inquisition licensing a Protestant tract to be sold at an auto-da-fé. Perhaps the *Journal*'s editor was simply giving him enough faggots to burn himself. But anyway, as you are unlikely to have seen that august publication, let me first summarise what his article had to say.

His thesis was that a striking change has begun to come over the public's attitude to medicine, without the public being aware of it. Until very recently the common assumption was that with the advances of medical science, quackery would gradually disappear; for only the gullible would continue to pay a fringe practitioner when they could get effective treatment free. But it is now the gullible who believe that orthodox medical treatment *is* effective. The hard-headed business man, the athlete, not seldom even the doctor, aware of the value of their time, go to their osteopath or acupuncturist or to a nature cure establishment, instead.

The reason for this trend is obvious. The belief that an organic cause for all forms of illness would eventually be found, and the appropriate remedy would follow, has dominated orthodox thinking for a century and more. Coupled with advances in hygiene and nutrition, it produced results striking enough to appear to justify faith in it. But what might be called the everyday disorders, ranging from colds and flu through headaches and backaches, bronchitis and asthma, to coronaries and cancer, have resisted this approach. The discovery of cause and cure is always 'just around the corner'; but the corner is never quite reached.

The fringe practitioner starts from a different premise. We should not think of diseases, he argues, in terms of felons breaking and entering, and laying us low. Most of our illnesses are self-inflicted. Not, of course, intentionally. They are the effect, or side-effect, of our life style. Our diet is unbalanced: we drink and smoke too much, take insufficient exercise, and suffer from a variety of social, economic and emotional stresses which we are not very good at dealing with. These conspire to make us illness-prone. At some point, the fuse goes, and we either get the illness we are particularly prone to – migraine say, or indigestion; or we pick up whatever bug is going around.

It is here that misunderstanding about the nature of illness is most common. When you take your symptoms to a doctor and, after consideration, he pronounces that you have a virus disorder, you will probably believe that this in some way exonerates you from responsibility. Not so. For a start, the chances are that he is using 'virus' in its original sense, of an unknown agent of disease. If he does not know what is the matter with you, it is a safe diagnostic ploy. But even if there is an identifiable virus, you may have caught it, rather than it catching you.

This is where the fringe practitioners hold the advantage. In the old days they used to specialise; the osteopath often dealing only with backaches, the naturopath with weight problems. More and more, they now use whatever treatment they think relevant: osteopathic manipulation, diet, acupuncture, psychotherapy, and various forms of healing; the object being not to attack the particular virus, whatever it may be, but to remove your proneness to virus attacks.

It is easy for a doctor to poke fun at these Jacks-of-all-therapies, medically qualified in none. Or, rather, it used to be easy, until the apotheosis of acupuncture. For years the acupuncturist, with his daft notion of curing people of a mixed bag of diseases by sticking needles into them, was orthodoxy's chief butt. Then, suddenly, the profession was confounded by the revelation that acupuncture worked. Television films, some taken by Western doctors, showed Chinese patients undergoing horrendous surgical operations, with only some needles between them and agony, yet remaining cheerful and chatty throughout.

Unable to tolerate the thought that it really could all be done by needles, orthodoxy has now grasped at an alternative explanation: that it is all done by some form of hypnosis. This is ironic, in view of the fact that the profession has never taken hypnosis seriously. It is also, from orthodoxy's point of view, a most damaging admission. For if it *is* hypnosis, it reveals that the mind has an even greater dominion over the body than has been recognised. In any case, so far as patients are concerned it matters little what the explanation is. If a method works well – as acupuncture does, for example, in childbirth – they will naturally want it.

Even people who go to a fringe practitioner, however, often do not appreciate that he can deal with illness in general, not just with a particular illness that doctors can't do much for, like rheumatism. The trouble is that we have been conditioned to think of diseases arising from germs and viruses as the work of criminals, requiring police – in the form of doctors – to handle. A better analogy is with football hooligans, who may be hard-working citizens during the week, breaking out only under the influence of hysteria or drink. Like hooligans, viruses cannot be all rounded up and executed. Drugs can palliate their symptoms, but little more. But we ourselves, given a 'lift', can render them innocuous.

To vary the analogy: as we plough through life's rough seas, waves come over the side, causing us to sink. Orthodoxy works by increasingly desperate pumping and baling. The fringe concentrates on providing buoyancy, so that the water doesn't come in, or is quickly disposed of. It is not a new idea; it is Hippocrates's *vis medicatrix naturae*, the exploitation of the body's own preservative and recuperative powers, coming back into fashion again, after so many years of neglect.

But this brings up a problem. An increasing number of doctors and, in my experience, of medical students are aware that orthodoxy has been beating its head against a cul-de-sac wall. But medical research throughout the world is dominated by the funds provided by the pharmaceutical industry, which depends for its profit on the continued sale of drugs; and even where government or charitable funds are available they are ordinarily administered by hospital consultants, who are barnacled in their own orthodoxy. So the direction of research does not change; and the medical curriculum, and hospital practice, change painfully slowly.

To take an obvious example. Many, perhaps most, GPs realise that osteopathic manipulation is on balance a much quicker and better way of dealing with backache than current orthopaedic practice (I understand that a recent retrospective survey carried out at a London hospital revealed that patients undergoing orthopaedic treatment there left worse off, on balance, than if they had had no treatment at all). Yet osteopathy is practised by only a few doctors, and available to very few patients on the NHS.

There is only one way out, the writer in the RCP *Journal* (who, I should admit, was myself) concluded: to introduce legislation which will enable suitably qualified – not necessarily medically qualified – practitioners to come into the NHS. It is ridiculous that highly skilled osteopaths and acupuncturists, whose abilities are generally recognised even within the medical profession, should remain outcasts. Unfortunately there are leading osteopaths and acupuncturists within the profession who object, claiming that only the medically qualified can be trusted (ironically, the fact they are so qualified limits their own opportunities; they cannot put their names in the *Yellow Pages*, as the unqualified can). But there are not enough of them, nor, given the ossification of the teaching hospitals, will there ever be. What is needed is a whole new category; a faculty for quacks.

Brian Inglis 15.10.1975

MY SON THE DOCTOR

'The most disgusting figure in modern civilization,' Shaw depicted us. Wrote Thackeray, 'Rakish young medical student, gallant, dashing, what is called "loudly" dressed, and (must it be owned?) somewhat dirty.' From Dickens came, 'A parcel of lazy, idle fellars, that are always smoking and drinking, and lounging.' The medical student image was indelibly drawn before the start of the century, a mixture of Flashman, Sir Francis Dashwood and a resurrectionist's lookout.

My invasion of the profession started the same spring Wednesday morning as Hitler's into the remains of Czechoslovakia. I rued my lack of the three qualities guaranteeing success: (1) Father a doctor, and from the same hospital. (2) Education at Epsom College, amid the sons of doctors. (3) Good at games. But I didn't drop my 'hs', I wore a clean white collar and I called everyone over 30 'Sir'. There were some educational requirements involving 'School Cert.', but nobody seemed to bother much about these.

The dean of my medical school was terrifying – big, pink, surgical and knighted. He asked a single, penetrating question: Could I pay the fees regularly? His practical mind recognized that detecting medical competence in bun-faced schoolboys was as diagnostically risky as foretelling the baby's sex on conception.

I later found the interview was anyway superfluous. The medical school secretary beyond the frosted glass door inspected all candidates closely through his pince-nez during their twenty minutes' wait, and told any who picked their noses, read volumes from the Left Book Club, asked him intelligent questions about the hospital's history, or showed other signs of social instability, that there were no vacancies and they had better try down the road at Guy's.

The dean's secretary is now displaced by UCCA, the monster in Cheltenham which has marred more adolescent summers than acne. Apart from requiring 'A'-levels above my ability – and I suspect of all my contemporaries now holding down consultant jobs – candidates today are grilled by a board including *one of the students*, who sit even on committees criticizing the teaching. In my time, this was as unthinkable as a midshipman being called in to help direct the Battle of Jutland.

My only knowledge of medicine came from the Boy Scouts' first aid manual and *The Citadel*, but I lived up to the student image without too painful self-consciousness. A young man who finds himself daily slicing his dead fellow beings down to the bone, whose stock in trade is the basic functioning of human body and mind, may be excused impatience with conventional affectations of dress and manners. We were rowdy, but even dear, gentle Bertie Wooster culled policemen's helmets on Boat Race night. Today, Bertie would be sent for Borstal training.

Society is transformed, the medical students hardly at all.

The only change in my hospital's rugby pavilion is the stolen roadmenders' lamps now shining yellow instead of red. Medical students are as mixed as any others, but they still seem middle-class, or not aggressively anything else. Like Evelyn Waugh's English county families of the Bollinger Club baying for broken glass, their roistering has none of the vindictive malice which has matched the spread of higher education since the end of World War II. They can still appreciate the delicate art of bad behaviour.

Nor do medicals take themselves and their opinions with the same ridiculous seriousness as the National Union of Students. Politically, they are as inert as argon. They neither sit-in, freak-out, howl down nor blow up. Authority is mocked and mimicked, but respected. In the medical schools, Greyfriars still keeps its terms.

Ours was a monkish society. The Privy Council admitted women before our hospital did. Now females get 40 per cent of the places. We enjoyed a terrible reputation towards them. Its cause was economic, not endocrinal.

With no prospect of a living wage under thirty, Sir William Osler's advice was Hobson's choice – to 'put your emotions in cold storage' until qualification. Emotions were one thing, nights out another. An indulgent girl in those decorous days understood that we could not make the customary repayment of keeping her in comfort for the rest of her life. This induced a wonderfully carefree attitude, lost in the medical student today.

Britain's 20,000 junior doctors now earn between £2,869 and £6,279 a year for a 44-hour week, and according to their spokesman in Glasgow are unsatisfied with it. It didn't matter how many hours we worked a week, because we weren't paid at all. And it didn't matter expressing dissatisfaction, because we should simply have been booted out. Our homes were our bleak housemen's rooms, our possessions a row of textbooks, two suits and a bottle-opener.

In a world crammed with wall-to-wall carpeting, washing machines and electric mixers, the youngest of doctors takes a wife so they can watch colour television together. Even first year students marry, to surround themselves with the same enviable consumer durables as the people in the colour supplements – cars, stereo and babies. Medical students are no longer sex mad. Just houseproud.

They are chivvied more about their work. Few of them smoke, even tobacco. There survive no longer the old medical lags, well dressed and worldly, cultured and charming, who endured the occasional lecture but came really to read the newspapers in the common room and take lunch, like any other gentlemen with their club.

Today's students are psychologically molly-coddled, each pressed to take personal problems before a battery of counsellors. Nobody gave a damn for our personal problems. Quite rightly, because in my knowledge they were generally awfully boring. Only one of my year committed suicide, by gassing himself in the lab. 'Extremely interesting,' observed the consultant professor hastily called to the scene. 'Notice, gentlemen, the characteristic cherry-red coloration of the skin from carboxyhaemoglobin. A *most* useful chance to familiarize yourselves with the fresh post mortem appearances.'

Medical students remain stable because medicine is a strictly disciplined profession. Not as an Army is disciplined, but from an unceasing responsibility for human life which makes everyone do as they're told as efficiently and promptly as possible without argument. Even the most flippant medical student embodies a tradition of unselfish service to the sick of all races, nations, political persuasions and personal tastes, with a considerably longer history than, say, the National and Local Government Officers' Association, or the National Union of Public Employees.

Richard Gordon 15.10.1975

SHOULD I GET A DOCTOR, DOCTOR?

The medical practitioner, as a repository for my blind trust, comes second only to motor mechanics and accountants. All right, third. Split hairs. Do you want this consultation or not? Let's have your shirt up.

All three, then, have this common appeal. I know that they know what they're doing, but I don't want to know what it is. Look elsewhere for this, say among the travel agencies or mail order houses, and you won't find it. I speak as a man recently assured by a top agency that only a £40 taxi could get him from one part of the Peloponnese to another, and learned too late that the bus ran twice daily at £1.90. Last week I was mailed a babycare catalogue under cover of a sickly letter starting, 'Dear Mother', and examples can doubtless be multiplied.

Don't write in, all the same. Your postcard from Fuengirola saying you've arrived safely at your unbuilt luxury hotel would be nice reading, and confirm my argument: likewise the note you wrote to kill waiting-time at the Jobcentre, about these Rover Vitesse brochures you keep getting, £14,950, number plates extra. It's a matter of fitting you in. Patients are under great pressure at present. I can only give each doctor five minutes.

And the pressure has got to the doctors. If you took your paper to the surgery the other Monday, as preferred reading to old copies of Country Life long worn to a mush, you've had the bad news already. It threatens to put my opening gambit, above, into the past tense. The update on our doctors is that they are off their rockers, stoned, hitting the hash, sick, topping the suicide ratings and generally unfit to practise, especially in the last bracket.

In saying generally I don't mean generally, either in the sense that the entire profession is unshaven, hallucinating and lurching around the intensive care department singing glees, or that any single healer runs the full gamut of disabilities at any one time. And when I say our doctors I naturally don't mean yours or mine, who could be traced back, and are sane, sober, in robust health, pop no personal pills and probably have sharpish lawyers.

The same is true of Dr Max Glatt, who has done his best to bolster my blind trust, calculating that no more than 3,000 doctors are drunks. He was touched off by Dr Allibone, another sure paragon, it's safe to say. I like to be safe. It was his article in the widely-titled *Journal of the Society of Administrators of Family Practitioner Services* that blew the whistle on this whole thing. He urged the General Medical Council to improve its machinery for quicker sightings of crazy, coked-up MRCPs, let alone FRCSs, before they start treating pink-eye with back liniment or sawing wrong legs off.

The council, I should say, has been on to the trouble for some time. But its screening system, 'designed to protect the public by providing early detection', has been too little and too late in Dr Allibone's view, allowing quantities of the afflicted to slip through. 'Doctors impaired by alcoholism, drug addiction or mental illness came to the council's attention only when they appeared before its disciplinary committee when they were liable to be suspended from practice or struck off the register': presumably for some other reason, such as dating wealthy widows. Widowers. I don't know. Anyway, it was only when they appeared, on whatever charges, and the board noticed that they were wearing their glasses upside-down or had a foot stuck in their medical bag, that serious disorders became evident.

I'm all for catching them early, particularly in view of the sudden trend towards stitching-back severed bits of the body. I happen to be intact myself, at the moment. But you never know. The last thing I want is to emerge from surgery with two ears on the same side of my head. Nor am I too happy with the news that doctors who do get a council going-over may be returned to circulation with 'some limitations, such as not prescribing certain drugs or not working alone'.

In a way, of course, I prefer my doctor to work alone. The man in the corner, affecting to read *Gray's Anatomy*, could be a second opinion. That's bad enough. If in fact he's there to see that the doctor isn't trying to listen to my chest-murmurs with the stethoscope stuck up his nose, where's your blind trust now? And what do you do, collecting your repeat castor oil from the chemist's and finding it's a menthol and benzoin inhalant? Apart from choke?

You can do something, if I read Dr Allibone aright. Well, you may be able to. I don't think I could. What is needed, he says, to sleuth out the medical man early in his self-medication, while he can still take the old amphetamines or leave them, is 'more local initiatives'. This can only mean that while my doctor is examining me, I'm examining him, noting such symptomatic give-aways as the slurred speech, dilated pupils, a tendency to fall over sideways, the blood-pressure tape strapped round his own biceps by mistake, an inability to focus a hypodermic on a virtually unmissable rump.

Hell. Could I do this, and report to Dr Allibone, the GMC, and Dr Max Glatt if time permitted? Frankly, no. In the first place, I shouldn't stay long enough. Once he's seeking my agreement to a hysterectomy, I'm out of there, personally shouting, 'Next!' In the second, I would feel compassion for this man, surrounded by easy, terrible temptations unknown to accountants and motor mechanics: they may be periodically seized with a wild lust for slamming off comically falsified tax statements just to relieve the stress, or having a quick go of anti-freeze behind the body-shop, but it takes time and guile, never mind losing the faith of the customer who revered their figures as holy writ, and never thought to see his Vitesse back from service with its rear spoiler dangling. What do they know, in even their wildest moments, of the raw alcohol and beckoning barbiturates so ready to my doctor's hand?

When I say my doctor I don't, of course, mean my doctor. Anyway, if I had the heart to examine him for the council, their spy in the surgery for God's sake, it's out of the question just now. He's on holiday. He deserves it. Even if his nurse did say on the phone that he's gone to Fuengirola.

But it's nothing serious I wanted to see him about today. This locum they've got should be able to handle it – though I shan't feel too much confidence until I'm shown in. If he's on the couch with his eyes rolled up showing the whites I may back out and drop the council a line after all. It isn't like sneaking on an old and trusted friend.

And like so many other ills of the flesh, when you come to think, flying ant-stings are apt to get well of their own accord. Without piling on the pressures of an already hard-pressed profession.

Basil Boothroyd 24.8.1983

BRITISH PATIENTS' JOURNAL

A NEW STEP FOR PATIENTS

The *British Medical Journal* is sent free to all members of the BMA to keep doctors up to date with the latest developments and to ensure a handy outlet for publicity and exposure on the media. No such service has ever existed for patients, who are perpetually in the dark concerning the latest research. But if doctors can be kept informed of their own problems (most of which are actually given them by patients), cannot we keep ourselves informed on our own problems (most of which are caused by doctors)?

Hence the birth of the *British Patients' Journal*. Each week we shall be bringing you articles and papers which will help you to understand many of the ailments and disabilities of our doctors, but more especially the troubles which they cause patients. We shall also act as a clearing-house for patients' requests and appointments. Above all we shall attempt, by the spread of knowledge, to dissipate the fear and ignorance attendant upon a visit to the doctor's. He is *not* an omniscient father-figure. He is a fallible, forgetful, fickle human being like everyone else. Only we can help to improve him.

M.R.C.S. AND BAR

We are often asked what causes the unsightly growth, after some doctors' names, of strings of letters, and whether it is infectious. Well, it *is* mildly infectious, but curiously enough can only be caught by other doctors; they believe, what's more, that it will help them to get better jobs and be better doctors. This is a harmless delusion that need not be discouraged. The only danger is if a patient falls for the same delusion and thinks he will do better with a doctor afflicted by letters. On the contrary; if a doctor has more than about fifteen letters attached he has probably spent far too long out of action acquiring these letters and not long enough practising medicine. He should be avoided.

THE GAIN DRAIN

Exact figures are not to hand, but it seems fairly certain that this country is losing some of its best qualified and best paid patients abroad. Not because medical treatment is necessarily any better abroad, but simply because the tax situation here does not allow our richest patients to devote the time and energy to their ailments in this country that they would like. In the last few months alone we have lost five of our most rewarding cases of incipient cirrhosis of the liver to Spain and the South of France. Take the case of a pop singer who prefers for tax reasons to call himself X.

'I been quite happy to work in England as a patient,' he says. 'I wouldn't call meself a specialist patient exactly, 'cos I've generalised over the years. I started out just with a drinking problem, but since then I've mucked around with a back injury, cartilage trouble and Parkinson's Disease – that's what we call loss of voice in show-biz. So I been working pretty hard not just with your actual GP but also a whole load of osteopaths and hypnotists and ortho-whatsits. See, I can't afford that anymore, and much as I'd love to go on working with them I'll have to take up this offer of medical treatment abroad. Course they don't want to see me go, but that's your bleedin' government for you.'

This constant draining of our best paid patients, many of whom display more advanced symptoms of new diseases than the average untrained patient, cannot but harm our medical system. One research unit in London, studying the effects of a new family of drugs, has had to close down merely because two pop groups left for America. Over to you, Mrs Castle.

THE DRUG HABIT

The fashion over the last ten or fifteen years among patients has been to let their doctor give them drugs of one sort or another and generally this has had the required effect – it has kept the doctor in a state of quiet satisfaction, and made him feel he is doing his job for the community, even though in many cases there is very little in the drugs to warrant such an effect. (Keeping doctors happy by letting them dispense harmless drugs is known as the placebo effect.)

There are alarming signs now, though, that many doctors are beginning to suffer from drug dependency and to become addicted to one or more large drug companies, and patients must begin to wonder if their treatment of doctors should not be revised in future. Typical side-effect symptoms are: the appearance of profuse brochures on the doctor's desk, the tendency to prescribe the same pill or capsule for different diseases, the temptation to use the patient as a test case for a new drug and the habit of persuading the patient that he is suffering from an ailment for which a new wonder tablet has just arrived.

But there are more serious effects. Some doctors, especially specialists, find themselves after a while linked in a financial arrangement with a drug company, which they thereafter find it very hard to escape from – indeed, they lose all will to do so – and thereby display all the classic symptoms of drug addiction.

Only the patient can help the doctor in a case like this. Refuse to take all but the simplest pills. Hide the brochures on which he is so unnaturally reliant. Insist on being given a linctus or ointment. If necessary, threaten to withdraw altogether from a doctor/patient situation. Above all, make sure the doctor knows that he is suffering from a dependency-state. There's none so blind as the doctor who thinks he's normal.

INCIDENCE OF PARANORMAL INVISIBILITY AMONG NHS DOCTORS: AN INCREASING SCOURGE

A correlation of reports from patients suggests that a new and baffling affliction may be affecting our doctors: a proneness to vanish. This usually takes the form of the patient being ushered into a waiting room or out-patients' hall and told, 'The doctor will see you in a moment,' and yet finding himself unable to physically see the doctor for anything up to two or three hours. There seems to be no particular explanation for this strange phenomenon, yet as it has been reported from all over the country it is obviously a widespread ailment. When the doctor does eventually materialise, he seems totally unaware that he has been in a state of disembodiment for an hour or two. If asked where he has been all this time, he tends to look blank and say that he has been delayed or very busy or, very often, completely unaware that the patient has been waiting. Occasionally he loses his temper and commands the patient to go elsewhere, but we still cannot be sure that irritability is a concomitant of invisibility.

Case Report

In what must admittedly be an extreme case, a 24-year-old patient in Newcastle reports the disappearance of a doctor *and subsequent failure to reappear*. He had been told to attend the hospital at 2.30 and was told on arrival that the doctor would see him in a minute. By 4.30 he began to get worried and told the staff that he was starting to feel better, and that if the doctor did not appear soon he might recover before they had had time to treat him. At 5.30 he was told that the doctor had been 'slightly delayed', 'called away on an emergency' and 'taken suddenly ill', all three excuses coming from different nurses, one of whom failed thereafter to rematerialise, and was asked to come back the following morning.

He did so, and was told that the doctor was 'unavailable', but that he would be dealt with by a new doctor, Dr Mendoza. Dr Mendoza duly appeared, two days later, and asked the patient what 'seemed' to be the trouble. The patient replied that the trouble 'seemed' to have gone; he was now interested only in the whereabouts of the missing doctor. Dr Mendoza said he did not know but he thought he was in Chicago by now. The doctor was never seen again.

Discussion

This case displays the classic symptoms of doctor dispersal, as this phenomenon is known; the repeated assurance by hospital staff that the doctor is about to come; the lack of any knowledge as to his real whereabouts; and the eventual appearance of a completely different doctor, always younger and usually foreign.

There seem to be three theories to account for this process. One is that the doctor does physically vanish. The second is that he changes in some mysterious way his total physical appearance over a period of hours, and that the younger man is none other than the missing doctor in a new guise, having lost in his transformation most of his medical knowledge and some of his command of English.

The third and most likely explanation is simply that when the hospital staff say 'the doctor will see you in a minute', they do not refer to a specific doctor, but to an idealised picture of a doctor who in a perfect world would turn up in the next minute. That is, hospital staff have hallucinated themselves into believing that (against all the known facts) there is always a doctor round the next corner. If so, and much more research is needed, there is no such thing as the problem of the vanishing doctor. Only the problem of the mass hallucination of hospital staff.

Readers are asked, if they find themselves in this position, to question the hospital staff more thoroughly. The following queries are recommended:

'What is the doctor's name?'

'Please describe him briefly so that I can be sure he has not changed his astral body meanwhile.'

'Can you send him soon to guard against the possibility that I, too, may vanish?'

'Will you swear by all that's sterilised that he is not on his way to Chicago?'

We look forward to hearing from you.

TEMPORARY GP AMNESIA

A short-lived and mild ailment which may nevertheless cause the doctor some embarrassment, GP Amnesia takes the form of the family doctor being completely unable to remember what a patient suffers from or even who he is. Normally a doctor can cure this himself by asking the patient who, after all, knows more about it than the doctor does, but when allied to residual pride it may cause the doctor to flounder around in some pain.

Case Report

'How's the trouble, Mr Porter?'

'Turnbull's the name.'

'Slip of the tongue. How's Porter's Trouble, Mr Turnbull?'

'Porter's Trouble?'

'New disease. Lot of it around. Haven't got it? Very lucky. How's the . . . the . . .'

'Wife?'

'That's it. Wife playing you up, is she?'

'No, it's the back again.'

'Back again?'

'Yes. Aren't you pleased to see me?'

'Of course. Just slip your jacket off and let's have a look at it.'

'There you are. Pure Harris tweed, and looks like new.'

'Good. Been having trouble with the back, have we?'

'No. *I* have. I've been taking the red pills, though.'

'Ah.'

'And the blue capsules three times a day, instead of meals.'

'Ah.'

'And the nose drops every day.'

'Does it? I'm sorry to hear that.'

'And everything seems all right now.'

'Good. Well, Mr Porter, I'm going to give you a clean bill of health now. There seems nothing wrong.'

'Turnbull.'

'Exactly. Sorry about the wife. Send her along if it gets any worse. Next please.'

Discussion
This doctor is now part of a very successful cabaret group.

A SICK BUSINESS

Doctors don't need to aspire to play God; once a man gets the protection of a well-ordered profession around him, the role comes quite naturally. Only the other night a doctor from my past preached at me from my television set. When we were students, no one would trust him with the price of a drink, not to mention the address of a girl friend. Yet there he was on my screen telling me why my twelve-year-old daughter should or shouldn't be on the Pill; I forget which it was but he said it very forcibly.

Authority like that doesn't come cheap; the price is subservience to a system of patronage that lies adjectivally somewhere between bizarre and Byzantine. Things have been slipping recently since Mrs Castle and those dreadful unions started to rock the boat but the hospital

life can still offer an insecure soul the protection of one of life's great brotherhoods. Once a chap has shown himself worthy of acceptance, he can progress atraumatically from student to houseman to registrar to consultant to retirement, provided he keeps his eyes down, his nose clean, and his thoughts and his flies buttoned up in public. The only irritants he will encounter along the way are those accursed patients. I suppose they are necessary.

The only step in his career that demands intelligent manoeuvring is the transition from houseman to registrar. To keep on good terms with the club's senior members and to stay in the running for eventual promotion to the club committee, a young doctor needs a registrar's job at one of those teaching hospitals which refer to themselves unselfconsciously as 'centres of excellence'. Applicants for jobs at these establishments must first determine what sort of candidate the hospital is after: a 'brain', a scrum-half, a freemason, or even the statutory black or woman whom teaching hospitals like to employ in these permissive days. Most likely the hospital will be after a decent chap known to one of the consultants (or his daughter) or recommended to him by another decent chap at another decent place.

Once accepted as a teaching hospital registrar, a young doctor (defined as anyone under 50) has established himself as a definitive decent chap and so he will remain as long as he attracts adjectives like sound and loyal and avoids ones like suspect, dubious or the dreaded 'too clever by half'. Although theoretically still 'in training' he will do most of the work in the hospital because his chief is likely to be busy elsewhere; not necessarily ringing up the till in private practice but attending committees or medical meetings where he can extend his acquaintance with men of influence and power. A professor of surgery who travelled a lot was once asked who did his work when he was away. He replied: 'The same people as do it when I am here.'

A teaching hospital registrar won't complain about doing much of his boss's work because of the chances he gets in the wards, the corridors or over the coffee cups to exchange a well-turned witticism or a deep insightful remark with some of medicine's most powerful patrons and to impress them, depending on which direction he aims his career, with his modesty, his commonsense, his zeal, or his healthy irreverence (confined, of course, within decent limits).

These contrived social situations are valuable because medicine's patrons have within their gift not only the best jobs but all the appurtenances that distinguish the gentlemen from the players. To the academically inclined they can offer access to research funds, consultancies to rich pharmaceutical companies and international agencies, and regular invitations to scientific congresses in such places as Florence, Tokyo, San Francisco or Barbados. For those keen to grub a living in private practice, they can arrange membership of dining clubs and specialist societies and appearances at post-graduate meetings which get a man's name known within the trade and are a more effective form of publicity, in terms of attracting referrals of private patients, than those appearances in the public prints so frowned on by the GMC. And for the unambitious man who desires nothing more than a quiet, pompous, professional life, the patrons can provide regular leg-ups on the beanstalk that springs from administrative and political committees and grows into the cloudborne land of the ermine, the mutual votes of thanks, the gold chains, and even the reassuring touch of the sword on the shoulder or the comforting snuggle of the coronet around the temples.

Like all good Establishments the system that distributes this patronage is not an organised network with a Mr Big skulking at its centre but an ill-defined scatter of well-meaning fellows, dropping a word here and a hint there, and earning each other's co-operation by lending support here, withdrawing it there. Many of them are unaware of the power they wield and take a paternal delight in the achievements of the decent young fellows they choose to smile upon. The network is so ephemeral in places that it would have perished long ago were it not protected by professional rules, which are usually paraded in the false though impressive clothes of Ethics.

Typical of these rules is the insistence on professional anonymity. Not so long ago the BMA 'noted with disquiet the increasing tendency for doctors to be named by the media'.

I can understand their apprehension. Things have really started to slide and not only in the media. Nowadays, as opposed to when I was a lad, too many hospital patients know the name of the doctor who is treating them. That's just a short step away from patients finding their way to kind, competent doctors without having to rely on guidance from within the brotherhood. And in such small ways can the authority of a great profession be undermined. Luckily, while hospital standards have declined, things have improved markedly in general practice. There, clever manipulation of appointment systems and deputising services can ensure that no patient knows the name of the doctor looking after him.

Professional rules are a negative way of protecting the system. Doctors are not ashamed to use more positive incentives or, as you lay persons like to call them, bribes. The most notorious are the merit awards which the NHS adds to some consultants' salaries in recognition, 'tis said, of distinguished work. They range from around £2,000 to £10,500 a year and the lucky prizewinners get them for the rest of their working lives. But because they are given in secret by a committee of doctors which considers the recommendations of other doctors, no one is sure who is getting what size award or why.

This secret handout of hard cash is such a shameless instrument of patronage, it might bring a blush to the cheek of a Mafiosa. Of course there's no evidence that anyone who bucks the system will be denied an award but the fear of what *might* happen makes doctors think twice before questioning authority, even when authority has put itself inarguably in the wrong.

No prizes, I fear, for guessing the grounds on which BMA spokesmen defend the secrecy. 'If people knew who got these awards,' said one recently, 'it would lead to difficult ethical situations tantamount to advertising.'

Much of this medical politicking is more worthy of a giggle than a snort of indignation. True, it ensures that medicine remains a conservative conformist profession but most patients, I suspect, would prefer to be treated by a conservative doctor than by a radical one. The real threat of the patronage network is the way it perpetuates mediocrity. Mediocre men with nothing to defend but their unmerited authority use patronage to repel all intrusion by imagination, initiative or enterprise.

Mediocrity can dominate a hospital for about twelve years but then it is usually overthrown in a palace revolution, because luckily the patronage system carries within it the seeds of its own subversion. Doctors who actually practise medicine – as opposed to those who play political games – spend a lot of their time not treating disease but unravelling the strands of life's rich entanglement. Occasionally a working clinician may succumb to flattery from his patients and begin to wonder whether a divine spark doesn't after all flicker somewhere about his person. But the evening when the divine robes are tried on for size is likely to be followed by the morning after when the boy whom he confidently diagnosed as having acute appendicitis mutters, just before he sinks under anaesthesia, that he forgot to mention he had eaten two pounds of green apples.

Not so long ago my nine-year-old niece asked her doctor father: 'Daddy, what is a lesbian?'

My brother-in-law, who had read Dr Spock, settled her in a comfortable chair and, eliminating emotional overtones, gave her a clear and detailed answer to her question. She listened intently, occasionally nodding her head in understanding. When he'd finished, my brother-in-law did what many a doctor does when he's pleased with himself. He went into the kitchen and told his wife. There he learned he'd been asked the question only because his daughter had been puzzled by the news that the family who have moved in next door were Wesleyans.

Stand up the Machiavelli who can devise a system to preserve our brotherhood's mystique at such a moment.

Michael O'Donnell 15.10.1975

DOCTOR ON THE BOARDS

Like many medical people, I am incurably stage-struck. I love to be the focal point of admiring eyes, mostly female, to bait the breath with my every movement, to sense the applause which is unheard and sweeter. To behave, in fact, like any surgeon any day in his operating theatre.

My appearances on the medical stage are now safely restricted to race meetings and cricket matches, my cue a plea over the Tannoy for a doctor. I respond like a pantomime demon popping through his trap-door. If anyone in sight falls over in the street, and does not scramble up again instantly, I am on the patient in a flash, administering the kiss of life.

This is a most unpleasant form of therapy at the operator's end. The number of beautiful young women to be kissed back to life is, statistically obviously, negligible compared with the fat old men whose smell is improved once they actually stop breathing. As most of the subjects are incorrigibly dead, deep-throated embraces with a corpse had chilly overtones of Poe, and would very much upset Freud. I now delegate the kiss bit to the nearest policeman, while performing the cardiac massage. This is repeated flat-palmed pressure, rather like a hand-off at rugby, which is less spectacular but you don't have to clean your teeth afterwards.

As a lad, I was determined to be an actor ever since Noel Coward sent me his autograph. My big break was the speech-day production, as Lady Macbeth. At the last minute, I decided to play it for laughs. Today, this might have landed me rave notices for Ortonesque grotesquery. It got me only the cane, instant expulsion from the cast, and I think from the school.

At medical school there was naturally an enthusiastic and enormous dramatic society. I fancy they found my style too vulgar for the Chekhov and Barrie. My chance came only at Christmas, when the students organised an itinerant revue. This was performed for the bedridden sufferers from ward to ward on Boxing Day, all patients likely to spoil the fun by snuffing it between scenes being tidied away into side-rooms.

These shows had a structure as rigidly formalised as the Nō theatre of Japan. The audience was unsatisfied, and even mystified, if the students failed to don Sisters' drag, with a dozen pairs of rugger socks down the bosom. Or if bedpans, bottles, vomit bowls and similar fundamental pieces of hospital furniture did not appear among the props. The script was mostly satire on the little professional and personal quirks of the consultants, who sat through it all with grins as steely as their scalpels. An operation scene was as obligatory as the barrel of beer backstage. Anaesthesia was always induced with a mallet, the surgeons shared a two-handed tree saw, and the patient's innards expelled any number of amusing articles, like bright red inner tubes, alarm clocks, hospital cutlery and (male wards only) a string of inflated contraceptives. It would have made Mrs Mary Whitehouse blush all over. But there is nothing like a stay in hospital to induce an earthy sense of humour.

I had a conjuring act, turning water into wine. After lunch on Boxing Day my aim was not at its steadiest, most of the fluid which was supposed to change colour from one jug to another hitting the mirror-like ward parquet. 'Nurse,' I heard the sister hiss. 'Fetch a mop and clear up that young man's mess instantly.' I continued jauntily with my patter, pretending that the earnest probationer swabbing round my feet was part of the turn. The following artiste did better. He started vomiting half way through *Tit Willow*, and won wild applause by singing it as a patient recovering from his anaesthetic. The next sketch was set in Out-patients', and when one of the actors passed out cold half way through, we carried on nonchalantly as though he had died suddenly in accordance with the plot. Thus I learned the most elusive of actors' arts, how to ad lib.

I was wildly excited when the director of the *Doctor* films offered me a small part. I played the anaesthetist, which was type-casting, as I had at the time just stopped being one. It also enabled him to muffle me from the gaze of the public in operating kit, showing only my eyes. (One of the actors told me they were quite beautiful, like a sick spaniel's.) As I sat at a hired anaesthetic trolley beside a hired operating table in a cardboard-walled operating theatre, amid gowned and masked figures curiously fingering the property instruments, another actor asked if I was a member of Equity. I asked him if he was a member of the British Medical Association. That seemed to resolve the problem. Today, I don't know what Vanessa Redgrave would have done to me. But my career as a film star never flourished. In the next *Doctor* picture I was

reduced to Man Walking Down Corridor, and in the one after to Man Walking Down Corridor Seen Through Glass. That's showbusiness, I suppose.

Two of my novels have been adapted for the stage by Ted Willis, though he turned down my suggested title, *Doc of Dixon Green*. The play of *Doctor in the House* opened in London with one of the students played by the unknown Edward Woodward, just as one of the passengers in the film of *Doctor at Sea* was played by an unknown titty French girl called Brigitte Bardot. The *Doctor at Sea* play opened later in London, and a very, very little later it closed in London. By then, I had discovered a fundamental principle of the British stage. It is not necessary for a piece to sniff the sweet smell of success in the sickly West End. Far more invigoratingly for the box-office blow the salty breezes of our seaside resorts.

I am indebted to the theatre for some delightful early season weeks in a variety of coastal towns from Lytham St Anne's to Lyme Regis, whose pleasures would otherwise have escaped me. I have been to Morecambe-on-Sea when it was so bitter they were catching the famous prawns already deep-frozen. I have visited Jersey, which was a mistake. The management overlooked the fact that in the Channel Isles the good things of life are duty-free, holidaymakers arriving not for artistic refreshment but a fortnight's sunny boozing. This summer we're at Great Yarmouth.

As I sat in the stalls on the opening night, digesting my bloater supper and wondering if I shouted 'Author!' afterwards anyone would take up the cry, I played my greatest role. The lady in the row behind me went into labour. I upstaged our entire splendid cast. I carried her out, laid her down, demanded ambulances, gave the impression that the happy event would coincide with the curtain calls. Everyone in the foyer was running about and calling me 'Doctor'. I admit, I hammed it up. But had it reached its finale, I can modestly claim in this particular drama to achieve a better delivery than Laurence Olivier.

Richard Gordon 27.8.1975

GRAHAM BARKER
Still Practising

DRS CAMERON & FINLAY,
ARDEN HOUSE
TANNOCHBRAE
November 5th 1984

To the Medical Officer of Health,

Dear Dr Snoddie,

Janet has just brought me the London *Times* today (a paper I rarely read, preferring the Journal of Urology for the spot-the-ball competition). Ye will, nae doot, hae seen the damn stuff and nonsense from the "Royal College of General Practitioners" (Sassenach busybodies) about refresher courses for us General Practitioners, implying that we spend on average only a few hours per week "updating ourselves".

Of course, young Finlay is cock-a-hoop. He's been trying for a long time to get me to come on one of those drug company binges with him — three days' debauchery on the Orient Express under the guise of postgraduate education.

He reckons that I do not expose mysel' enough tae modern medical methods of diagnosis and treatment. He says commonsense and the prescription pad is not enough nowadays.

He forgets that every week the drug companies send some bonnie wee lassie representative, w' a briefcase, short kiltie, an' legs up tae her armpits, to sit on ma desk and tell me of her latest developments — and if you think that alters my prescribing habits one little jot — then you're absolutely right.

Finlay and his generation do not always realise that I am often reading and informing mysel'. Sometimes he forgets that my car windscreen is covered wi' medical details on the back of cards saying: "DOCTOR VISITING — back in 15 guineas". And when I am lighting the garden fire with all that mail from the DHSS, it is impossible to avoid reading a sentence or two, or even a whole paragraph on a windy day.

My patients dinna want all this modern medical stuff, they want a friendly word and sympathetic handling — something Finlay sadly lacks for all his seminars and conferences. Last week, the McBurnie girl from over the council estate, a sad case to be sure, told Finlay that every year she goes to Spain for her holiday she comes back pregnant. She asked him if he thought it was due to something in the sea air. "Aye," snapped Finlay. "Your legs."

Finlay comes back from these meetings for GPs in Edinburgh, his head full of blood tests, ECGs and scans, and the patients cannot unburden themselves to him without rolling their sleeves up first and losing a pint o' blood. Take Mistress Niven's youngest niece, a frail young lassie who married 30 stone Jamie McTavish the hammer thrower; she came to me in tears. She could nae get Finlay tae listen tae her problem. Apparently, McTavish lacked a little finesse in his approach on their wedding night, for she asked me: "Surely, Dr Cameron, there must be more to foreplay than shouting 'Brace yourself?'"

Lately Finlay's gone machine mad. Three weeks away from the practice on a programming course and then he comes back and spends the earth on a computer. He tells me I need an age/sex register, screening programs, blood pressure monitoring service etc. Folks don't want medicine thrust on them — they will come to the surgery when they have something worth showing. Imagine, the waiting room full of healthy people. He's going quietly cuckoo. To cap it all, Finlay upset the Minister's wife last Sunday at the wine and cheese by reminding her, in a loud voice, that her cervical smear was due and a check for warts on her vulva. She told him, in no uncertain terms, that she had never bought a Swedish or any foreign motor car.

And the infernal word processor means the end of those quick referral letters to the hospital — gone are the days of a couple of indecipherables on the back of a fag packet — now a letter to our local surgeon looks like a *Reader's Digest* circular. It takes so long to write them — not like "Tired? Blood" or "Cough? Lungs" in the good old days.

So there is no need to put me down for any of those refresher courses you have arranged. You'll not be getting me up to the Infirmary to let those wet-behind-the-ears professors tell me how to practise medicine. I may not know the difference between Altzheimer's Disease and pre-senile dementia (and may even suffer myself from both), but at least I can manage my patients with kindness and tact.

Unlike Finlay, MRCGP, of course. Tact, he's never heard of the word. Last month, when McDonald came home from working on the oil rigs for a year, he found his wife pregnant. He stormed up to see Finlay. Instead of giving him the usual story of long gestation and wrong dates, he came out with it to McDonald's face: "It's a grudge pregnancy." "What's a grudge pregnancy?" asked the furious McDonald, and Finlay replied: "Someone had it in for you."

Aye, a little knowledge is a dangerous thing, or so they say,

Yours as ever,

Cameron.

PHYSICIAN, SPOOL THYSELF

Overworked doctors may soon be playing tapes on health matters to people in their waiting-rooms.

Daily Mail

'Morning, morning!'

The afflicted benches murmured a minimum response as the healer hurried in. Cheerfulness was a watchword with Dr Sweatband. Spying a patient across the road he would cry, 'Hello, you're looking well!' It often cut down the waiting-room crowd, though not always. This morning, for instance, having just praised the healthy appearance of Mrs Dewly, he realised that she had followed him up the hygienically scrubbed steps and was waiting for someone to move up and make a place.

Old Josher Cackworth was back again, he noticed, and the Walker girl with her single-parent twins, their handprints already visible on the glass of the midget aquarium. Dr Sweatband had been the first in the neighbourhood to calm his clientele with goldfish. He wasn't sure that they did anything, but they were tax-deductible. So was the music. Broken only by coughs, sneezes and the occasional groan, if only of impatience, selections from *Gigi* were now seeping through the close air.

These were cut off as he shut the surgery door behind him and slumped in his chair. Cheerfulness took its toll. He wished a patient or two would tell him how well he looked one of these days. Though it was doubtful, he reflected, whether it would stop his jumping cheek spasm or slight giddiness after running up steps.

He had a good ten minutes in hand. It was his policy to be early. It was his patients' policy to be earlier: and Nurse Gulling's, from behind her glass hatch, to keep a strict watch over the first-come, first-served principle. 'Now then, Major,' she would say, sliding back the window and rapping sharply with a heavy expectorant bottle, 'you know better than that.' Major Fox-Lucas, on the pretext of changing a 1982 colour supplement for a 1983 at the literature table, was notorious for gaining a seat or two's precedence if he could.

This brief spell before the rush started was Dr Sweatband's quiet time. Surgery hours were still discernible on the plate outside, despite forty years' application of Brasso to the affected part. Today he wondered for a moment whether to take his blood pressure, but knew it would only rise again with the struggle to get all that tubing back in the box.

Instead he turned wearily to Nurse Gulling's clipboard of repeat prescriptions. Sign them now? Wait? Make a start and leave the rest? He was getting worse lately at making decisions. The only course, once he felt his irresolution clouding judgement, was to come down smartly one way or the other so that people wouldn't notice. It was true he'd been wrong about the lump on the Vicar's neck. Those things happened. In his own case he was undecided whether even to worry about his two middle fingernails having stopped growing since the summer before last. At medical conferences he now kept the hands lightly curled, unless shaking. Shaking those of other doctors. Otherwise he tried to forget the stationary nails, except when filing the others.

The tape-player clicked off. He turned the cassette over. *Waltztime in Old Vienna.* He brought up his own volume control slightly for that. Why should those devils outside have all the best tunes?

Automatically sweeping the day's stack of drughouse samples off his blotter into the desk-side waste-bin he gave them the usual no glance. Even such personally relevant breakthroughs as 'Spasmojump', 'Gronails' and 'Giddistairs' went unregarded, though he paused for a second, undecided, over a bottle of 'Decide-o!' tablets, their rattle muffled by promotional literature from a leading psychiatric establishment.

Last among the brightly-coloured packages, however, one of unusual shape caught his eye. It was from the same firm, and was flat, sharply rectangular.

'Dear Dr Sweetbang,' began the sales pitch, on chunkily embossed paper worth a guinea a sheet. 'Are you losing your voice, your patience, your enthusiasm? Do you sometimes tire of that constant repetition of advice and solace so conscientiously yet exhaustingly expended on daily visitors to your surgery? Here at Mind Medication International, Dr Sweltgland, we feel we have the answer. The enclosed EQ-120² RT-400gm Low-Noise Cassette . . .'

His attitude towards this kind of thing was one of screw-up and forget. But he had to admire, this time, the electronically matched accord between the type-weight of the message and his inserted name. This wasn't right, of course, but commendably closer than usual. He faded out the Strauss and snapped in the MMI EQ-120². At least it was a change. As good as a rest. Curious, he spooled the fast-forward, taking a test scan.

'So much for Alopecia, Apoplexy and lumps in the Armpit. Don't worry, you may not have them. But never ignore symptoms. Next, Asthma. Much easier to identify. If the breathing, particularly in young babies . . .'

He whirred on into the B's. The Blood Pressure item held him for a half-minute. Not bad, if short on cheerfulness. He felt that Boils needn't have enlarged into Carbuncles. He wouldn't do that, with Mrs Dewly and Major Fox-Lucas. The item on Bowels was under the broad, generic heading. He let it run with approval. Laxatives would as usual be high on the day's prescriptions. The recorded voice was studiously classless, but earnest.

'. . . so even though the daily motion is desirable, remember that up to five days of waste matter in the food tract . . .'

Good God! He peered at his watch. The Major. Mrs Dewly. The names echoed back. Late, late, late. With good coordination for a man of his age he simultaneously buttoned-off the tape and pressed his first-patient buzzer, summoning up his brightness as the door opened. Nurse Gulling appeared. She had her hat on.

'All went, doctor. Mr Cackworth on the lumpy armpits. Miss Walker and the twins on the asthma. The boils had Mrs Dewly and the Major jammed in the doorway, and the rest all cleared on the bowels.'

Dr Sweatband strummed his catarrh and groped for a phrase. 'You're looking well.'

Nurse Gulling paused at the surgery door before slamming it.

'Not what I bloody feel,' she said, going.

He himself thought he felt better.

But it was often a thing he couldn't make up his mind on.

Basil Boothroyd 5.9.1984

DOCTOR WHAT

The trouble with these bogus doctors is that they show us real ones up. Every time one of them gets nicked, there's suddenly a queue of patients ready to swear holes in pewter pots that the bogus doctor is the kindest, gentlest, most considerate medic on earth – like a sort of Albert Schweitzer only younger and more saintly.

If the newspaper reports are anything to go by (and they aren't) then bogus doctors are cool and confident, helpful and humane, decisive and charismatic – honest, decent and truthful but not, unfortunately, legal. Bogus doctors make up their minds quickly, bogus doctors don't stand around fumfering and umming and erring and sticking their ties in their mouths and scratching their heads. Unhampered by facts and conflicting editorials in *The Lancet* and *BMJ*, bogus doctors can make management decisions based on whim, fancy, prejudice, drug adverts on blotters, Tarot cards or the I Ching. As most of us would like to – if we didn't feel so guilty.

The simple fact of the matter is that bogus doctors have the ease and *savoir faire* of the actor inhabiting a fantasy world. In the same way that some of us (ie, me) might practise being an airplane pilot in the bath and enjoy going roger-sierra-orange-delta-three-greens-decimal-five-zero-and-holding-on-flight-path etc etc and might be tempted to swagger into a briefing room if the door was left open just to see, so these guys have the practised ease of the fantasising faker. A practised ease that genuine practitioners often lack.

No wonder the patients prefer the bogus

article – even if he's set their ankles horizontally or hitched a prolapse to a parathyroid or similar. It's the confidence of the confidence trickster that the punters have always loved – and they still do. (Viz reflexology and coffee enemas – to which my main objection is that it makes the coffee taste so awful afterwards.)

However, let us focus on the central issue – what are we non-bogus doctors to make of it all? Should we view the bogus boys as a threat, likely to bring the medical profession into disrepute and disgrace? I say not – I think that we are now being offered a unique opportunity to get ahead – if we only have the firmness of purpose, courage and grit, tinged with a hint of psychopathic recklessness.

What I think we should do is hail the bogus doctors as the leading edge of the alternative medicine movement and welcome them warmly. (On the basis that 'alternative' qualifications and skills could be more broadly defined to include 'none at all'.)

Think of it this way – we now know that up to a third of medical consultations are for symptoms not attributable to organic disease or organ failure. Seen from the conventional post-war training point of view, people with these symptoms are bogus patients. We know they don't take kindly to being sent to psychiatrists, so why don't we send them to bogus doctors? It's fast, convenient and above all, cheap.

We could establish an entire Bogus National Health Service at a fraction of the cost of the real one. After all, bogus doctors are simpler to train (average bogus-medical training time = 7–9 minutes), cheaper to equip (just let them steal a white coat, someone else's name-badge and a Fisher-Price Playdoc stethoscope) and they don't need superannuation or married accommodation. Or a salary come to that.

Of course, the whole bogus medical network would have to be set up properly; there would have to be a Bogus finals exam at which candidates would either have to pass or successfully forge a certificate. And for the really advanced ones there'd be the coveted Bog. Phil. (subject to the parole officer's report). Naturally, there would still remain the snobbery and nepotism so beloved of our profession – the best bogus doctors vying for places at RADA (like their fathers) while the riff-raff slog through Oldham rep.

But just think what this would do for the real NHS. For a start we would put an end to the need for tightened security. When hospitals are periodically searched for bogus doctors to root out the incompetent, bungling imposters, they always end up grilling the same old professor of endocrinology anyway, so that would save some effort and expense. Then, with bogus doctors properly licensed, we could establish a new bogus pharmacopoeia with hundreds of different placebos. Then the drugs companies could go wild producing me-too placebos, and that would cut down iatrogenic disease and help reduce waiting lists too. Simple, no?

Perhaps I have gone too fast for you – after all we are a conservative profession (in any sense of either of those words). You may feel like turning your back on anything as radical as what I am suggesting here, but before you get too sniffy about the terrible and lethal things that bogus doctors might get up to if left to their own devices, let me remind you of one thing.

Hawley Crippen wasn't a bogus doctor – he was one of us.

Robert Buckman 30.11.1983

David Taylor
talks to
CHRISTIAAN
BARNARD, MD

Dr Barnard was heppy as a sendboy. In the United States he was quite heppy to be living there, until one day he went to see *Out of Africa* and those plains, those flamingoes, it all made him feel a little unheppy that he was not back at home in Cape Town, but in Oklahoma City instead. Now things are not so heppy in South Africa besides. But we do not speak of that yet, until in a moment or so.

In Oklahoma City, at the Baptist Medical Center, Christiaan Neethling Barnard MD is a scientist in residence, no more a surgeon because of his arthritis which has become

role and the influence of some substances called Glycosphingolipids, which we may abbreviate to GSL to make them somewhat easier to say.

Blow them down if GSL did not seem to have some strange effects upon the genetic memories of skin cells, such as to repair, if not to renew them. Now maybe this will become the tip of an iceberg. There are, after all, many kinds of GSL which could do many kinds of things, perhaps even be the antigens of certain kinds of cancer.

No, no please – no specific claims at all. What is to be stated only is that in skin tissue studies, comparing young skin with old skin, it was revealed that while GSL is active and abundant in young skin, the quantity is rapidly diminished with age. So perhaps we should try to put some back! It can be got from a natural source, like the heart of a cow. Isn't it so?

Wait a moment, suggested some colleagues of Christiaan Barnard MD, there is after all some commercial value in such a notion if some form of GSL were to be put into a range of cosmetics. He did not begin this process, let us be sure of that. He is not required directly to endorse the cosmetics, but only the efficacy of some GSL. If the two quite separate things do somehow become confused in some people's eyes, it is a thing which just happens perhaps and he is not able to prevent it.

Of course not. Of course it will not make Christiaan Barnard MD into a millionaire. Certainly it is true that the cosmetics are expensive. Certainly it is true that in a few months during which they are sold in America, they have sold some twelve million dollars' worth of such cosmetics. But for Christiaan Barnard MD there is only 5 per cent of 3.5 per cent of the royalties from Glycel, made in Switzerland by America's Alfin Fragrance.

There are absolutely not any specific medical claims, of course not. The chronology of skin results from sundry factors such as genetic background to begin with, then some personal habits or environment, the climate where one is, the emotional stresses of life also – all such factors can contribute to the look of skin, or complexion. To take care of the skin can contribute much to the quality of life and in this respect GSL may represent a scientific breakthrough, exclaims Christiaan Barnard MD.

Of course yes, Christiaan Barnard has made

severe. And no longer so young because in fact he will be 64 in November, which also makes him feel somewhat unheppy.

He'd like so much to be young. He'd wish to have the prowess which he had when he was a young man in his youth. Who wouldn't be so heppy to have their youth again or to have it last for them a little longer? Any person would wish that. They might not wish to say that they would, but he thinks that in truth they would wish it to be so. It is a thing he has been looking at. And thereby hangs a tale, as we shall see in a moment or so.

Christiaan Barnard MD was doing some research into this subject of ageing and the effect of ageing upon the quality of a person's life when he was for some time in Basel, which is in Switzerland, at the Schaefer Institute, where such things are conducted. This was after his retirement from doing the heart surgery, for which he was so known, and after for a while when he was running some Italian restaurants to keep the pot boiling. And so to Switzerland.

One time the scientists were looking at the

some use of such products on his own skin. People say to him now that he looks very young for one of his age. Certainly he feels very young for one of his age and is quite heppy to have with him by his side a young companion of only 22 years and exquisite beauty besides, a quality which all his life he has greatly admired and wished to be with. He will joke that maybe he is kinky or something, but for him some young and beautiful girls are irresistible and he feels good with them as a man who is still very interested in sexual orientation with very beautiful women, such as his companion, who is a model and is called Karen.

Some doubting people will assert that it is only because of Karen that Christiaan Barnard MD now feels so zesty and so virile and all of these things have nothing whatever to do with whatever it is that they put into the cosmetics of which he spoke. But to them he suggests that they try some. After all, the proof of the pudding is in the eating, claims Christiaan Barnard MD.

Of course there are. Of course there are difficulties for South Africa, although perhaps not so much as a person might envisage from seeing South Africa all the time from television and not living there. But he told them. Fifteen years ago he told them that they must dismantle Apartheid and he was at the time widely condemned for saying that in South Africa.

Just the other day, there were some MPs in South Africa to whom he was talking and he told them, look, you know that one of the first signs of insanity is when a person is not prepared to face up to the realities? That is the first sign of what doctors will call a psychosis. Very well. The ANC is now a reality and it does not matter one jot what you think of them, they are a reality just the same.

Now, by the same token, Mandela is considered their leader and that, too, is a reality so that you cannot go on pretending that it isn't so, rather you must face up to the reality and let him loose so that you can deal with it.

But you know South Africa has now embarked on a course to dismantle Apartheid and it is no good for Sir Geoffrey Howe to go there and say you must do this and you must do that because the Afrikaner is a stubborn sort, with a lot of Dutch blood in him, who does not take kindly to being told what to do and so will turn on Sir Geoffrey and tell him to get stuffed.

There is the wrong approach inside South Africa and there is the wrong approach outside South Africa, that is the nature of the present tragedy. But nevertheless it is to South Africa that a South African, born in Cape Province, must return in a moment or so, towards the final stages of life, even a life regenerated by Glycosphingolipids maybe, he muses with amusement. He will farm some cashmere goats, or maybe still write some more books like *Your Healthy Heart* or *The Living Body* or *Christiaan Barnard's Program For Living With Arthritis* or *The Faith* (a novel) which he wrote already.

Of course yes – to have so many things of interest to surmount is the thing. It helps to keep you young and heppy.

16.7.1986

5

Teeth 'n' Smiles

'You have lovely teeth. You should take
anti-depressants more often.'

Patient (to Dentist). 'EXCUSE MY TAKING MY COAT OFF.
PAIN MAKES ME SO IRRITABLE, I'M SURE TO STRUGGLE A BIT.'

Evergreen Buck (to Dentist, who is making him a
complete set). 'BY THE WAY! REMEMBER! NO WISDOM
TEETH!'

A REGULAR TURK.
Tommy (who has just been operated on). 'I
MEAN TO BE A DENTIST, WHEN I GROW UP.'
Aunt Annie. 'WHY, DEAR?'
Tommy. 'TO HAVE REVENGE!'

Dentist. 'ANYONE IN THE WAITING-ROOM?'
Maid. 'YES, SIR, A GENTLEMAN; BUT HE'S LOCKED HISSELF IN.'

A LITTLE TOUCH OF HALI (IN THE NIGHT)

It was the evening of the day that Diana arrived back from her skiing holiday in Italy.

'Darling,' she said, as we were finishing supper, 'what have you been eating while I have been away?'

'Eating?' I said, 'I don't know. Why?'

'Well,' she said, 'I hate to say this, but you have just a teeny-weeny –'

'Yes.'

'Touch of the hali.'

'Hali?'

''tosis.'

'Oh, *no*,' I said, 'how *awful*!'

'It's only a touch. But I thought you ought to know.'

'When did you first notice it?'

'This morning at the airport.'

'Why didn't you say then?'

'I thought it might go. I didn't want to fuss you.'

'Dear God! How long have we been married?'

'Twenty years, isn't it?'

'And is this the first time?'

'Absolutely.'

'I wonder what's caused it.'

'Teeth, do you think?'

'Or tummy. I've heard some people say it can be the tummy.'

'Why don't you check up?'

'Of course,' I said, 'right away.'

Next morning I rang the dentist and asked for an early appointment.

'I'm sorry, Mr Blunt,' the receptionist said, 'but we're fully booked for the next two weeks.'

'Oh, I must see him before then,' I said, 'it's urgent.'

'Are you in pain?'

'Not exactly.'

'Has a filling come out?'

Perhaps it had; perhaps that was the trouble.

'I think so,' I said.

I heard her leafing through the engagement book.

'I've just had a cancellation for four o'clock on Tuesday. Could you come then?'

Tuesday was three days off. 'Is that the earliest?' I said.

'Yes, it is, Mr Blunt.' Did I notice a touch of exasperation in her voice? 'We'll expect you then. Good-bye.'

Next day I was lunching with my wine-merchant, an old friend. I'd have put him off but his office didn't know where he was. Half-way through the meal he said, 'Charles, are you feeling all right?'

'Fine,' I muttered, 'why?'

'Well, generally when we meet, you talk nineteen to the dozen, so that I hardly ever get a word in. Today you've been mumbling monosyllables into that handkerchief as though you'd got lock-jaw, and you've never once looked me in the face.'

'I'm sorry,' I said.

'It's so unlike you. Do you know what I'd say if it was anyone but you. I'd say you'd got a drop of the old hali and were trying to cover it up.'

He gave a huge belly laugh, clearly expecting me to join in. I did my best, but it died a quick death in the handkerchief.

That night I said to Diana. 'Still there?'

'Breathe,' she said.

I did.

'Just a touch.'

At the dentist's I sat in the chair and took a swill of the pink mouth-wash. I really believed my troubles would soon be over. The dentist was wearing his plastic visor, and I wondered whether this was protection against his patient's hali or for them against his own.

'Lost a filling, have you?' he said.

'I'm not sure,' I said, 'but something's happened. My wife tells me I have bad breath.'

He didn't seem much interested. 'Open your mouth,' he said, 'and we'll have a good look round.' He made my mouth sound like an art gallery. Presently he said, 'You've got quite a lot of tartar. Maybe that's what's doing it. I'll clean it up.'

He chipped away at the tartar with a miniature spade, then covered a brush with toothpaste, inserted it into the drill and whisked it round. It was ticklish on the gums.

'There,' he said, 'let's hope that will do the trick.'

At home that evening I opened my mouth at Diana. She smiled and said, 'Not a trace. Just dentist's toothpaste. I believe he's done it.'

'Oh, hurray,' I said and hugged her tight. 'We'll go out to dinner to celebrate.'

We went to Vecchio's. The bill was fifty pounds and I didn't grudge a penny. But when we were undressing for bed Diana said,

'Darling?'

'Yes.'

'I'm afraid it's come back.'

Next day I told my troubles to the family doctor.

'Do you suffer at all from flatulence?' he said.

It's not a word I use myself, so I wasn't too sure of his drift.

'Belching and farting, you mean?' I said.

He blanched. 'Yes.'

'No.'

'Get on the couch, will you?' he said, 'and lift up your shirt.' I did, and he went over my tummy like a baker kneading dough.

'Sore anywhere?' he asked.

'No.'

When I had dressed, he said, 'Well, I don't quite know what to make of it. You seem healthy enough and you say your teeth are in good order. It could be some temporary gastric upset, in which case it'll pass. Get yourself some Listerine mouthwash, and if it hasn't cleared up in a month, come and see me again.'

But it didn't clear up, or rather when it did, it was only briefly. As the days passed I became increasingly self-conscious and miserable. Determined not to inflict my infirmity on others (for having been on the receiving end several times in my life I knew how grim it could be) I refused all invitations to lunch or dinner, developed a habit of speaking out of the corner of my mouth, and spent long hours alone, reading or looking at the telly.

My sex-life suffered too. Normally Diana and I would make love two or three times a week, but now the thought of blasting her with the fumes made me totally inhibited. She was wonderfully understanding about it, yet the feeling I was letting her down increased my sense of inadequacy.

'Oh, Charles,' she said, 'don't be silly. As if that really mattered.'

Another worry was that Diana was the only person in a position to tell me the state of play, and when she went away for a day or two to visit her sick mother, I had no one to turn to. It would have made all the difference if our children had been at home, but Simon was spending a year in Australia before going to university, and Kate was looking after a diplomat's children in Washington. Sometimes in the evenings and early mornings, which Diana said was the worst time, I would blow into my cupped hands and then sniff, as I had once seen a badly-afflicted boy at school do; but it told me nothing.

I discovered the cause accidentally. Coming home from the office one evening, I found a note from Diana on the hall table saying her mother had had a stroke and been taken to hospital. She was leaving at once to join her, and would ring me later.

I had a couple of drinks, cooked and ate some scrambled eggs, then wandered into the little room where we keep the television set. There didn't seem to be anything worth watching, and I was looking idly round the room when my eye lit on Diana's pen, lying opened on her desk, and next to it her cheque-book and a neat pile of bills. I assumed she must have been about to write out the cheques when news of her mother came. Then I noticed, half tucked into one of the pigeon-holes, a letter in her own hand.

Curiosity got the better of me, and I pulled it out and started reading. It began: 'My own darling Giuseppe.' It went on to say how much she had been missing her darling Giuseppe, how he filled her thoughts night and day, how she could not wait until she was in his arms again.

Then I turned the page and read this:

'You ask me, darling, if I have been really faithful to you, as I promised I would, and the answer is, Yes, I have. You say, how is it possible for me to be faithful when I have such a demanding and energetic husband. All I can tell you is *I have*. As to *how*, that must remain my little secret until we next meet. And I hope, my love, that will be very, very soon.'

Later that evening Diana rang up from the hospital.

'Good news,' she said, 'Mummy's on the mend.'

'Splendid,' I said, 'and I've got good news too.'

'Oh?' she said. She sounded genuinely interested. 'What is it?'

'My hali's cured,' I said.

There was a noticeable pause, and then Diana said, 'Oh, I am glad. But, well –'

'How do I know?'

'Yes.'

'Ah,' I said, 'that must remain my little secret. Until we next meet.'

And in the long silence that followed I added, 'And I hope, my love, that will be very, very soon.'

Ludovic Kennedy 29.10.1980

'. . . *upper right seven buccal filling . . . upper right six mesial filling with palatal extension . . .*'

ffolkes:
'A WOMAN IS A TOOTHSOME THING'

(Anon)

'This probably contravenes the Code of Practice but . . .'

'Well that's over, Mrs Chwast. You can start gnashing them now.'

'Mrs Henderson says she can't keep her appointment. Scorpio is ascending.'

'Funny thing is, I'm terribly brave about having babies.'

HERE COMES A CHOPPER

I've lost them. Close friends for over half a century, champers of caviare in Astrakhan, grinders of grits in Arkansas, chewers of chops in Redcar, masticators of muesli in that good, cheapish place in Gstaad, squashers of squashes in Cape Town – there they lie in a porcelain dish like spat out cherrystones waiting for the trash can. Adieu old mates.

Still numb. Fingering an upper lip is like testing fresh putty on next-door's window-pane. Still bleeding though not as much as I'd prepared myself for – no blood-spattered corridor lies behind me – I'm led upstairs. Prosthetics is what it says on the door. I know that word. I've been here before. It's from the Greek. And it means making up for deficiencies. And what it boils down to is False Teeth.

As with doctors so it is with dentists. Both professions are suckers for fashion. Doctors in the 1930s, for example, had one phrase only when you mentioned your appendix: out with it. If you went in so that they could inspect your duodenal they'd whip your little endpiece out as well just for the hell of it. But now you can say you have this bellyache and go down on your knees to them for an appendectomy but the wormlike bit stays where it is. Doctors have switched to liking appendices the way academics like them after having written their long boring books on odious little men like Stendhal or Hardy.

The dentists' approach to the false teeth question has also quite changed from when my mother was sentenced to a top set. The pulling out went much the same way then as now, but post-operational tactics have quite altered. She was immediately sent home for three weeks. She kept herself as incommunicado as possible and went about when she had to with her face swathed as if she was an ayatollah's number one wife, with only the nostrils showing. The gums – this was the tale she was told – had to be given time to *harden*.

How different, in the later stages, the experience undergone by my goodself (dear God, what an expression). Oral surgery came first, and that was on the ground floor. Nothing much to this really. A beefy young chap jabbed me, numbed me (counting up to 250 for the full effect to establish itself), and then hey for the long pulls and the strong pulls. I remember thinking, my head underneath his arm as if it was a rugger-ball: next Saturday afternoon this sinewy toughie will be practising his shot-putt and debating whether he follow Follows to Uncle Lenin-land and the Karl Marx Olympic Village (KGB *veilleuse* and bubbling samovar on every landing).

Then suddenly, in no time at all, he crammed my oral orifice with bandage-wads, wound up the reclining-chair, turned off his headlight, and said to a willowy, white-clad girl who was altogether a great comfort, 'Lead him off.' This is where I was at the final stage, and this is where the changed methods in dental practice came into play, grim play as you shall hear.

Down into another reclining chair first off. Then out came the bloody wads with me staring intensely into the headlight, and in went the upper section of the mantrap quick as light.

– Close and bite.

I closed and bit. There was absolutely nothing to it. The mid-upper acreage of my face was still as unfeeling as the cold nose of an iceberg grinding against a rocky promontory along the northern edge of Spitzbergen.

—All right?

—Hn. Hn. Hn.

A swift follow-up inspection date was arranged. Any day, any day: I was ready to agree to anything. Then I was out in the street a bit dumbfounded. Numbness prevailed in the same areas. I felt partially invisible but nobody looked round. A one-yellow-line district it was and a predatory warden had passed that way, careless of the ding-dong that had been going on on ground and first floors. What did six cut-price pounds matter set against the considerably more than six work-weary choppers I'd lived a life with? I pulled the flappy document from under the wiper and ran it along my upper lip. I heard a rasping sound but felt nothing. Eerie. Then I got in, barged my way into the tailback, wholly disregarding the discordant toots and those contemptuous, pitying headshakes that all drivers get the trick of immediately after the de-L-isation. One truculent trucker from Gateshead even stuck his head out of his cab to enquire why they had ever issued a licence to a bloody nootcase?

—Hn. Hn. Hn, I said.

I was a long time getting back. Numbness gradually wore off. I was spitting blood a bit, but no bright red gush, so steady, I thought. Normal. Hove to against a traffic light stuck on red I discovered that clenching the teeth was no way this time to resist pain because it brought it on in swift bounds. The Book of Revelation I've always found on the whole better at obscuring than revealing, but by the time I'd drawn up outside my North Finchley mansion I knew with sharp certainty what the Patmos visionary had meant by Out of his mouth went a sharp two-edged sword. How, I wondered, had the Patmos health authority been on prosthetics?

My wife immediately said it was a great improvement. It had taken years off me, she said.

—Hn. Hn. I flailed with my arms. She backed away.

—I've got something soft for lunch. Scrambled egg on toast. I don't expect you'll feel like much for an hour or two.

—Gruel, I tried to say.

—Don't keep saying Hn Hn. And don't make unnecessary fuss. There are people who *sleep* with double your lot.

I sliced off a corner of scrambled egg on toast and popped it in the way I'd been doing since before the war.

This was the moment of truth. Had she beaten the shards of broken bottles into the eggstuff? Had I married a descendant of one of those Victorian female poisoners whose creepy goings on are pointed up to make six fifty-minute slots on the telly? And were the genes now belatedly surfacing in her like crocodiles out of procreative slime? I had come down smartly on a crusted snippet in the careless unthinking way the decades had taught me. What I need really at this point in time is a simile on Homeric lines. As when the presses squeeze the bulbous grape, And juices run all red, and unoiled wheels, Scream at the sight of bloody business done, SO I, SO ME, AND SO ON.

—Look at all this wasted. Do you know the price of farmfresh eggs as fixed by the CAP? So unnecessary. In two days you won't know you've got them in.

—Hn, I said. Hn. Hn.

It's been going on like this for not two days but an age. Lines from our tiniest poet laureate, Alfred Austin, have been running through my head. Austin isn't quoted much now on any exchange, stock or literary, because he really was tiny, that man, poetically as well as physically. If only he'd had the knack of keeping a horse balanced he could have ridden on the flat, but he could only manage written on the flat which is nothing like as profitable. You didn't find Lester Piggott bothering with odes when he had a Minstrel. Anyway little Austin felt it incumbent upon him to get down to an ode when Edward VII was having one of his bad turns, and it's from this piece that I now quote:

Across the wires the electric message came:
'He is no better, he is much the same.'

Though I laughed at the time, I see now why my mother went around all swathed for three weeks: she was giving her gums time to harden, like the chap said. But his descendants today don't see it like that at all: cram them in because that way the gums won't shrink. Ah, what the hell. Hardening, shrinking—they have you either way.

Excuse me now. I'm off to collect my fifth replacement order for GUMSOOTHE. It's

£2.99 per tube and so far, like presidents of the United States, gets no results. I've also tried EASIGUM at £3.99 per spraygun, but that wasn't any good either. I keep thinking of those spat out cherrystones in the porcelain dish. Where are you now? as Amy Woodford-Findon queried about the pale hands she had loved.

Ground up for fertiliser? Couldn't say: one thing I can say though. There's no putting the old uns back, as Kant said. Or was it Kierkegaard? Some foreign commentator on the human predicament anyway.

David Williams 23.7.1980

Doctor. 'YOU WOULD PROBABLY FEEL MUCH BETTER IF YOU HAD ALL YOUR TEETH OUT.'
Patient. 'YES, I SHOULD, DOCTOR. THIS LOT NEVER FITTED FROM THE DAY THEY WERE PUT IN.'

TEETHING TROUBLES

What I got for Christmas was my two front teeth; filed down to little tusks, to be precise, like those egregious African dandies who hop out of the scrub and gnash you, and you don't get *that* in the shops.

An operation of infinite tedium, this filing business, but lah! my dears, now it's over, far from hunting out a clump to lurk in like my precursors in the Bush, I shall be adopting a conspicuously high profile. You'll know me when you see me: a swirl of broadcloth, a lambent glittering smile, the faintest hint of expensive mouthwash, and – pouf! – I'll be gone, leaving only a lingering after-image of something rather wonderful, and a flurry of discomfited folk rushing for the Pepsodent.

A crowning glory, if you follow me. Onto my attenuated dentition, two porcelain prostheses have been clamped; between them, suspended by golden cantilevers and guyed with platinum hawser, a third tooth is now positioned where previously there was none; the void which has disfigured me for so long is filled. It feels queer at first, since over the preceding months I have learned to champ a mean gum; but I'm going at it doggedly: yesterday a marshmallow, today the breakfast bacon fried *al dente*, working up to the big one, the celebratory Crunchy Dinner, spare ribs, *crème brulée*, Bath Olivers, beaks, bones and shells. Tomorrow? Next week? Soon, anyway; soups and possets have come to pall.

That was my big present, this Christmas: bridgework. And by no means unromantic; gastronomic considerations apart, and forgetting for the moment the precious materials involved, there's the spin-off; my wife, insistent donor of this orthodontic *cadeau*, was expressing proleptic gratification at the thought of my dental Renaissance as far back as last summer, and I can confidently expect some benefits from *that* quarter.

Drinking, too, will be less of a hazard. Blotting up a peaceful Scotch-and-soda becomes a rare experience when one is gap-toothed. The assumption of fellow-drinkers seems to be that one has lost one's tooth as a result of aggression and violence, that one is a desperate fella, that one should be watched, d'you hear me, don't turn your back on him for a moment or he'll be onto you, fists, knives, the lot, how d'you think he lost his tooth, if I were you I'd belt him one before he's noticed you, the best method of defence is attack d'you know . . .

Other benefits: being able to smile again (I know Wernet's DentuFix does that as well, but you need something to stick in with it, no good just clogging up your gap with glue, that won't fool anyone). Being able to clench my pipe like a proper Englishman instead of having to hold it like a pansy. Not whiffling when I speak. Increased probability of women flirting with me at parties. Possibility of women even, um, how do I put this? It's not that one *would*, do you see, it's merely that it's nice to know that one could, or rather that one might be allowed or even encouraged to, *if one wanted to*, a circumstance which, the minute one displays a maw with all the visual allure of a Mississippi stump field, recedes into the realms of improbability normally inhabited by Government economic theories.

But why, you may be asking, am I telling you all this? Shouldn't I keep my orifices to myself? Not at all. For what I am latching you into is a *trend*, something to cut out and keep for next Christmas when those two great theological questions come round again: (1) How did God assume the nature of Mankind while simultaneously retaining His divinity? and (2): What the hell can we give Uncle Ignatius?

As always, the Americans provide the answer to both questions, as follows.

(1) 'Well that's a very good point there from the gentleman in the kinda kaftan and the neat pointy hat, but before we ask *you*, the *audience*, what *you* think, a word about Auricular Odour, the Hidden Enemy. Try STAPES, the nature-fresh ear deodorant which is kind to the Earth. Contains no propellants. And now, back to our audience at the Hymie FitzBeelzebub Shopping Mall, Modesto, for part two of the Make Yourself Look An Utter Prick And Win $10,000 Show – and today's Theme is Mediaeval Scholasticism, where we ask our audience the Big Prize Question: if Duns Scotus had had the

"He's wonderful with children . . ."

benefit of modern Personal Hygiene Technology, would he have written the *Opus Oxoniense* or would he have been out having a good time like you lovely folks here . . .?'

(2) 'Give him Spare Parts.' Yes, really. 'It's the ultra-fun chic gift idea that's swept the upper echelons of American high society this year – his 'n' hers facelifts, plastic surgery vouchers redeemable at all participating clinics for the operation of your choice, ranging from an all-in package deal to lift your sagging boobs, hitch up your drooping bum, unhook your nose, debag your eyes, unjug your ears and disembowel your paunchy ruptured belly (for that Very Special Person) to a simple facial epidermal degreasing (for a maiden aunt or a business colleague some way down on the Gift List). Why let your wife walk round looking like an Elephant Man? Just phone in your Master-Card number and we do the rest . . .'

True. Would I lie to you? And you can see the attraction. Why waste time having your beloved's initials Stamped By Wizened Craftsmen onto This Chippendale-Style Leather-Look Corkscrew Case when you can waste money having Ava Gardner's 'face' Stamped By Wizened Plastic Surgeons onto Your California-Style Leather-Look Wife?

Want to try before you buy? Nothing could be easier; in flashy Beverly Hills there lives a plastic surgeon who exercises his vulgar tasteless craft upon the person of his wife. You want to see a sample, you see his wife. Perhaps she was once as homely as a mud fence; perhaps he's very greedy and she's very stupid; whatever, he's slit, cut, tacked, tucked and filled-in every available inch of this 'woman' until she looks like a spun-sugar death's-head, an old drumskin, a scorched Goth.

In short, the ultimate personalised present. 'Guess what!' chortles fond hubby, the syringe behind his back. 'Honey-pie,' squeals delighted wifey, as she claws negligently at her new Halston bandages. 'Togetherness,' gurgle the mum-mified pair, as they breathe through their mouths to save wear on their new nostrils. ('Wave Goodbye To Ugly Coke-Sniffers' Nose! Our Special Yuletide His 'n' Hers Nasal Septa Twin-Pak Means No More Sodden Hankies, No More Tuxedo Stains, No More Unexpected Breathing Through The Ears!!!')

It could catch on here, too, along with Genuine English luxury hand-crafted accessories. How about a made-to-measure glass eye, for the man who hasn't quite got everything ('It cockles when I do – grunt – this.' 'Never mind, Sir, it'll ride up with wear . . .')? There was a bit about them in one of the Sunday supplements. You can find them in the Yellow Pages, under Artificial Eye Makers – Human, as opposed, presumably, to Artificial Eye Makers – Unsympathetic and Beastly. The man says you can't tell it from a real eye; but I bet I could, if you came up behind me and bunged one in when I wasn't expecting it.

A difficult present, in fact, to make really attractive. A gleaming optic wrapped in a hanky has a certain *cachet* but perhaps not the immediate appeal of a box of Prestat truffles; same goes, too, for that ultimate stocking-filler, the bespoke false leg, still to be had from that Schiaparelli of monopedes, Dessoutter of Roehampton.

But the actual presentation is merely a detail, and you've got nearly a year to work on it. The thing is to get in now. If this craze catches on there'll be queues by September. It'll be worse than *E.T.* (and there's a candidate for reconstruction if ever I saw one. Treacly insinuating little reptile). Have a close look at your friends and family. There's not one of them, I bet, that couldn't be improved by a little judicious plying of the knife. They'll be thinking the same about you, too.

After all, it's the thought that counts.

Michael Bywater 5. 1. 1983

6

Comic Cuts

IN AN IDEAL WORLD . . .

'He was here a moment ago when I was preparing his injection.'

Basil Boothroyd
MEDICAL REPORT

Commentators on our record 1985 summer give no figures for the rainfall in hospital car parks, which have been as full of water as of cars.

Why the weatherman has missed this, racked as he must be for an injection of variation into the bad news, I don't know. Either his wife hasn't been inside, warm and dry and hanging by the leg from bed-end scaffolding, or he can get out of his car faster and run quicker than I can, not getting drenched to the Y-fronts.

I am not yet good at that. When you're finally wedged in the last space, at the bottom of the slope, listing heavily to port, it's an adroit manoeuvre disembarking to starboard carrying a frilly nightdress, two more flower vases, funny cards from wellwishers, David Cecil's *Melbourne* and a bag of bananas, while trying to open a lady's umbrella caught by the hook-end under the passenger seat. Backwards is the only way. But it means that the force of gravity keeps shutting the door on your calf, and I may well finish with a leg hanging from scaffolding, though at least warm and dry.

One wants to look one's best on visits, not like a monster from the sea. One wants to laugh at the funny cards. Not easy even when spruce, since they are mostly jokes about people in bed with their legs up.

All this is at our present hospital. I say our without misgiving. As things stand, by the time we're out of the place we shall have bought it. The car park at the other one was level, but farther from the door you had to go in by, which opened outwards, calling for adroitness again with two armfuls of wet requisites and an umbrella you needed a third hand to furl. And there were more spaces in the park. Most of them, it's true, marked staff only, doctors only, ambulances only, disabled only. Only proper, that. Though panting, and with one knee gone funny from the long walk, I had scruples over claiming disablement in the clinically accepted sense.

You can't expect doctors to suffer any hardship. They have to be on the spot when needed. We needed ours for forty minutes before he showed, but he was jolly, young, cheerful, curly-haired and quick to comfort and diagnose. We took to him. Felt in good hands. A friend.

'My last day here,' he said, as my wife, shuddering on a trolley, gave a list of her bangles, baubles and beads to a lady official, who wouldn't put 'gold' for any of them. Yellow metal. 'New job tomorrow. Winchester.' So we were sorry. He was in high spirits himself, looking in later to say goodbye to the staff, pinch their bottoms, and drag his clipboard along the radiators with a rousing effect, particularly for a patient in her first sedated doze, that momentarily drowned out the ecstatic audience laughter on the TV sitcom.

We liked the consultant, too, who couldn't come for a day or two. But he had that easy confidence of a man fully in charge of all destinies, and we felt we were lucky. He gave instructions for the leg-scaffolding, dissented, if obliquely, from curly-hair's estimate of a discharge in 48 hours with your jewellery back in a plastic bag marked NHS PATIENT'S PROPERTY. SAFETY FIRST. KEEP AWAY FROM BABIES and YOUNG CHILDREN – and said he was off to Scotland for three weeks. Serious outbreak of salmon, I think.

Goodness, those nurses are marvellous; not only ministering angels when pain and anguish wring the brow or other affected parts, but structural engineers skilled in wing-nuts and interlocking metal-work. This only struck me on the third day. Owing to some communications failure between the consultant and the ward, that was when they got around to erecting the scaffolding. I wouldn't have known where to start, quite frankly. If you've ever tried assembling a light-alloy hammock support, arriving by mail order in eleven pieces and a bag of bolts, you'll have some idea.

It's no sort of work for girls. No wonder, when they finally got it up, the top bar fell on the patient's affected part. Tubular-bell and scream effect, which drew sharp looks and shushings from several old lady patients, a Bob Monkhouse gag having been killed stone dead.

My wife apologised. The nurses too, give them credit. Lucky for them Sister didn't see it. Not that we saw her much. Though one evening she did trumpet from her little glass office, 'Did you have visitors this afternoon?' Nobody owned up. All but one stayed stuck on Wogan. But she was the one. The shame of it, when Sister came out to read the name on the temperature chart and personalised the question. 'Tell them in future to take their chairs back where they came from.'

It killed a Wogan gag but there was no shushing. You get to know your place. Also where to get the chairs from, and put them back, after a few visits. It can be a tough search at first, though. I got into trouble for finding one with wheels and a lavatory seat, and can't say I was sorry. You feel an idiot, caught with your trousers up.

Still, we've removed to this hospital now. Snug little old-world cottage type. Chain-pull loos, one telephone line and a vase shortage. But carnations are carnations, even strangled in a gents' specimen bottle. I keep splashing off to the other hospital from a week's habit, but am getting better. If that early jolly prognosis about a 48-hour stay hadn't given us the excuse not to confess to BUPA we would have removed before. If it is BUPA. PPB, is it? Plutocrat Pay Bed?

I can't find the documents. I don't know if we're covered for septic legs. Unless perhaps removed. But then I can't find anything. The clothes line (hall cupboard). For what it's worth, this weather. The gas manual, still missing, after I'd cloaked every radiator in the house with wet washing and the heating wouldn't come on. And never thought of hunting for the ironing board in the garage behind the step-ladders. Though ready-assembled when found it was worse than a hammock frame to get it open, and I had it flat on the kitchen floor twice, raping it in a frilly nightdress.

We can always sell the house. What's money, I tell the patient, if you have your health? Freedom from compulsory game-shows is a snip at £120 a day. We signed the form right off, X-rays extra, what the hell. The nurses here are just as marvellous, but a lot fewer. We hear all this talk about pressures on the NHS. Nothing on the brave struggles of the NPB girls, who are marvellous. Polite knocks on the room door. Cups of tea. Apologies for only sprouts again with the shepherd's grey pie, or for the new consultant, promised at six, me there at five in case early, didn't come at all. 'They aren't very good timekeepers,' said the nurse reverently. I think she was a nurse. The scanty hierarchy is puzzling. Ask a nurse for a new light bulb, she says just a sec, she'll ask nurse, who comes right off, or in twenty minutes. Apologising.

And their sympathy never flags. Last Thursday, by the wet light of dawn – I only know what I'm told when I bring the bananas and things – the door opened without a knock and a man with staring eyes and a striped dressing-gown cried, 'Hello, hello! And could you oblige me with the correct time, my fair lady?' Followed by a smart military salute and disappearance.

The night nurse's sympathy was unflagging when she heard about it and made a cup of tea. Some flaw in the paperwork. 'He shouldn't really be in this ward,' she said. 'It's terribly distressing for him.'

We like her enormously. She's leaving on Saturday.

However, I'm now trying to find some nail varnish, and have got as far as the set of mixed herb phials, top shelf beside the cooker. A request like that is a sure sign of a fair lady's good progress. The consultant, what's more, who has squeezed us in several times now, promises a promotion to crutches next weekend. Home before September.

After all, it's not London Clinic prices. One way and another, everything could be worse. Apart, I mean, from the weather.

21.8.1985

A LOT OF THEM ABOUT

The first thing which happens when a surgeon or physician is admitted to hospital as a patient himself (after he has made a vow never to write a piece about his experiences called 'Wrong Side of the Sheets' or 'How My Eyes Were Opened – bastard surgeon changes view on human race') is that he is taken into Sister's Office. To the plaintive beat of a Staff Nurse's side drum, the senior consultant present rips off your name badge, plucks off your white coat buttons, throws your bleeper to the floor and finally snaps your stethoscope over his knee. You are led out, reduced to the ranks, to don the new uniform of a squaddie – striped winceyette from Marks and Spencer.

However, like any busted sergeant, they can take your stripes away but not the knowledge and guile. As GBS revealed, old soldiers carry in their ammunition pouches not bullets but grub, thus the busted surgeon also knows a few tricks of the trade.

My first concern when admitted for a recent back operation in a world-famous neurosurgical unit was not as you would think. Not for me the telephoning home, the buying of newspapers at the League of Friends shop, chatting up the nurses to ensure good meals etc. – no indeed – the first move was off with the wrist-watch and

on with the plastic nameband, with a treble check of the details. The chance of a patient being confused with another is very remote in British hospitals but there is always a tiny chance (about one in three). However, when you are on a neurosurgical ward with half your fellows on the Nutcracker suite, it is hard to forget *One Flew Over the Cuckoo's Nest*. Coming back from the operating theatre with a Mohican haircut and staring eyes, instead of a neat line over the lumbar area, is well worth avoiding. It is best to conform, keeping one's own nameband on, and not, for devilment, swapping it with a man one has met in the TV room, just to test the system.

In addition, most hospitals utilise the simple precaution of labelling the affected part to be operated upon with a large arrow, daubed on with a felt-tipped marker – particularly when the operation is to be one side or another or even both. As a lowly house surgeon, the task used to fall to me. When I gazed at those bare, arrowed hernias and varicose veins, they pleaded to me for embellishment. However, my added comments like, 'Cut along the dotted line' or 'This Way Up', met with a perpetual frosty silence when viewed by the consultant surgeon for whom I worked in theatre. Once, before an operation, he stared over his gold half-moons at a young lady patient from Tooting on the operating table, with apparent disbelief. He then gave me an incriminating stare, his eyebrows, not dissimilar from those of the late George Woodcock, rising up and down like angry hornets just about to fly across and sting me. After he requested me to confine my literary efforts to 'pulp journalism', I pointed out that my felt-tip was not to blame. Some years previously the young lady had taken it upon herself to have tattooed across her more than ample breasts in large letters: 'ALL FOR YOU, SYD.'

At the end of six months' loyal service to that surgeon he wrote my testimonial. It consisted of one sentence: 'This doctor pushes doors marked Pull.'

However, as our medical defence unions and societies point out, genuine cases of mistaken identity in hospital can occur – sometimes with disastrous results. I remember, as a resident surgical officer, being in theatre and spotting that a young woman anaesthetised on the table had been brought up from the wards in error. Two adjacent patients on the operating list, Jones and Jonas, were mistaken. A minor slip which, had I not spotted it, would have led to us checking the fertility of a patient with four children already and wishing to be sterilised, and us sterilising a patient with no children and wishing to have her infertility investigated. Hardly a therapeutic triumph.

Occasionally even the staff need to be checked. Last year a hairdresser 'worked' as a doctor in several London teaching hospitals, including my own, mainly in Casualty where his real identity was slow to be discovered. Of course, one could argue that a scalp laceration might be more carefully sewn up by one's coiffeur (remembering the old barber surgeons) than by a Rugby-football-playing casualty officer, botching it up quickly in order to get back to his kebab, chips and *Match of the Day*. There was also the bogus theatre porter in Redhill whose orthopaedic surgery was quite good except that he occasionally left hip replacements with legs facing in opposite directions. This was apparently spotted by a patient's tailor and the bogus surgeon exposed. I gather NHS hospitals now make some enquiries about their potential surgical staff before employing them.

In my own speciality of gynaecology and obstetrics (a gynaecologist is a man who wallpapers his entrance hall through the letterbox), we have taken on a new identity protection – that of the prospective father. Gone are the days when the spouse paced the smoke-laden 'Visitors' Room' outside the labour suites until the door burst open and a portly midwife roared out in a voice loud enough to render a birth announcement in the *Daily Telegraph* superfluous: 'Mr Thatcher, twins, one boy, one girl' and dragged the trembling fellow to his wife's bedside, several hours, in fact, after the happy event.

The father-to-be initially came under the capacious wing of the midwife-in-charge. Seizing her opportunity to punish mankind in general for the pains of women with both talons, she clad the poor unfortunate in a white gown, taped at the back, over his day clothes, blue pantomime overshoes and a large bouffant paper hat – a cross between Mrs Mopp and a third-class drag artiste. To stop him giving his wife a kiss, or

any other filthy, unhygienic tricks, he had to wear a surgical mask. Thus dressed, he was placed in the labour ward at a temperature of 90°F and ordered to relax. Even the dimmest potential father, noticing that his wife did not wear a surgical mask and that many of the medical staff waltzed in and out of the same room in ordinary clothes, would have been suspicious that the sterile technique to which he had been subjected was being used as retribution for getting his wife pregnant in the first place.

In the United Kingdom, pantomime overclothes for labouring fathers are becoming a thing of the past as hospital deliveries become more homely, but in the United States, having a baby remains a full surgical procedure. They are currently trying to find ways of autoclaving potted palms and houseplants to make their delivery rooms look less like tiled slaughterhouses but just as sterile (pronounced sterrull). But here in Merrie England we do have a new problem. Many of us like to perform Caesarean Sections under epidural anaesthesia (much safer and nicer than with general anaesthesia) in which the mother is awake and experiences the new-born baby immediately with her husband by her side, and not, like the Duke of Edinburgh, playing squash and enjoying himself, however sensible that might be. In many units, these operations are performed in the main operating suite of theatres. The fathers dress up in theatre pyjamas, mask, hat and boots – just as theatre staff do. In the past, senior theatre Sisters, who rule the roost in a manner that makes even our own dear Prime Minister appear benign, would grasp an extra man in theatre clothes wandering around the theatre block, admonish him for laziness and set him to work cleaning floors or washing instruments. Occasionally he would be too busy to watch his wife's Caesarean.

We have largely overcome this problem now by assigning a medical student to accompany the father into the theatre and to act as his ombudsman. Even he or she might not be flak-proof and I have rescued both father and medical student from scrubbing the corridor under the 'Eagle Eye'. Another improvement is to pin a large sign marked 'FATHER' on the unfortunate man's theatre shirt to offer more protection. The jocular temptation for me to label other members of the theatre staff with: 'LETCH' for the anaesthetist, 'SLASH HARRY' for myself and 'RIGHT LITTLE STRUMPET' for one of the student nurses, could not be resisted on several occasions, and was followed by the usual letter of complaint to the 'Theatre Users Committee'.

In many other medical and surgical fields the use of telescopes, flexible endoscopes and microscopes on patients who are awake during these procedures has led to requests that closed circuit video be used so that patients too can see what is happening. In our teaching hospitals the use of monitor screens allows students to view clearly what the operator is seeing and doing down the endoscopes. If an additional monitor is used outside the screens or room, then the students need not actually be with the patient and so embarrassment is reduced.

In gynaecology, we are making increased use of colposcopy to investigate and treat women with abnormal cervical smears. A low-powered binocular microscope is inserted into the patient's vagina (colpos) in order to inspect the cervix and take biopsies. The term colposcope therefore means looking into the colpos – a Greek word for bay; a glance at a map of the Greek Islands coast-line will confirm – with plenty of colpoi to be seen around the coasts, especially in summer.

During colposcopy the lady takes off her underclothes, lies back on an hydraulic couch and raises her legs apart, to be supported vertically in stirrups – rather like a stiff jockey who has fallen backwards from his horse. This inelegant position is achieved with tact and decorum from the surgeon and his nurse. Privacy is desirable and the closed circuit video idea assists with this. An enlightened gynaecological friend at another hospital in London has no objections to acompanying husbands looking at the video monitor. One such was notably uneasy as his wife stripped, climbed into the ungainly position and underwent the colposcopy with pan-views, close-ups and a few 35mm stills for the record. As she was getting dressed afterwards, her 'husband' thought it prudent to let the gynaecologist know that he was grateful for the viewing but that he was just a neighbour who had given her a lift to the hospital.

Graham Parker 23.1.1985

'I never dreamed the bed shortage was so acute.'

*'It's millions of years since **He** created the perfect machine and we're still waiting for a comprehensive spare part service.'*

'I understand Mr Scott's going to be with us for a while!'

BANX

'It was only a matter of time before BUPA got in on the act.'

'That bleeping sound you hear is nature's way of
telling us something is wrong.'

'Every hospital has one. I'm Her.'

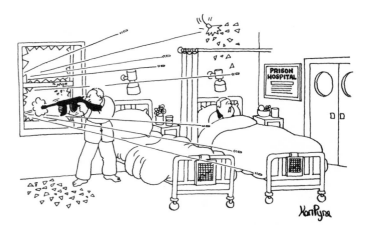

'Nurse! He's out of bed again!'

'It was such a lovely evening I thought I'd just toddle down and have
my ears syringed.'

'That's right. We've moved Mr Robinson from the intensive care
unit to the insensitive no-one-gives-a-damn unit!'

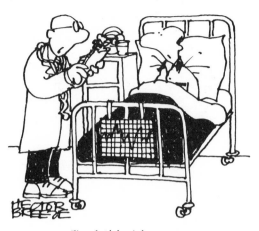

'I'm afraid there's been an error,
Mr Thackley – you've been cured in
mistake for another patient.'

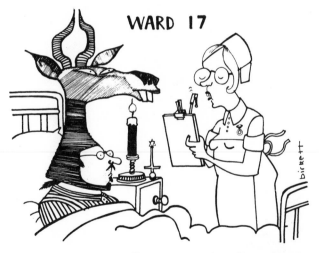

'If you can't give me a sensible answer, Mr Mathers, I'll just put you
down as C of E.'

Butcher. 'I OFTEN THINK, MADAM, I MADE A
GREAT MISTAKE IN MY CHOICE OF A PROFESSION. I'M
SURE I SHOULD HAVE MADE A FEARLESS SURGEON.'

'They only come over here to use our National Health . . .'

'You've certainly got to hand it to these Manchester United
supporters – they're game right to the end.'

KING SOLOMON'S BITS

A scheme to bulk-buy kidneys and other human spare parts for transplant surgery is being mounted by an eminent British doctor. Dr Gordon Kells plans to embark on a massive shopping expedition offering to buy up the organs for hard cash from poor people overseas.

Sunday People

J. Gordon Bennett,
New York Herald, NYC.

June 18

Dear Editor:

I have today safely arrived in Zanzibar, despite an unpleasant incident off the Horn. A slight attack of mal-de-mer had taken me to the ship's infirmary in search of a palliative, and the ship's doctor, in the course of what he claimed was the taking of a routine history, enquired as to whether I had ever suffered any kidney trouble. Upon my replying in the negative, he then offered to exchange one of my kidneys for a digital Omega in a 9-carat case. I told him that I could not see the point in having a wristwatch hanging inside me, and left.

The swine's ambitions did not, of course, escape me: clearly, the East African market flourishes. I took this as a heartening sign that our quarry is still alive, and in business. A further indication was afforded this afternoon as I disembarked: an urchin scuttled up to me on the very waterfront and offered me his grandmother, assuring me that she was both cheap and free from disease!

When I expressed my shock and also my view that matrimony was a sacred state, the wretch looked puzzled. His grandmother, he said, had been run over by a truck three days earlier, and was now in the deep-freeze his family had received last month in return for his uncle's pancreas. While her lungs had been snapped up and a deposit had been paid on her heart, there had as yet been no firm offers on her liver, which

he was prepared to let me have for five hundred pounds, to include handsome carrying-case.

Clearly, my dear Bennett, I am on the right track. Tomorrow, I leave for the interior.

Yours in haste,
Henry Morton Stanley.

J. Gordon Bennett,
New York Herald, NYC.

June 24

Dear Editor:

A poor start we had of it, I'm afraid. Of the twelve porters I selected, eight fell down the hotel steps, three collapsed on the pavement, and the last died while attempting to lift my typewriter. I came out after settling my bill to find local Arab surgeons disputing the corpses with the vultures. Apparently, the porters had all given blood that morning, in exchange for a special offer on Dave Lee Travis LP's, and I doubt that there was more than a pint or so left inside the lot of them. It took two further days before I could assemble enough able bodies to carry my gear, and even these are fearfully scarred and, in many cases, missing hands; though whether as the result of judicial action (the penalty for stealing organs is amputation) or whether they have simply been cutting them off themselves to sell to medical school travelling representatives, it is impossible to say. Indeed, it may actually be a combination of the two, since the penalty for cutting off *other* people's hands to sell to medical schools is also amputation. If, however, you cut off someone else's hand to sell to a thief to replace the hand he has had cut off for criminal activity, then the penalty is to have a foot amputated; a thief, on the other hand (as it were) who receives a hand knowing it to be stolen, in order to replace a hand he has had cut off for criminal activity, has his *other* hand cut off.

Sadly, this trade in hands is somewhat academic, since there is as yet no way of grafting on a new hand; but these are simple people. Indeed, many unfortunate thieves spend their entire waking lives in exchanging hands, in the forlorn hope of eventually getting their own hand back.

I set out, at last, on the 21st; arriving, after five days forced marching, at Ngogi, an up-country settlement whose hundred or so inhabitants were all attached to a huge saline drip set up in the village square, and watching *It's A Knockout* on a new Sony colour set. I enquired of the head man as to whether they had seen 'a tall white man him got ears belong stethoscope', and was told that he had passed through a month before and bought everyone's intestines.

This was indeed encouraging news! Our man is known to favour bowelgraft in ulcer therapy, and the likelihood that it was he is very strong. Thus encouraged, we pushed on and made camp; but the day which had begun so well ended badly when, shortly after midnight, I was awoken by screams from the porters' bivouac. Rushing thither, I learned that, Arab organ-traders being in the neighbourhood, our chief porter had run off to join them, taking with him the spleens of two of his colleagues, summarily (though expertly) removed with the aid of machete, and a bag of assorted ears. Dressing the wounds as best I could (the men being highly suspicious of my own motives in approaching them with my first-aid kit), I sat up the rest of the night with my Henri-Martini cocked and ready.

I am sending this back with a runner. Or, to be accurate, hopper.

> Your obedient employee,
> Henry Morton Stanley.

J. Gordon Bennett,
New York Herald, NYC.

June 30

Dear Editor:

Upon arriving at the Great M'shanga Plain this forenoon, a bizarre and unsettling sight met my astonished eyes!

There, in the middle of some two hundred square miles of open scrub, stood the territory's one tree, with a new 1.3 Marina wrapped around it! My surviving porters instantly fell, not unexpectedly, to the ground and began beating their breasts and keening, having naturally taken the thing to be some sort of sign: since several of them, having sold the organs of their nearest and dearest, had invested the money in British Leyland shares, their immediate reaction was that here was an ill-omen sent by their gods to indicate that half-year profits were once again drastically down on forecasts.

But upon my interrogating the leader of a Bedou camel caravan driving north with a cargo of mitral valves and bladders, I discovered that the vehicle had been airlifted in on the instructions of a tall bearded British surgeon, in payment for graft-material he had taken from the local tribal chief. Unfortunately, that material had consisted of the Chief's corneas, which went some way towards explaining the accident; although my informant went on to explain that when the Chief's remains were levered out of the glove compartment, he was smiling; so perhaps all is for the best, after all. It is not, my dear sir, the brief of a mere reporter to analyse the myriad and mysterious workings of the Almighty!

This afternoon we pushed on quickly, so as to be clear of the territory of the Ngweeni before nightfall. Being pygmies, they have found that their tiny organs have almost no commercial value whatever, and have, in consequence, become a sour and malevolent folk, embittered by the knowledge that video recorders, waste disposal units, and Swiss bank accounts will never be their lot. I was deeply grateful that, by dusk, a dozen miles of dense jungle stood between us.

> Yours ever,
> Henry Morton Stanley.

J. Gordon Bennett,
New York Herald, NYC.

July 15

My dear Editor:

At last, the news for which we, and the world have craved for so long! Though not, it should be quickly said, in quite the form for which we had, I think, prepared ourselves.

Shortly before mid-day, my weary party and I arrived at the outskirts of a hamlet called Ujiji; noticing that the village women were sitting in a circle on the banks of the river, scrubbing their new Hoovermatics and banging their tumble-dryers with large flat stones, I felt my heart skip a beat – this, surely, was the place! And when a scrawny youth in a long green coat and surgical mask trotted up to hand us a slate indicating current secondhand prices and the starred bargain offers *du jour*, I knew that the arduous quest was finally over.

I asked to see the head man. The boy

explained (with what was clearly commercial chagrin) that while they had an excellent heart man, a highly recommended kidney man, and an obstetric unit fit to rank with any on the Ovary Coast, the transplantation of heads was, as yet, proving something of a dead end. A scalpectomy, however, *was* possible, and if I happened to be a $7\frac{3}{8}$, I might be just the chap Elton John had been looking for.

Once again, I was forced to demur; and managing, at last, to communicate my actual wishes, I was led to a large mud building at the edge of a suspiciously hummocked clearing. Above it hung the hand-lettered legend: UJIJI ORGANMART. TOP PRICES PAID. SCRAP OFFAL COLLECTED DAILY. LET US QUOTE YOU.

I walked forward, tentatively, heart pounding, wiping my hand on my shorts.

A figure rose, in the gloom of the building's interior. He stepped on to the porch. He was gowned and masked. I took off my topee. I held out my hand.

'Doctor Livingstone, I presume?' I said.

The surgeon paused. A cricket burped. A leaf fell.

'Hum,' he said. 'Dat all dependin' on de way you lookin' at it.'

He took off his mask. He was remarkably black, for a Lanarkshire man.

'Ah,' I said. 'I see I am not looking at David Livingstone.'

'You lookin' at his pump, all right,' said the surgeon, tapping his huge chest. 'Also his kiddleys. Plus one or two other choice bits it gittin a bit damn pussonal to mention, heh-heh-heh!' He stroked his chin. 'You lookin' at about twenty per cent o' Doctor Livingstone, basically.'

I licked dry lips.

'And the, er, other eighty per cent?'

'We ate 'im.'

I staggered. Despite the heat, my skin chilled.

'But – but that's *cannibalism!*'

The surgeon beamed.

'You a damn illogical buggah, honkie!' he cried, slapping his thigh. 'Round heah we calls it a oral transplant!'

I trust, my dear Editor, that I myself shall be with you not long after you receive this, my last letter; although I am troubled by drear forebodings. This evening, I came upon the surgeon with a group of his young registrars: they were passing a Stanley knife around, laughing helplessly the while, and shrieking in a language which I did not understand.

Yours ever,
Henry Morton Stanley.

Alan Coren 2.4.1980

Doctor. 'WHAT DID YOU OPERATE ON JONES FOR?'
Surgeon. 'A HUNDRED POUNDS.'
Doctor. 'NO, I MEAN WHAT HAD HE GOT?'
Surgeon. 'A HUNDRED POUNDS.'

'Would you prefer to have your operation featured on television or in a colour supplement?'

'I'm afraid, gentlemen, it's more virulent than we first thought.'

'What with flu, transport problems, ancillaries on strike . . . scalpel!'

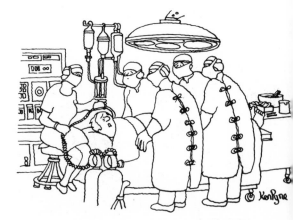

'Do you think you could perhaps make one small mistake? – I need the money.'

'He contains artificial flavouring, vegetable colouring,
albumen, plus additives . . .'

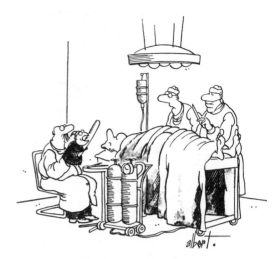

'How long were you at the government
re-training centre?'

'We are aware of your unqualified success in the
hospital panto, Dobson . . .'

'The brain surgeon's done a marvellous job – go ahead
and ask me something difficult!'

WHAT SURGERY?

THE MONTHLY MAGAZINE FOR THE HOME OPERATIONS ENTHUSIAST

EDITORIAL

SCALPEL FREAKS

The guys who write this mag and all of you out there who keep us in business are regarded as fanatics. O.K., so we're fanatics. Your Mr Average is quite content with the occasional corn removal, ham-fisted acupuncture, and maybe a cartilage when he's really in the mood.

Time will tell. As with Hi-Fi, photography, or any other new leisure activity, purism eventually becomes the norm. And we're not about to start in as missionaries. We're quite happy for time to take its course.

But although we're fanatics, we don't hurt anyone, right? And it's important that the scene doesn't get a bad name, right? So this month can I ask you to keep an eye out for scalpel freaks in your neighbourhood. You know the type—quick transplant—he's got two left hands—she's got two right ones—pigs' t*st*cl*s—that sort of kink.

It gives us a bad image. And damn right, too. It's not NATURAL. It's messing around with God's handiwork. I mean, what sort of a buzz do these guys get?

We'll campaign against it, but you can help to stamp it out.

See you,
Hank.

EQUIPMENT REVIEW

BATTLE OF THE GIANTS.
STANLEY v. SPEAR AND JACKSON

STANLEY PD 403(SS)
SPEAR AND JACKSON 970 MA

As you'd expect from these manufacturers, both scalpels are well-made, well-finished and well-packaged. The Stanley features a curved aluminium grip holding a welded, stainless steel blade. The S & J is a one-piece, molybdenum/aluminium alloy, claimed to be eversharp and corrosion-proof.

PANEL TESTS

As the Stanley arrived somewhat late for tests, we were unable to put it through major operational vortexes. However, it seems to cut straight and fine, handlability was (as usual with Stanleys) excellent, and we were particularly impressed with its performance in fat tissue.

The S & J scores equally well on these points, but with its smaller blade proved more manoeuvrable in delicate work. However, we did feel that the grip wasn't all it could be. Slip factor was inferior to the recommended 0.2ym for close-to-the-artery stuff. Furthermore, the alloy comes in a highly polished finish which looks great but tends to give a confusing reflection when operating on yourself.

There was thus no clear recommendation. The Stanley seems the best bet in terms of safety, although it's not going to prove adequate for intricate tasks. A good, no-nonsense, all-purpose scalpel. The S & J is much more refined, but they'll have to sort out one or two design factors before we can encourage our readers to invest.

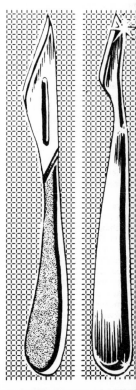

STANLEY
LIKES: Matt finish.
　　　　Grip security.
　　　　Clean cut.
DISLIKES: Clumsy blade.

S & J
LIKES: Size of blade
　　　　Appearance.
DISLIKES: Reflectability.
　　　　　Grip security.

OPERATION OF THE MONTH

This month's operation is suitable for amateurs and professionals alike. Techniques are basic, but it still offers a challenge to skill, for a perfect finish is never easy.

THE BROKEN WRIST
1. Break left wrist. (Lefties break right wrist).
2. Take X-Ray.
3. Study X-Ray to discover location of break. (Those who have done the operation before may well be able to by-pass this stage, working by feel. However, it's always satisfying to go through the rituals.)

4. Wash hands. (Difficult under the circumstances, but essential for the enthusiast. It feels right.)
5. Inject with local anaesthetic.
6. Wait until pain subsides, then gently move forearm around until you hear a solid click. (Be careful not to confuse with splintering noise. Can be tricky the first time, but practice makes perfect.)
7. Mix plaster of Paris and apply liberally. (Don't forget the Vaseline.)
8. Allow to dry.
9. Wait 3 weeks, then remove plaster.
10. Normal physio.

If the results aren't completely A1 for straightness, the operation can always be repeated until perfect. One of the beauties of this op: mistakes can be rectified.

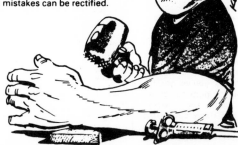

EWS IN BRIEF

aho

A group in this picturesque state
ve pushed the frontiers of home
rgery an important step further.
ue, the group's co-ordinator, said,
Ve felt that home surgery could
 an exciting addition to social
e. Something more than ex-
anging tips or borrowing brain
ans. So we decided to organise a
ll-bladder swapping party. 20
ople turned up, and the fun went
 to the early hours. It was such a
ccess that we'll be organising
milar events soon."

I. Other groups take note.

alifornia

The annual "Close it up" com-
tition will be held in November
 Sacramento. There are three
ain classes this year.
 Abdominal surgery—judges are
interested in symmetry and
neatness of scar tissue.
 Exotic transplants—originality
is all-important.
 Family class—open to families
with two or more children.
Variety and tastefulness are the
keynotes here.

icago

Jane-John Jones, 25, has been
tablishing a considerable repu-
tion in Chicago's clubland with
s/her unique cabaret. Calling
m/herself "The Fastest Change
 Show-Biz", Jane-John can be
ught four nights a week.
esdays and Thursdays she/he
rforms the op: to change himself
o a woman. Wednesdays and
days are vice-versa nights. "I'm
st an ordinary guy," she told us
 the phone.

ADERS' LETTERS

'our mag is aimed at
ginner's. What about a feature
open-heart?
Tim

*Look. This isn't a hobby for
nboys. Learn some humility and
e out your apostrophes.*

ar Hank,
'our readers might be interested
 a tip we found useful in artificial
 work. Unless you've got the
ney for the platinum-coated re-
cement units—and who's
ward Hughes these days?—the
adium alloy units do take a little
e to run in. We thought, hey, a

---

body works on the same principles
as auto engines, so we tried a little
SAE 90. It did the trick! Don was
able to throw away the crutches
after only 11 weeks, and he's now
on Physio Grade 5 after just
two months. He's delighted, for his
"ball and sockets" are certain to
last longer than the originals.
Linda

*Ed. Thanks! Ingenuity like yours
moves the whole waggon along.
The Technical boys are checking it
out. More next month.*

Dear Sir,
 Your recent review of our portable heart/lung unit (March) was,
we feel, more than a little inac-
curate. Pump flow stability and
oxygenating levels are much
superior to those you found. Was
there a gremlin somewhere? We
would be only too pleased to supply another model for re-testing,
for we feel it would be a pity were
your readers discouraged from
availing themselves of the latest
technology which would greatly
enhance their leisure enjoyment.
Barnard & Barnard

*Ed. Which? found the same as
we did. It's down to your quality
control, buster!*

READERS' MART

**1977 Harman-Bower sterilis-
ation unit.** Fully portable. 1
owner from new. £275 ono.
BOX 110.
Unwanted gift. Drip with trolley
and several plasma, various blood
groups. BOX 210.
Pacemaker. 2 years old. Light
use. Genuine reason for sale.
Successful transplant. BOX 320.
Double volume. 'Layman's
Gray's Anatomy'. Good as new.
BOX 410.
Complete home theatre. Table,
lamps, instruments, anaesthetic
eqpt. Owner going abroad. Serious
offers only. Box 510.
Genuine 1872 surgeon's outfit.
Lovingly restored. £100. BOX 610.

PERSONAL

Guy, (26), shy, sensitive. Long, delicate
fingers. Seeks artistic girl for mutual research. BOX 190.
Gay, (39). O.K. I'm balding. Take it as a
challenge. Anything considered. BOX
290.
Divorced, (35), lady, gallstones developing, seeks mature man, preferably
with hernia or similar. Serious. BOX
390.
Black, (28), male, (very), into discos,
jazz, ebony, country walks and neuro-
surgery seeks soul mate. BOX 490.
Ugly girl, (19), seeks understanding guy
into plastic surgery to turn her into a
princess. BOX 590

*'We'll have to postpone your
operation – there's nowhere to put you if
it goes wrong.'*

"Doctors may soon hold surgeries in High Street department stores under a scheme being considered by the British Medical Association. The idea was put forward by the Debenhams group, which believes it would reap commercial advantage from attracting patients into the store who might then make purchases in other departments." *Daily Telegraph*

IT'S A SNIP!

ONLY £25

Because of a cancelled export order, we can now offer, FOR A LIMITED PERIOD ONLY, five thousand vasectomies at a knock-down drag-out price!

Yes, it's true! At this time of year, British surgeons traditionally flock to Iran to perform this wonderful little operation, bringing valuable foreign currency into their hip pockets. But as the result of the new regime, vasectomies have been banned as contrary to the Koran's stipulations. You may now take advantage of this surprise cancellation!

GIVE MUM A BREAK THIS WEEKEND—AND SAVE £££'s FOR YOURSELF!

Only **£25** (no cheques) at all branches of Marks & Woolly, W. H. Tesco, and Fine Boots, where anyone showing his scar will be entitled to FIVE POUNDS OFF any other purchase over £50!

OLD DRUG STOCK LUCKY DIP!

Hundreds of Wonderful Bargains!

Due to a Grand Clearance of Bathroom Cabinets, literally millions of fine pills have come on to the market at virtually giveaway prices! Many brand name birth pills, tranquillizers, emetics, analgesics, diuretics, worm pills, pile shrinkers, laxatives, pep pills and many, many more, *all mixed up so that you can take POT LUCK!*
THERE MAY WELL BE RARE TREASURES HERE! EVEN *WE* DON'T KNOW!

JUST LOOK AT THESE BARGAINS—

500 Pills of the British Empire £2.50
200 Colourful Pills of Africa £1.75
500 Pills of King George V £5.00

At all large branches of Timothy Dyas & Hollingsworth's, or by post (include 12p for p & p). Personal callers are invited to visit our garden furniture department, where there is a 10% discount for diabetics on all folding tables.

FROM STOCK NOW!

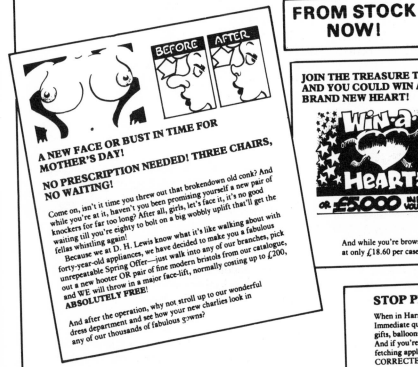

BEFORE | **AFTER**

A NEW FACE OR BUST IN TIME FOR MOTHER'S DAY!

NO PRESCRIPTION NEEDED! THREE CHAIRS, NO WAITING!

Come on, isn't it time you threw out that brokendown old conk? And while you're at it, haven't you been promising yourself a new pair of knockers for far too long? After all, girls, let's face it, it's no good waiting till you're eighty to bolt on a big wobbly uplift that'll get the fellas whistling again!

Because we at D. H. Lewis know what it's like walking about with forty-year-old appliances, we have decided to make you a fabulous unrepeatable Spring Offer—just walk into any of our branches, pick out a new hooter OR pair of fine modern bristols from our catalogue, and WE will throw in a major face-lift, normally costing up to £200, **ABSOLUTELY FREE!**

And after the operation, why not stroll up to our wonderful dress department and see how your new charlies look in any of our thousands of fabulous gowns?

JOIN THE TREASURE TRAIL AND YOU COULD WIN A BRAND NEW HEART!

WIN-a-HEART! OR £5,000 IN BUPA VOUCHERS

Amazing, yes, but true! At all Augustus Oddbinn Surgeries until May 31, anyone having a boil lanced will be entitled to an entry coupon for our Lucky Organ Draw. The winner will receive a new heart OR £5,000 in BUPA vouchers to spend just how she or he likes in any British clinic, there are ten livers (or £1,000) to the immediate runners-up, and the first five hundred entrants opened will be entitled to minor surgery worth up to £50 (sorry, no dental work!).

THOUSANDS OF OTHER FINE ORGANS FOR THE LUCKY RUNNERS-UP!

And while you're browsing, may we recommend the '76 Chateau Mouton-Benghazi, at only £18.60 per case?

STOP PRESS!

When in Harridges, why not stop by our new **HERNIA BOUTIQUE?** Immediate quotations, qualified staff, rock music, open sandwiches, gifts, balloons and lollipops for dependants under 12, lifts to all floors. And if you're beyond surgery, why not try on our wide range of fetching appliances? Remember our motto: WE STAND CORRECTED!

BMA The Price Busters!

THEATRE OF THE ABSURD

Everyone wants to be a surgeon. It is a job with the status of a disc jockey, the salary of an airline pilot and the sexiness of a ski instructor. Do not be deterred by the stuffy doctors' union, demanding you spend years and years studying such irrelevant and boring topics as biochemistry, microbiology, geriatrics, dermatology and psychoanalysis. You could be operating tomorrow!

Every year, real surgical enthusiasts – meat salesmen, hospital cleaners, young clergymen, impatient medical students – take the direct route to the operating theatre. All you want is a Chester Barrie suit and a well typed reference. Offer yourself as a locum at a busy hospital in August, and nobody is going to risk losing your services by checking it.

HOW TO BE A BOGUS SURGEON

The only skill you need is at handling small pieces of greasy machinery in awkward corners under intolerable working conditions. Have you replaced the chain-drive of your motor mower, lying on the lawn in blazing sunshine? Then you can operate.

First, remove your suit in the surgeons' room, taking care to leave nothing of value in the pockets. Slip into anything clean and white lying about. Let a nurse dress you up in a green gown. Donning rubber gloves is the most difficult part of the operation. Entering the theatre with ten teats on your hands invites suspicion. If in serious trouble, hurl successive pairs to the floor, with increasingly loud complaints of punctures.

You will find the operating theatre overcrowded with anonymous masked figures in gowns. Those with bumps on their chests are likely to be nursing staff. Control them all with the cheery firmness of a captain his team, or producer his cast. Slyly play on their touchiness about their own importance over the others.

The one surrounded with pipes and glittering machinery is the anaesthetist. His presence is vital, to indicate which end of the heavily towelled patient is the head.

Principles of Surgery
There are two classes of operation –
  (1) Cutting it off.
  (2) Cutting it out.
The necessity for (1) is obvious through an inviting lump, gangrene, impaled gear lever etc. If a search of the area reveals nothing of this nature, proceed to (2).

The Incision
The cutlery provided may be confusing, but need cause no worse embarrassment than deciding how you should eat asparagus. Hold knife and forceps as though enjoying a tender, rare fillet steak.

If you pick from the display an instrument outrageously wrong, the nurse in charge may exclaim, 'Surely you're not going to use a cleft palate knife on a haemorrhoidectomy?' Inspect the instrument for some seconds, replying, 'I'm surprised you still sterilize these, sister – they went out in World War II.' Or simply drop it on the floor and bark, 'Blunt!' Or fix her with your eye, rasping 'Hackenbusch's lithotriptoscope – quick!' When she says hastily she hasn't one sterile, snap over your outstretched palm, 'Oh, it doesn't matter. I'll make do with the Wurtenburg-Mayo cholecystoduodenostomy anastomosis clamp instead.' She will give no further trouble.

Surgical Anatomy
Make a large slit, as though opening a paper sack of cement. Do not worry about the bleeding. Someone will busy himself stopping it. At first glance, the inside may seem confusing. But the human abdomen contains only two organs of concern to the amateur operator.

The stuff like pink bicycle inner tube sloshing about in the middle is the *gut*. At the top end, resembling the leather wine flask used by Spanish road workers, is the *stomach*. The gut is about 10 yards long. It does not matter how much of this you care to remove; humans can exist happily with hardly more than would make a good serving of *tripe à la mode de Caen*.

The liver is at the end nearer the anaesthetists, 8 pounds of it, looking like the stuff you fry up with bacon. With the pancreas, kidney, adrenals and other goodies deep in the abdominal bran tub, it is best left to the inquisitive fingers of the professionals.

Towards the end of the gut, under the right pocket of the jeans, is the star of surgical drama, the appendix. It resembles a four-inch worm, and like the Aldwych Tube leads nowhere. If a brisk rummage discovers nothing exciting enough to cut out, remove the appendix. This will cause no comment, the normal appendix being frequently removed in error.

Sewing Up

Stitching human tissues is no different from sewing on shirt buttons or darning socks, and the needles come ready threaded. Buy *The Vogue Sewing Book*. Practise gathering and shirring, French whipped seams, gussetting and mitering. Do not worry if you leave your patient branded like a Wild West steer. He will strip his sleeve and show his scars as proudly as a Crispin's day veteran. Without a good scar, he hardly feels he has had an operation. It is like the decent suntan which proclaims that he enjoyed his holiday.

X Rays

Inspection of the X-rays is useful when wondering what the devil to do next. X-rays are easy to read, because their shadows invite as many contrasting opinions as the Turin shroud. If uncertain whether the picture represents a fractured rib or a swallowed four-inch nail, emit a low whistle and exclaim, 'My word, that *is* a whopper, isn't it?' As you are the surgeon, everyone will nod in humble agreement.

Heart Transplants

This is the glamour surgery, attracting so much delightful and profitable publicity, the amateur is as desperate to perform it as the fully-qualified professor.

The operation is as simple as changing the wheel on your car. The difficulty is its necessitating, like sex, two people for its consummation. The recipient is no problem. Donors are difficult. There are innumerable healthy hearts in the country, but their processors seem loath to

perform an organ voluntary at the enthusiastic surgeon's request. The best technique is buying a reliable portable life-support apparatus, and parking behind a hedge at a sign saying ACCIDENT BLACK SPOT. The Government are most creditably encouraging this exciting branch of surgery, by refusing to legislate the compulsory wearing of seat belts.

Orthopaedic Surgery

A firm favourite with d-i-y surgical buffs, because it is only warm carpentry. The chisels, hammers, saws, Black and Deckers etc are exactly the same in the operating theatre as in the garage. *Home Woodworking* will see you right. Many professional orthopaedic surgeons exercise their skill with equal energy at home as at hospital, though patients do not qualify for a Government improvement grant.

Aftercare

The operation is but a single spectacular act in the programme of surgical treatment. Once you have knotted the last stitch, turn to your first assistant – the one so fussy about stopping the bleeding – and say condescendingly, 'I leave the postoperative management wholly in your care, with the utmost confidence.' His head will so swell, you need make no further contribution to the case beyond bellowing, 'And where's the coffee, then?'

Forensic Medicine

Protagonists of the closed shop are as savage towards surgical amateurs – who perform valuable service by relieving the overworked surgeons of the NHS – as towards blacklegs in any other nationalised industry. Though it is a cherished principle of trade unionists that the law holds no sway in their activities, 'cowboy' surgeons may find themselves involved in tedious legal wrangles.

If you do get put inside, why not study my companion work, *How To Be A Bogus Judge*? This job, too, allows dressing up and the psychological expression of infantile omnipotence. It is performed in greater comfort, sitting down, and you can call the tea breaks when you like. Less intelligence need be shown, there being twelve other people to reach all the painful decisions for you.

Carry on cutting! Remember – *If In Doubt Cut It Out*, and *ars longa vita brevis* was Hippocrates' way of saying that Vita walks nearer the ground since the plastic surgery on her bum.

Richard Gordon 1.8.1979

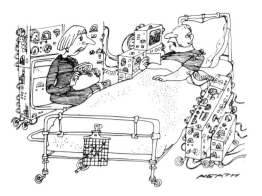

'*Look, I'm as sorry about this as you are, but my new heart belongs to somebody called Doreen Grimditch.*'

'*Can we fit in a quick nose job on the Duke?*'

'*Other men take their working-clothes off when they come home!*'

DUNCAN COMIC CUTS

Hospitals hire 'MASH' theatres

By DAVID FLETCHER
Health Service
Correspondent

CASH-STARVED health authorities are renting mobile operating theatres as a cheap way of clearing long lists of patients waiting for operations, it is disclosed today.

'For God's sake hurry, man, before the Chancellor introduces new cuts.'

'All he said was, "Hand me the scalpel, Hotlips!"'

'In this game you have to have a sense of humour or else you go under.'

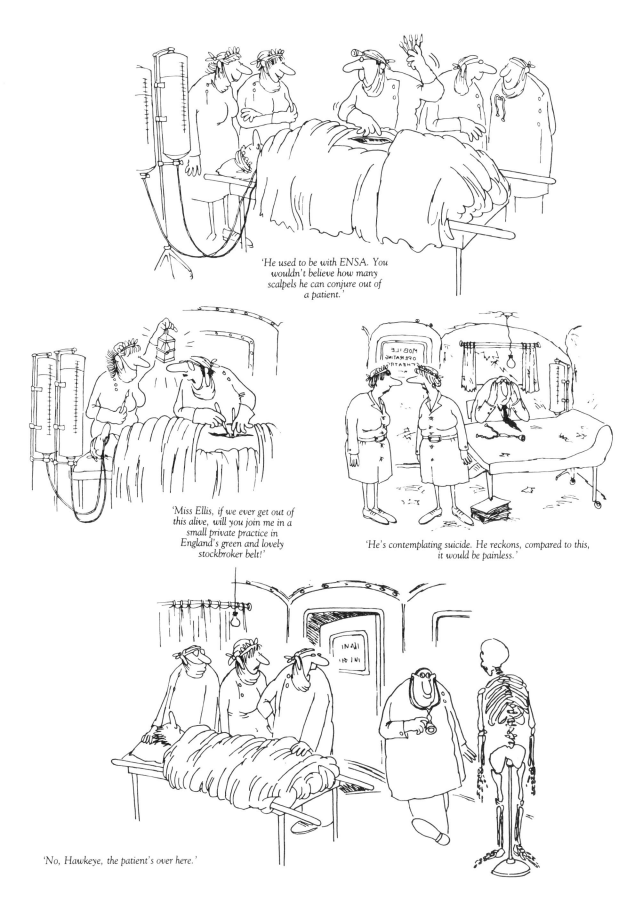

'He used to be with ENSA. You wouldn't believe how many scalpels he can conjure out of a patient.'

'Miss Ellis, if we ever get out of this alive, will you join me in a small private practice in England's green and lovely stockbroker belt!'

'He's contemplating suicide. He reckons, compared to this, it would be painless.'

'No, Hawkeye, the patient's over here.'

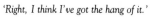

'Right, I think I've got the hang of it.'

7

Shuffling Off

'First the good news. His temperature has gone down.'

DOC BRIEF
Robert Buckman on
AGEING

THE AGEING PROCESS

The ageing process is one of the least understood biological mechanisms, though it is regarded by some anthropologists (usually the older ones) as nature's only alternative to dying young. What is even more astounding is the way that some animal species seem virtually immune to the ageing process, e.g. bush babies, shrimps, kippers, certain waterfowl, including Donald Duck, and other fictional characters, e.g. Michael Heseltine, Desmond Morris etc. Whereas, by contrast, other species seem to adjust to it brilliantly and never actually suffer from the effects of it or die of it, e.g. giant turtles, Stilton, the Swiss, etc.

However in the case of *Homo sapiens*, we know that, as ageing progresses, certain things go up, e.g. blood pressure, serum cholesterol, insurance premiums, number of wives, number of newspapers you own etc. While simultaneously many other parameters come down, e.g. haemorrhoids, memory, number of your friends in the Cabinet, number of newspapers you can understand etc. While, thirdly, some other equally important biophysical processes neither go up nor down (see Impotence below, but try not to get upset). However, the question that most people have written in to ask me is whether we know when the ageing process actually begins in man. The answer is yes, we do know, and it always begins in about five years time.

CELLULAR AGEING

Human beings are composed of cells in exactly the same way as many other biological organisms

are, e.g. prisons. And in exactly the same way that a prison is said to be ageing if its cells are old and it's difficult to keep clean and mucked out and important things keep escaping, so it is with our bodies. Although when, as we get older, important things escape, we don't try and recapture them. Except youth maybe – which, if you pursue it enough, will eventually land you in prison, thereby proving the validity of my analogy. Ah. I seem to have got lost. Well, the point is that the cells of which we humans and journalists are composed become older. As we do – in fact, we do *because* they do.

So how do cells age? Well, the answer lies in things called lysosomes, which are small intracellular packets of proteolytic enzymes situated within the cytoplasm like the packet of soy sauce in a Chinese take-out. Except lighter brown and more smelly. No one knows precisely what lysosomes do (mind you, nobody really knows what soy sauce does either – except your stomach, and it won't talk). So what happens as a human cell gets older is that its lysosomes become leaky and release their enzymes, just like the soy sauce leaking all over your sweet-and-sour prawn-balls (no tasteless remarks here please, wait till the next paragraph). So what makes these lysosomes leak and cause the cell to age? Well, we know the answer to that – which is that they become leaky due to a biological process called 'ageing'. And nobody knows what causes that. Though in my opinion, when you're looking for the causes of ageing, it must have something to do with Chinese take-out, especially when you look at the people who sell it to you.

BALDNESS & IMPOTENCE

Actually, research into impotence has never aroused much interest. Perhaps when it comes to the psycho-social aspects of declining sexuality, social anthropologists simply fail to grasp the point. Which is that impotence and baldness are exact opposites, in that impotence is associated with decreasing testosterone levels, whereas baldness is caused by high testosterone levels and is thus a symptom of a healthy, virile masculine scalp. It is not known what evolutionary function baldness serves – although there are some tribes of animals in which bald-

ness is a signal of veneration and wisdom, e.g. teddy bears, octopuses and caviar.

It might be imagined that in such animal societies, the bald venerable elders of the tribe would be admired and allowed to sire many children which would be similarly wise and bald. In which case, how would that work for impotence? In fact, how does anything work for impotence? I mean, everybody knows how to cure baldness – what you do is allow your three remaining hairs to grow to eleven feet in length and then coil them over your scalp, spray with a light epoxy-resin lacquer and emigrate to a place where the wind never blows. But would that succeed for impotence? Probably not, but it would make failure more amusing.

OTHER ASPECTS OF AGEING

Of course not all aspects of ageing are negative. For instance, one positive aspect is that as you get older, your in-laws get older still. And there are many ways in which older people can enhance the values and inter-relationships of our modern society – by losing at arm-wrestling, for instance. And of course there are many other aspects of ageing that I forgot to mention – forgetting things was one of them, and I can't recall the others. That happens to me quite a lot now – forgetting recent *things*, I mean. But I can remember the golden days no problem – when Britain ruled huge tracts of the world, e.g. Fleet Street, when *Punch* was hilarious and *Hansard* was serious. That's the worrying thing about this whole ageing business – I don't mind what it's doing to me, but look what it's doing to the world.

THE DOCTOR ANSWERS YOUR QUESTIONS

Q: My friends say that I'm very gullible and far too inclined to believe everything that anybody tells me. Is there a cure for this sort of thing?

A: Certainly. Send me £100 for a course of curative tablets and handy hints.

Q: I don't believe you.

A: You see, they're working already. Make that £200.

WHEN YOU'VE GOT TO GO

A few grave digs from HEATH

The oldest student in the world even when dead, refused to do as everyone else, and had to be beaten into the coffin with a heavy rock LP. Luckily the burial was free, as a grant covered all expenses. He was buried with ceremonial pumps or bumpers, and prayers were said to the martyrs St Oz and St It and children's crusader Richard Neville.

The Supermart Owner. Trussed up and frozen in an airtight plastic bag the Supermarket Owner can die as he lived. There is four pence off this funeral as it is considered a loss leader by 'Multi Undertakers' who specialise in dealing with the little man on the corner.

It would be nice if everybody had a good cry as I'm sure I will be missed. The thought of the crowds (after all I am the Rudolf Valentino of the cartoon world) sobbing around my grave quite brings a lump to my throat.

O DEATH WHERE IS THY STING-A-LING-A-LING

Vincent Mulchrone laughs all the way to the grave

The first bribe I ever took as a reporter was half-a-crown. I was seventeen, and he was dead.

'Would you like to have a look at him?' the widow asked. Office instructions on the point were explicit. I looked.

The other women in the little West Riding kitchen gathered round as the handkerchief was lifted from his face for the umpteenth time.

He was my first corpse, and for the first time I heard what was to become a familiar litany – 'Ee, doesn't he look lovely? . . . Better in death than in life, Sarah Jane . . . Doesn't he look like himself?'

I was backing out when the widow reached under the tea caddy on the mantelpiece and handed me the half-dollar. I composed my pimply features and explained that there was no fee. This, I said, was journalism.

But I must take it. *He* had left it for me. But he didn't know me. She knew that.

'Before he died,' she explained, 'he said "When I've gone, they'll be sending somebody round from t'Observer. Tell him to have a pint wi' me – and tell him to get t'bloody thing right."'

By chance I came across his funeral tea. They were burying him with ham at the Co-op Hall. There was tea – great, steaming, practically untouched urns of it.

The Co-op was run by Primmers, but the janitor wasn't one, and winked an eye at the bottles smuggled in from the pub over the road. The therapy stopped short of a knees-up. But I've been to worse *parties*.

The feast was splendid. The widow, who conceded that I'd 'got it right,' explained that, as well as the insurance, she'd had him in a club. There are still scores of burial clubs listed with the Registrar of Friendly Societies, survivors of hundreds started in Lancashire early in the nineteenth century to avoid a pauper's grave and provide a bit of a do for the mourners.

The Friendly Funeral Society, founded 1815, offered the relatives a benefit of 48s. – *and 2s.* more 'provided they have beer to the amount of 4s. where the collecting box is'. The link between pubs and funerals is an old one.

A funeral used to be an occasion, sometimes grand, sometimes boozy, generally a great display but always, one might almost say, full of life. Corpses were always 'beautiful', funerals always 'lovely'. Now it's twenty-five minutes at the crematorium (and a 'fine' if the clergyman runs over time), a peek at the flowers on the way to the gate, and a cup of tea in the parlour.

Where we used to see them off with ham, now we do it with high speed gas. An ad. in the funeral trade press says 'High Speed Gas – chosen by over ninety-six per cent of Britain's crematoria.' Where, one wonders, are the leisurely four per cent?

A man used to lie in his own church and be buried in his own churchyard. Now the body goes to a 'chapel of rest' and its disposal becomes an embarrassing sanitary exercise set to Muzak.

Well, say the undertakers – 3,500 of them run a £60 million-a-year industry – we offer chapels of rest because vicars can't afford to heat churches for just a few hours.

And because so many families are out of touch with the church the undertakers frequently hire a clergyman most mourners have never seen before and may never see again.

He will officiate for as little as a guinea. The only briefing he needs if the crematorium, too, is strange, is on the location of the button that will send old Fred sliding stage Right to the Gas Board's special pride.

The great majority of those who go – 600,000 of us every year – no longer believe in that damnation which gave point to the fear of death. Why, then, the antiseptic ritual, the bottling of emotions, the conspiracy to pretend that death has not occurred and nobody is grieving?

Death, it seems, has superseded sex as the last taboo. In his book *Death, Grief and Mourning*, Geoffrey Gorer convincingly concluded . . . 'death and mourning are treated with much the same prudery as sexual impulses were a century ago.'

Certainly our squeamishness about death and the mechanics of disposing of the body is utterly irrational. We try to deny the facts of death and loss. The Victorian convention of giving up social activities for a time has almost gone. Unlike mourners in Europe, we have stopped wearing full mourning.

'Must keep busy,' we say. 'Think of the future. Life must go on.' Occasionally the dead themselves anticipate this and insist on paying for a last round for the boys from the coffin.

An old Yorkshireman recently left instructions for his cortège to stop outside the George and Dragon, where he had left a fiver for the purpose. Said his son 'As he was a happy man who looked on this as his last joke, we played it out.'

André Simon, the wine writer, ordered champagne for his memorial service. A Cheshire publisher arranged his own funeral stag party. His son said 'Father had a wonderful sense of humour.'

Old men, you see, with a glint in their eye, and memories of funerals as they used to be. The publisher expressly directed that there should be no wailing women at his funeral.

A Halifax widow, certainly no boozer, felt so strongly about the misery of modern funerals that she forbade mourners to come near hers. Instead, said her Will '. . . after my coffin has been removed I want my friends and neighbours to drink three bottles of champagne, provided by me.'

Not that drink is essential to give a funeral a bit of a lift, a touch of style. One of the handsomest funerals of this year was that of an old farmer who insisted on being buried in his own garden alongside the graves of his dogs.

In Caerphilly there's a bricklayer who makes them his hobby. He got hooked on his mother-in-law's funeral fourteen years ago and now goes whenever he can, whether he knew the corpse or not.

'Sometimes he comes home a bit depressed,' says his wife. 'But nothing, not even cricket on the telly, his other big love, keeps him here if there's a funeral on.'

The amateur mourner himself says 'I don't like fussy funerals. I can't stand all the crying. I like the ones in the Order of Buffaloes best. There's always some good, strong singing, and people looking happy.'

When that grand old engineer, William Foden, departed at the age of ninety-five a few years back, he rode out on Pride of Edwin, a steam traction engine he built himself in 1916. Marching ahead of the coffin, blaring in blazing scarlet, went the Foden Motor Works championship brass band. Now *there's* a way to go.

You don't get the *racy* funerals of old any more. It's ten years now since Johnny 'Scarface' Carter, Sid the Con, Nick the Ape and Freddy the Fly were at a funeral together down Camberwell way.

The deceased was a motor trader whose £6,000 Cadillac crashed in flames near Tower Bridge, and so many of the lads turned out that the cortège stretched for a mile. The best wreath, by general consent, was a four-foot billiard table with six legs of red carnations, a green moss surface, and a set of ivory balls and a cue. Lovely funeral.

They can be happy affairs. I was at Pandit Nehru's funeral along with about half a million others, and that was quite a gay scene, with vendors selling chupattis and pop in the crowd. They watched his body pass and smiled fondly because they do not make our mistake of equating the corpse with the life that was in it. There was no hush. How could there be, when everybody wanted to say goodbye?

The English scoff at the Irish wake, not appreciating that it has nothing to do with dogma or superstition, and very little (apart from a prayer or two) with the corpse, but a great deal to do with sustaining and cheering the living.

I survived one in West Cork earlier this year. Then his friends, as is the pleasant custom, dug the old sailor's grave, but not too deep, for they soon struck another coffin. He barely got below ground, and in the hush a voice said 'Jaysus, he hasn't got six inches of freeboard.' Everybody smiled. Why wouldn't they? They loved him.

Our funerals have become mean, miserable, embarrassing affairs with, at crematoria, as much style as a production line. Dammit, the Chinese hire men to bang gongs and carry crazy floats. We go with a hum of tyres and a hiss of gas. Taped music, an optional extra, is used for solace the way the big jets use it just before landing.

When I go, give me a Basin Street funeral band, Belgian black horses with plumes, a stop at the tap room of The Hermit, and lots of ham. It won't bother me, mate. But it might just take that miserable look off *your* face.

30.12.1970

'I'd like a second opinion.'

'I think we can dispense with the formalities, for a plumber.'

'I'm here against medical advice, of course.'

'I've pencilled you in for next Wednesday.'

'Oh, super – après life!'

'This wasn't supposed to come as a surprise to you but, unfortunately, there's been a walkout of harbingers.'

'The insurance money didn't amount to much then?'

FUN AT THE RUE MORGUE

It's not that no-one believes me: I don't actually believe anybody else. If someone says they're going to Paris for a week, however terrible their state of physical decay, general enfeeblement or holy homelife, I cannot entirely banish from the outermost provinces of my mind the suspicion they are Up to Something. More so, at least, than if they were off to Swansea, say, or Wolverhampton. But sitting at my typewriter, translating away on the fourth floor front, watching the lights go on at dusk in the new block of the Hôpital Cochin as they lock the gates to the morgue, I can't help feeling how unfair it is that anyone should suspect me of it.

My own experience of the Hôpital Cochin – setting aside its current lustre as the temporary resting place of Jacques Chirac after his recent road accident – has never exactly formed part of the richly-encrusted treasure of Parisian memories, formed in the molten heat of ecstasy, that underlies, I suppose, my present suspicious attitude to other people's Business Trips.

My first encounter with the Hôpital Cochin was at half-past three in the morning, accompanying a fellow English actor at the Théâtre National Populaire who was convinced he was dying: we had dinner at a rather expensive restaurant in the Rue de Sèvres. I imagine it was the oysters. Symptoms developed shortly afterwards, and he disappeared, dull-eyed and fumbling erratically with his clothing, to lock himself in the lavatory halfway up the wooden stairs of the cheap hotel where we were both staying, in the picturesque old quarter between the Boulevard St Germain and the river.

I went up half an hour or so later to ask how he was getting on: he said, very faintly through the door, that he'd definitely been poisoned, and could I get an ambulance? It was now well after midnight, everyone in Paris except the tourists had been asleep at least an hour and a half: I pressed every bell I could find behind the desk downstairs, but no-one came. Eventually I uncovered a list of emergency numbers, and rang the hotel doctor. No answer. I went back and tapped on the brown-painted door: the situation seemed to have deteriorated. Barely a whisper; could I dial 999?

I had never dialled 999 before, even in England – I can't even remember whether it's the same three figures in France – but it wasn't a success. A high-pitched klaxon in the earpiece, followed by an urgent French voice – recorded – telling me I'd dialled the Fire Brigade and was under no circumstances to hang up. Then another klaxon and the same message over again. It occurred to me, even amid the washing-machine whirl of nerves in the solar plexus, that if the hotel had been burning down, the klaxon and recorded message would not have been much help. *'Vous avez téléphoné aux Sapeurs-Pompiers: ne quittez pas!'*

It was certainly over a minute before I had the courage to do so: I looked at the Directory again, and redialled. The same klaxon, the same urgent recorded voice: then I realised it was the same actor and practically the same text, but the Ambulance Service. So it was that we arrived at the Hôpital Cochin, three-quarters of a mile south of the scene of the accident, at half-past three in the morning, at the suggestion of a phlegmatic taxi-driver I finally found in the street. The Casualty Department. A great deal of filling in forms, soft feet pattering away through hygienic white-tiled corridors to fetch the doctor on duty, by which time the dead had awakened, been perfunctorily sick, and was talking rather sourly about going home.

The drive back in the early light was very pretty, the only event *en route* being a seaside-postcard tart who had blocked the entrance to the Rue Jacob with her Mercedes in order to conclude a discussion with a client, who remained in his car while she stood with her hands on her hips in a tiger-skin mini-skirt, handbag dangling from a length of gold chain and high-heeled shoes planted some way apart, waiting to hear his side of the argument.

This week the Hôpital Cochin has provided me with the same kind of life-giving stimulus it gave my poisoned friend. Its less successful cases, it seems, are stored in an architect-designed concrete cube – I say architect-designed because it has one tiny deep-silled window at floor level of no use to any living soul and clearly of none to the occupants – about sixty feet square at the base of the modern block, across the road from the room I work in. In front there is a small walled car-park. The gates open at nine, and bodies are collected, at times with very little ceremony: a green-painted Volkswagen van bounces in, reverses up to the door, the driver jumps out in dungarees, smoking a cigarette and waving a piece of paper, an old man in a white coat takes it and goes inside, and after a bit the coffin is carried out, loaded in the back of the van, doors slam, and off they go. More alluring, for my money – and I suppose we should all be putting aside the odd bob for just such an eventuality – are the *Pompes Funèbres*.

The men from the *Pompes Funèbres* – known locally as *les croque-morts* – arrive at about half-past eight, some in the hearse and some on mopeds, bundled up against the cold, and the gates are closed behind them. From my position on the fourth floor I am able to watch their preparations as they shake out the black and silver drapes, exchanging gruff jokes, stamping their boots, and puffing on their cigarette stubs, to arrange a dignified silver-fringed awning over the concrete entrance. The last touch is a silver-framed initial, placed centrally above the door.

On the stroke of nine cigarettes are stubbed out: curtain, as it were, up. The gates are opened, the mourners arrive in cars of various colours, park in the street outside, and enter the compound in bewildered knots to watch the Beloved borne out through the black velvet maw softening the hard edges of the concrete. The *croque-morts*, out of their moped wrappings by now and into double-breasted uniforms and shiny-peaked caps, settle them in the nice shiny hearse with the Deceased, and off we go at a more seemly pace. This morning's lucky initial is 'O'. *Fin*, I suppose, of another *Histoire*.

John Wells 14.3.1979

ETERNITY ON DEMAND

David Harper entered Hospital in the late afternoon of November 21st, passing briefly through Accident and Emergency before transfer to the Coronary Care Unit. He was forty-eight years old, overweight and a heavy smoker, and his wife was to say later how often she had asked, though nagged may well have been a better word, him to cut down, not only on the cigarettes but also on the work that seemed to take so much out of him these days.

'I'm only surprised,' she said, 'that this didn't happen before.' Such is the beauty of hindsight.

The traffic was heavy, as it always seems to be on rainy days in London, and he slipped the gearshift into neutral for the hundredth time, letting the engine idle unevenly at the traffic lights by Fenchurch Street. Rivulets of water trickled down the screen, blown at obtuse angles by the wind gusting between the high buildings. He sat hypnotised by the wiper blades whining back and forth, carving wide arcs through the raindrops until a horn blared behind, shaking him awake, aware now that the lights had

changed, the traffic ahead pulling away down Gracechurch Street. Past Adelaide House and onto London Bridge, he followed the slow-moving tail-lights. It was getting dark but the inevitable tourists still leaned over the parapet, frantically snapping Tower Bridge and H.M.S. *Belfast*, grey as the river, in the fading light.

The first vague pains which caused him to grimace and fumble for indigestion tablets were not what they appeared to be. Coronary artery occlusion and the pain of Ischaemic heart muscle is often confused with peptic ulceration or indigestion, and Harper, who had missed breakfast, but lunched heavily, was prone to indigestion and consequently ignored the warning signs. He could find no antacid tablets and he grunted, belched uncomfortably and lit a Marlboro instead. The nicotine relaxed him a little and he tapped the steering wheel rim lightly in time to the radio, across the bridge now and caught up in Borough High Street swirl; stop, start, red light, wayward pedestrians. On the right, the vegetable market, lorries disgorging tons of potatoes and cabbages up muddy side streets, on the left an alcohol-steeped tramp slumped in a shop doorway, soiled fly agape, muttering incoherent obscenities that no one wanted to hear, studiously ignored by hurrying umbrella-carrying passers-by, station bound.

It was 5.17 p.m., he had been up since six-thirty and felt jaded, grubby. With luck, he thought, I will be home in forty minutes, barring road works in Camberwell or a set of traffic lights out on the Walworth Road. He thought of the hot bath, and how good the first gin and tonic of the evening always tastes. And he thought of Elizabeth, who had spent her day, no doubt, complaining about the leaky washing machine or some such trivia, over endless cups of coffee with other bored housewives, waiting to greet him at the door, telling him how awful he looked, wishing he would slow down, not work every hour the Almighty sent, though God knows she didn't mind spending the fruits of his labours. And he thought of how later, in bed, she would hastily remove his questing hand from beneath the nightdress and tell him to act his age. Life goes on.

When the pain hit him again, it was multiplied tenfold, a hundredfold and he braked sharply, was all but rear-ended by a tailing taxi. He pawed at shirt buttons that suddenly constricted, gasped for air that seemed syrup-thick, clenched and unclenched a left hand in time to the waves of numbing pain that swept along the inner surface of the arm. Trembling fingers found the hornpush and the strident tone rose above the shouts from angry drivers and concerned onlookers, a distress call echoing along the grey street.

The infarction was large, probably full thickness, and the insult to the heart muscle considerable. That much was evident from the first hurried E.C.G. performed in the small emergency treatment room by an overworked casualty officer who fervently wished the resuscitation team would get its collective arse in gear. The patient, unconscious on arrival, went into cardiac arrest as the team made dramatic entrance, and launching immediately into their faultlessly rehearsed routine they managed to kickstart the injured heart on the second application of the D.C. electrodes.

At 6.25 Harper was placed in a bed surrounded by expensive micro-circuitry, and staff were busily occupied calculating electrolyte regimes and monitoring available information, particularly aware of the possibility of fibrillation setting in, that unco-ordinated, disorderly contraction of the heart muscle fibres that reduces cardiac output to practically zero. On the front of one of the machines was a pulse monitor with flashing amber light, above a small cathode-ray screen across which an E.C.G. trace flickered impatiently. Some thirty wires and tubes connected Harper with the realities of the technological 20th Century.

At 6.48 p.m. the amber light stopped flashing and the trace on the screen collapsed into static.

Consciousness returned almost at the very instant the light ceased its regular tell-tale, and the warning buzzer built into the instrument sounded loudly at his side. Harper leaned across the bed and stared intently at the stationary needle on the pulse meter. It seemed to him, newly awakened but strangely composed, that something was not right, that a device so obviously designed to register vital signs should not just stop doing so on a mere electronic whim, National Health or no National Health. He felt sure that he'd suffered a heart attack in

the car, but had no idea how long ago that had been, nevertheless he was surprised at how well he felt, obviously the attack had only been minor. Slowly, by way of experiment, he sat upright, swung his legs over the edge of the bed and with little apparent effort stood up. Strange, there was no sensation of bare feet on chill linoleum and the few exploratory steps away from the bed had a curious airiness about them, a not unpleasant sensation, if a little confusing. Looking down at himself he realised with horror that he was totally naked and he quickly turned, intent on getting back into bed before anyone noticed. It was then he saw that somebody else had arrived there before him, and not only that, was surrounded by agitated medical staff. Perplexed, he raised a hand to attract the attention of a pretty young nurse who stood nearby. She stared at him without the remotest sign of recognition.

'What's happening?' He spoke, but the words seemed only to sound inside him, and though he could hear the voices of the others, they were indistinct, fluffy. Clearly in all the confusion they had forgotten him. Better, he thought, to keep out of the way, perhaps look for a dressing gown or something. He resolved to keep a low profile, and return when the crisis, whatever it was, had ended and he could regain his bed. There was a door at the far end of the room.

Walking seemed effortless, and so engrossed was he in the sensation he seemed to pass through the door without any conscious design. Simply one moment he was on one side, the next standing in a wide, brightly lit corridor which must have been singularly long for try as he did he could make out neither where it ended nor where it began. At intervals along the uniformly white walls there were other doors, with no number or identification, and all closed. He strained his ears for any sound, but there was nothing, not even the familiar background hum of air-conditioning, or the distant murmur of voices, activity of any sort. Poised in the corridor for fully two minutes, he strove desperately to make a decision, acutely aware of the sort of things that might be in progress behind any one of those doors, post-mortems, gynaecological examinations, God knows what else. Somehow he felt the third door on the left would be a good choice, and he walked over to it and gently knocked. The door opened smoothly inward revealing a bare rectangular room, a window on the far wall beneath which stood a low desk of glass and tubular steel. Two chairs faced each other across the desk-top, one was occupied.

'I'm so sorry, I was looking for a dressing gown, pyjamas or something.' The man in the chair beckoned him to sit down, nodded by way of greeting. Meekly, Harper lowered himself into a chair which looked awfully uncomfortable but which proved quite the reverse. He squinted in the fierce sunlight that flooded through the window, obscuring anything one would normally have been able to see. At no time did he think it strange that such light should be evident in November.

'Does the glare bother you?' The voice was mellow, soft and round, accent-free and perfectly articulated.

'Yes, a little.' Even as he said it, the light that blurred his view of the man, forming diffraction spectra in the glass desk, began to fade as if some change in polarisation had taken place within the very substance of the window.

'Is that better?'

'Yes. Thank you.'

The diminished brightness afforded a better study of this enigmatic person. A tall man, this much was obvious even though he remained seated. Dressed in a plain white coat over light coloured shirt and tie, the face kind yet imperious, with a high forehead and neutrally styled grey hair. The nose was vaguely Etruscan, but delicately so and not out of place, the lower jaw firmly set and clean shaven. But it was the eyes that formed the focal point, eyes of the palest limpid blue, the colour of liquid oxygen, orbs that barely moved and never blinked, the very epicentre of the persona.

'I'm glad you came. So often one doesn't get the opportunity for this kind of meeting.'

'I beg your pardon. I'm not sure I understand. You see, I was in bed up until a short while ago but, well, I had to leave. I know I shouldn't have really, but I feel fine.'

There was a pause. The eyes appraised him.

'Yes I see. Perhaps I had better explain.'

'Explain what exactly?'

The man examined his elegantly manicured fingernails for a moment. Harper waited patiently.

'Are you a religious man, Mr Harper?'

Somehow it didn't seem strange that this man would refer to him by name.

'Not in any orthodox sense.'

'I see. Then this must seem all the more confusing. Let me instead ask you another question. Are you a happy person, contented with life?'

'Excluding emergency admission to hospitals I would say life has been relatively kind to me, yes.'

'Excuse me, but that's not quite what I asked. Passing through life with comparative ease does not necessarily imply happiness. What I want are your personal feelings, whether or not you enjoy life.'

Not an easy question. Can one distill down a half-century of emotion and experience, misery and joy into a simple essence, enjoyment or not enjoyment, pleasure or displeasure?

'Does all this have any bearing on my case. I mean what exactly is wrong with me?'

'You are very ill, Mr Harper. In fact I think it is a fair statement to make that you are at death's door. Literally.'

'That is a considered medical opinion? Odd then that I feel so well, peculiar that one so moribund walks with such ease.'

The man sat back in his chair, brushed a non-existent fleck from his trouser leg.

'The transition from mortality to immortality is a perplexing time, often a person may reach the very brink of death during some medical crisis, only to be snatched back. Are you aware, Mr Harper, of the extraordinary experiences so many people relate when they regain consciousness after such crises?'

'I've heard one or two stories, yes.'

'But you did not believe them, you attributed them to drug-induced flights of fancy perhaps. Wishful thinking even.'

'If I bothered to give them that much consideration, then yes, I suppose you're right. I would have put it down to hallucination.'

Was there a hint of a wry smile, even a little smugness in that noble face? Harper began to feel vaguely uncomfortable.

'Do you then suppose you are hallucinating at this moment?' There was a suitable pause, during which his discomfort increased. Carefully he shook his head.

'Oh, come now, Mr Harper. You have just suffered a severe heart attack, yet you wander naked from your bed feeling seventeen again, and blankly accept all you see without question, though it is all unquestionably bizarre. Hardly rational, sentient behaviour.'

'Yes, all right. I do feel well, *and* young again, but apart from that nothing's changed. I still think the same, have the same memory. I know who I am, where I live, what I do. That's not dreaming.'

'Well, what can be happening then?'

What indeed? 'I don't know.'

'Then I will tell you, and whether or not you choose to believe is entirely your own affair. Where you have come from there is still a body, a corporeal entity. It is you, or at least what you have always considered to be you and it is on the brink, the very edge of termination. So you, that is the "you" to whom I am speaking, have left, because you cannot remain inside a dead corporeal, instead, you the ethereal must separate. It is very difficult for you to accept this idea, for the concept is totally alien to your beliefs and because all the awareness you have ever known has been inescapably intertwined with the existence of your organic body. Except perhaps in your dreams, but then dreams are but insignificant extensions of the subconscious mind. Or are they, Mr Harper?'

'I really don't know. The whole thing sounds contrived and preposterous. Is it some new form of psychiatric treatment, have I gone mad as well?'

The man gestured a little impatiently as if to one he considered intellectually inferior. Harper felt a little like he had done so many times at school, in front of the master's desk.

'Surely you can see that one does not necessarily cease to exist merely because one's clumsy body breaks down, wears out; the organism per se is only transient. It is the etheric, the soul that is important.'

'I see now why you asked me about religion.'

Again the slightly impatient air.

'Religion is quite unimportant, simply a convenient gift-wrapping for the truth, a neat preparation for the inevitable, bare facts of existence, namely that life does go on after so-called death.'

'What about all the rest of it, the triumph of Good over Evil and all that, the meek shall inherit the earth, you know the whole Christianity affair?'

'Window dressing.'

They both sat for a while, digesting this latest remark.

'Disappointed?' A rather offhand sort of question, considering the import. Almost the way one might discuss a football result.

'Hardly, since I expected nothing and have been shown that there is something after all. I imagine it's the religious ones that are most disillusioned. They're the ones that have staked the most on the outcome, so to speak.'

He smiled. 'On the contrary, it is the so-called philosophers who object most, they seem to take it as a personal affront to be proved so devastatingly wrong after a lifetime of preaching in favour of death being an end in itself. Truth only hurts those who deny it.' He paused for a second, as if phrasing his next remark carefully in his mind.

'You know the decision you have to make now, don't you?'

He nodded. 'About going back you mean? Is it really entirely my decision?'

'The doctors can only revive your body if the spirit is intact. If you return, perhaps they will extend your corporeal existence; that I cannot predict. You must make up your own mind as to whether or not a continuation is desirable or worthwhile, and act accordingly. Go now, if you wish.'

Harper stood, looked down at the seated figure.

'How can I possibly make such a decision? You've told me absolutely nothing, offered me a choice which is no choice at all, between something about which I haven't a faintest concept, and life, with which I am intimately acquainted.'

'I see; better the Devil you know?'

'An unfortunate phraseology, but yes. Life may not be all a bed of roses but how am I to know that what you're offering is any better?'

Again the impatient turn of the mouth, the speech becoming a little abrupt.

'Mr Harper, I am not offering you anything. I'm not a salesman; when your life is over you will find out these things for yourself, that is inevitable. I am merely presenting you with the facts.'

'Hardly.'

'There used to be a saying in certain so-called exclusive London shops, jewellers and the like, that if you needed to know the price of the merchandise, then you couldn't afford it.' There was a pause. 'Can you afford it, Mr Harper?'

'You mean can I afford the risk?'

The man shrugged.

'Perhaps there is no risk after all. Only you have the ability to find out. All you have to do is turn your back on the body out there.'

Harper stood quietly. Behind him lay the door, which if taken, would lead him once again to the ward, to his bed. To his life. He considered his work, his indigestion, his overdraft. If he survived would he be a cardiac cripple? No more alcohol, cigarettes, rich food. Perhaps he would have to retire, condemned to life on a meagre pension.

What alternatives, thus far concealed, could be worse than that? For a brief moment the way seemed clear, but in that instant he saw, in his mind's eye, a wife in her moments of tenderness, a son in his flashes of filial intimacy and it seemed such a cop-out, a rat deserting a sinking ship, that not to return became unthinkable; to die when one has no choice in the matter is one thing, but this, this seemed simply suicide. He moved to the door. The pale blue eyes followed him quizzically.

'I'm going back now,' he examined those eyes, expecting to read disappointment, but saw only impassivity.

'As you wish. You know the way.'

Pausing at the door he turned again, thinking to apologise, but the eyes said no need, and as he moved again he found himself once more in the long white corridor, and the way back to reality seemed plainly marked.

The ward was unchanged, a crowd of people round his bed. As he approached his visual senses became distorted and it seemed to him he was now looking down at himself, as if suspended from the ceiling though no transition had been consciously engineered, it was merely a shift of emphasis, like the passing through of closed doors. Beneath him hands worked quickly and efficiently, applying intra-cardiac adrenalin, plugging in electrodes. Slowly he sank downwards, closer and closer to the inert body that lay invitingly, passively below. An odd sense of anticipation pervaded his thoughts, he keenly felt the right motives behind his decision and eagerly he reached down, embraced his poor diseased body and in doing so mingled with it, was enveloped by it, became one with it, revelled in the intense pleasure.

The body arched in a spasm of direct current and there was only blackness.

'It was a terrible shock. I thought he died years ago.'

The woman sat quietly in a corner of the bright waiting room, an unattended cigarette burned in the heavy glass ashtray, spirals of grey smoke curling lazily to the tiled ceiling. The doctor entered and she looked up, hurriedly stubbing out the cigarette, and then stood, handbag clutched tightly in both hands. A tall woman, once strikingly attractive, who now bore lines of worry and age on her face. The doctor paused before her, hands thrust deep inside the pockets of his white coat.

'I'm very sorry Mrs Harper. We did everything we could, but your husband never regained consciousness apart from one very brief moment.'

She stared at the floor, a numbness crept over her, and she thought of how he was when they first met, but somehow the memory kept fading, going out of focus.

'Can I get you something Mrs Harper?'

She shook her head.

'No. No thank you Doctor. And thank you for all you have done. You've all been so kind.' A pause.

'At least he knew nothing about it, I'm sure he would have wanted it that way.'

Richard Beioley 6.8.1980

WHOSE DEATH IS IT ANYWAY?

'Good morning doctor. What I'm going to say is going to shock you.'

'Impossible. We doctors are shockproof. Far more than any Roman Catholic fathers, and you don't have to blurt it all out in such an uncomfortable and cramped posture. Paedophilia, pot, porn, pouffs, Pakibashers . . . in our infinite Freudian compassion, we see such matters as interesting, often amusing, quirks of human behaviour.'

'Things are going badly, doctor. The wife's run off with a younger man. Both the kids are in Borstal. Business is poor – I make decimal currency converters, and there doesn't seem much call for them these days. The TV tube's gone.

I'm a lifelong Chelsea supporter. I'm so utterly wretched, I'm thinking of ending it all.'

'Jolly good idea.'

'You're not offended? Honestly? Snuffing the sacred flame of life?'

'There's a lot of euthanasia about this time of year. It's all the fashion – we have them in medicine, you know, like in economics and architecture. They cause hallucinations quite as powerfully as LSD, until displaced from our minds by the next lot, which in time are discovered to be equally disastrous. Fifty years ago, constipation was the cause of everything from dyspepsia to kleptomania. Forty years ago, surgeons attacked the sinuses with hammer and chisel, to cure headaches and halitosis . . . but I digress. So you're going to kill yourself? How?'

'I've thought about all sorts of ways, but none of them strikes my fancy.'

'Ay, there's the rub. Read any Dorothy Parker? *Guns aren't lawful; Nooses give; Gas smells awful; You might as well live.* Why not shuffle this mortal coil off Beachy Head? It's instant, once you make splashdown.'

'Fact is, doctor, I took a single ticket to Eastbourne. But I had to come home, I've such a terrible head for heights. Could you suggest something less dangerous?'

'My dear chap, for generations the medical profession has been making suicide painless, if not unnoticeable. You can do it by eating. Sixty years ago, clever actuaries in life insurance calculated that anyone much over ten stone had a progressively shorter life ahead. If you eat four square meals a day, with hamburgers, bars of dairy milk and bags of prawn-cocktail-flavoured crisps in between, you'll be dead in no time.'

'Trouble is, doctor, I'm so miserable I've lost my appetite.'

'Luckily, modern medicine means precise treatment. No need to gorge indiscriminately. Stick to cholesterol. Quite deadly, makes Dynorod jobs of your arteries in no time. All the really lovely dishes are swimming in it – bacon and eggs, fish and chips, bread and butter, steak and kidney, strawberries and cream, roly-poly and custard, cheese and pickles, cockles and mussels . . . you're making me feel quite suicidal. Simpler still, stop eating fibre.'

'That a way of saying, stop chewing the rag?'

'Fibre comes in bran, brown bread, brown

rice. Terrific for the liver and prolonging life in general. Though you'd better hurry up, before we doctors discover we're wrong, and every packet of muesli carries a Government Health Warning. You smoke, I suppose?'

'Never fancied it, doctor, since I got the cane at school.'

'Take it up. Fags, naturally. Havanas are probably just as dangerous, but not enough smokers can afford them to provide reliable statistics. You drive? Never wear a seat belt. That gives you a thousand extra chances of death a year, without even breaking the traffic laws. Odd how MPs, and even ordinary balanced people, react so angrily against simple measures to keep them alive. You're not the only one. Freud was right, the whole world's drunk on thanatos, which isn't a tonic wine but the death wish.'

'I've got one of those cars which makes a rude noise if your belt's unclipped.'

'We must find something else. As Webster said, *Death hath ten thousand several doors for men to take their exits*. We need no society of self-important busybodies to show us them. Why not change your job? Men used to die from mule-spinners' cancer in Lancashire and hatters' shakes in Luton, but I expect modern technology's changed all that. I believe mining and trawling are still dreadfully dangerous.'

'I suffer from claustrophobia and seasickness.'

'I expect there are occupations more comfortable and as risky. The Atomic Energy Authority might be able to offer you something. Been on holiday?'

'I thought I might allow myself a nice break somewhere sunny, before doing it.'

'Excellent notion. Go to Spain. Catch legionnaires' disease. Often fatal. Like Scotland? Take a fortnight on Gruinard Island, just off Wester Ross. It was salted experimentally with anthrax by the germ warfare boys in 1940, and they can't get rid of the spores. Though perhaps a fortnight would be a bit long. The incubation period's seven days, and it can kill you with dreadful agony in the following three.'

'As you say, doctor, though I must confess, I'm really an old stay-at-home.'

'There's no place like it. More accidents occur there than anywhere else. Just sit around, waiting for one to happen.'

'There's one thing I find worrying about suicide. Supposing it doesn't work? Supposing I wake up in a nice clean bed in hospital?'

'Nowhere is more reliable for ending your life as swiftly as possible. They needn't even give you the wrong drugs. Modern drugs cure all diseases, but with so many side-effects they kill you first. Hospitals are understandably crawling with antibiotic resistant germs, because people bring them there specially. They so fiddle with your internal organs with needles, and tickle the inside of your heart with plastic piping, modern hospitals are as deadly as Scutari under Florence Nightingale. It's called iatrogenic disease, because you catch it from a doctor.'

'Dear me! Death's more complicated than I imagined.'

'It's the simplest thing in life. You can commit suicide by doing nothing more lethal than breathing. Second-hand cigarette smoke can be almost as nasty as your own. And lead! You're breathing it this minute, spewing from every exhaust-pipe in the country, just to profit the oil companies. You know why the modern generation of children is thick-witted and inclined to graffiti, insubordination and vandalism? Lead poisoning, everyone says so. Well, everyone who hasn't any oil shares. Surely you've some asbestos about the house? A few deep breaths in its direction on the hour will surely do the trick.'

'Doctor, this is making me more miserable than ever.'

'Suicide can be *fun*! Have sex. Get the syph, in ten years' time you'll die believing you're the King of Siam.'

'Don't think I can wait ten years to die from anything. The missus might come back.'

'Then disappear with a pack of sleeping pills and a bottle of whisky, somewhere they can't find you for twenty-four hours.'

'I don't drink, doctor.'

'Neither did the first patient I gave that advice. He took the whisky first and the world looked so much better he decided to remain in it. He's now on three bottles of single malt a day, and pushing eighty-four. Otherwise, I can only suggest you go and live in Belfast or Beirut. Good morning.'

Richard Gordon 27.5.1981

'I warned him not to let that property
developer in.'

ABSOLUTE
HEAVEN

by HEATH

'He committed every sin in the book,
but he's got such charm.'

'He's only the third this week –
we're going to have to lower the
standards.'

TALKIN' WID DE LORD

The problem, as I see it, is not theological at all, but social: when, that is, the Almighty shakes whatever it is I have for a hand (a wing? a flipper? an ectoplasmic pod?), informs me that He is pleased to meet me, and offers me a plate of little sausages on sticks, do I reply: 'I will give thanks unto thee, for I am fearfully and wonderfully made' or 'I see QPR played another blinder, then'?

If, of course, He would ever say He was pleased to meet me. Leaving aside such metaphysical imponderabilia as whether He already knows me even as I am known, how do we begin to make sensible guesses about divine etiquette? After all, what class is God? Is He a toff? Lower middle? Senior executive? Working? Not – marginally possible – English at all, but someone who will simply click his heels and snap 'Entzückt!' or (shaking His Rastafarian locks) cry 'Gimme some skin!'?

Perhaps He doesn't shake hands at all. Many foreigners (if He will forgive me, and there is every reason to believe that He will, this being a trespass of minor proportions) embrace; Eskimoes rub noses; some Melanesians, according to Margaret Mead, pull one another's ears on meeting. It is possible He does all of these, and more.

Though, on balance of probability, not. With a million people dying every week, there would never be time for anything but the most cursory of greetings: three people every two seconds pouring into Reception from geriatric wards, DC-10's, Cambodian bunkers, fogbound motorways, imploded tankers, KKK rallies, inept barbershops, East End casinos, potholes, scaffolds, free fall parachute displays – many of them, too, still somewhat bewildered and in no shape to have their ears pulled by the Almighty.

Unless time is different There, mind. A thousand ages in His sight are, as I understand it, like an evening gone: Crossing Over may well be like going into Italy and suddenly finding small change with 1,000 written on it. You may get anything up to six eternal months to the hour

sterling, Over There.

It's a complicated business, eternity.

I shouldn't have got myself enmeshed in its boggling coils at all, had it not been for Glenda Jackson, Willie Whitelaw, Flora Robson and, of course, Richard Baker. They, and 596 like them, are why I am standing here today, just inside the pearly gates, wondering if I ought to be wearing a dinner jacket. For those six hundred eminences have just presented a petition to the General Synod of the Church of England, asking for the restoration to normal worship of the Book of Common Prayer and the Authorised Version of the Bible, and have thus set a cat among the liturgical pigeons more than likely, as such things traditionally do, to leave the loft full of bloodstained feathers and beak-torn fur.

Now, I must point out immediately (since I have no wish to spend whatever mortal time I have left writing mollifying letters to millions of apoplectic readers whose temple-veins begin to throb like lugworms whenever they feel that the Litany is under the cosh) that I care not a whit how people worship, or, indeed, whether they worship at all. With the gas-boiler on the blink and the lawn full of moss and a phone-bill just in that makes the National Debt look like Bob Cratchit's take-home pay after stoppages, I have scant inclination to worry about other people's immortal souls; and in fact should have paid no attention to my own, had it not been for a remark passed on this morning's *Today* programme, while I was shaving, by a hired torpedo sent along by the General Synod to stick up for his employers' desperate tinkerings. 'It's all about,' he murmured, 'finding a comfortable way of talking to God.'

Which, as it was bound to do, left me for some minutes staring, motionless, at that soap-girt face which in the fullness of time, or (who knows?) its shallowness, may, if the General Synod, Richard Baker, and numerous other unimpeachable authorities are to be credited, be staring at its Maker and murmuring rubbish about how nice it is to be here.

Because how *will* one talk to Him?

The manner will be the least of one's worries. Personally, though I risk offending against Glenda Jackson and incurring the wrath of Willie Whitelaw, I shall probably stick to the vernacular, since I should feel a fool, upon shaking hands/rubbing noses, if I were to say: 'O God our heavenly Father, who by thy gracious providence dost cause the former and the latter rain to fall upon the earth, that it may bring forth fruit in the use of man, we give thee humble thanks that it hath pleased thee . . .' and so on. I do not talk like that, and should anyway have a job sustaining it when the conversation turned to whether He had enjoyed *Annie Hall*.

Which is where we approach the nub: for while the Synod and the Chartists currently lock horns on how God is to be addressed, I am chiefly exercised over the fraught business of what we shall actually talk *about*. What, in short, is He interested in?

I am assuming that He and I will not have a great deal of time together, but at the same time assuming that He will try to get around and have a word with everyone, since He is not called the Lord of Hosts for nothing. I suppose I see the occasion as a sort of huge Divine Garden Party, with the newly dead pouring in constantly through one gate, having a drink and a bridge-roll and a quick chat, and then pouring out again through another, towards some further desti-nation as yet unspecified. We shall all thus have only a very few minutes to make an impression; and if that seems a somewhat worldly and ignoble ambition, I have to say in my defence that that is part of my nature and I do not wish to be fobbed off with a nod and a smile and promptly forgotten by the Almighty. I shall, after all, have waited a long time (the longer, if He will once again forgive me, the better) for this chance, I shall have to have popped my very clogs for the opportunity, and I have no inten-tion of being no more than a brief fuzzed face in the crowd, instantly shoved out of sight again as a mob comes in from the latest Kurdish uprising.

I had, as a matter of fact, a sort of dress rehearsal for it, once, and I do not intend to let the like happen again. I was at a Royal wedding reception, almost certainly through a misad-dressed envelope, when HM the Q, such were the peristaltic convulsions of the huge crowd, suddenly appeared in front of me, as in some bizarre Paul Jones. She smiled (radiantly, I believe the word is), and I glanced down deferentially, frantically framing some extra-ordinarily clever epigram about its being remarkably warm for the time of year, and when

I looked up again, she had turned into Bernard Levin. I watched her smile being borne away through the mob with an expression on my own stricken face which led the solicitous Bernard to clutch my forearm and enquire whether I wan-ted a glass of water.

I have no intention of letting that happen Over There. Much as I should enjoy Bernard's scintillating company for (if Einstein will forgive me this time) the duration, I do not plan to move from the celestial spot until God and I have chewed the fat for an adequate spell.

But how to go about it?

Normal cocktail-party opening gambits are, of course, quite useless. 'Have you ever noticed . . .?' or 'Has it ever struck you as peculiar that . . .' or 'I bet you didn't realise that . . .?' are quite obviously out of the question. Indeed, omniscience itself could well prove to be an unclearable hurdle, since it would patently come as no surprise to the Almighty that Clem-ent Freud once held the record of 105 omelettes in half an hour or that the male rabbit, if startled, will eat its own children. Facts are the one thing calculated to make the divine eye glaze and wander.

Likewise, jokes. Bizarre though it may be to ponder it, God has heard something like eighteen million jokes, including over two hun-dred about a man who went into a chemist's shop. Worse than that, and still more bizarre, is that – omnipotency being the thing it is – He also tells them better than anybody else.

We may well be on safer ground with opinions. Assuming that theologians have got it right in framing the concept of Free Will and weren't just cobbling any old thing together to make some sort of logical sense out of life's contradictory lunacies, I think we may take it that our opinions are our own and have not all been previously covered by God. He may, that is to say, be fascinated by our view that the new Lancia reminds us of the old Fiat, intrigued by our suggestion that it is better, when trying to get to Maidenhead from Barnes, to avoid the M4 altogether, and surprised to learn that we felt *Tinker, Tailor* to be incomprehensible cobblers (enabling us, perhaps, to get in some snappy riposte, such as 'It's all right for you, Almighty, you knew who the mole was all the time, har-har-har!')

Not, mind, that there might not be dire pitfalls even here. We do not, for example, know whether the Almighty Himself holds views; is there any point in having opinions when You are in a position to alter the conditions under which You hold them (if there are any Jesuits out there, my number is ex-directory)? Indeed, especially for those who do not cleave to the Free Will dogma, it may be that the facts *are* God's opinions, i.e., He feels that the tallest mountain in the world should be exactly 29,002 feet high and that Elton John should go bald, which means that you could be on very unsteady ground if you were to use your precious minutes over the elysial Babycham in saying that, in your opinion, the First World War was a bad thing. He might have enjoyed the Somme enormously, the supernal equivalent of blow-football, and meet your small talk with a very stoney eye indeed.

Which, now I come to think further upon it, may well be the reason that Willie and Glenda and Richard and all the rest are in favour of sticking to the frequently unfathomable 1662 version; because when all is said, done, and tastefully interred, would it not be better, at that great encounter in the sky, for me to grasp my Maker firmly by the hand, look unwaveringly into His welcoming eye, and cry, with Psalm 147: 'HE HATH NO PLEASURE IN THE STRENGTH OF AN HORSE: NEITHER DELIGHTETH HE IN ANY MAN'S LEGS'?

Which will not only resonate wonderfully over the surrounding hubbub, but also baffle even Him so effectively that He will still be wondering what it was that clever little soul meant long after I have passed through the further gate, and gone.

Alan Coren 14.11.1979

'Some kind of foul-up, I'm afraid – science gets all the money, and you each receive one-third of his corpse.'

'Apparently he had a strong belief in reincarnation.'